The Intellectual Discourse of Interwar Egypt:
Globalization of Ideas Amidst Winds of Change

Giora Eliraz

The Intellectual Discourse of Interwar Egypt:
Globalization of Ideas Amidst Winds of Change

Giora Eliraz

Published by ISRAEL ACADEMIC PRESS, New York
(A subsidiary of MultiEducator, Inc.)
553 North Avenue • New Rochelle, NY 10801
Email: nhkobrin@Israelacademicpress.com

ISBN # 978-1-885881-68-7
© 2018 Israel Academic Press

© 2018 All rights reserved
by the author Giora Eliraz

Cover: (Front panel) *Old Street Cafe in Cairo, Egypt c. 1900s. Street Scenes Photography.* (Top left) *Singapore, Hil Street. c. 1920;* (Bottom left) *Rue Lepic seen from the Place Blanche, Paris c. 1920s.*

The right of Giora Eliraz to be identified as authors of this work has been asserted (with exceptions in the case of the reading excerpts that are reprinted here with permission) in accordance with the US 1976 Copyright 2007 Act and Israel's חוק זכויות יוצרים, תשס"ח. No part of this book may be reproduced or utilized in any form or by any means, electronic or mechanical, or by any information storage and retrieval system without the prior permission of the publisher. The only exception to this prohibition is "fair use" as defined by U.S. copyright law.

For
my beloved wife,
Bati,
and my two dear daughters,
Orly and Liat

Table of Contents

Acknowledgements 7

CHAPTER ONE
Introduction 9

CHAPTER TWO
Facing Westernization: Navigating between "old" and "new" 21
- *Cultural confusion and fear amidst a fast changing world* 21
- *Apologetic approach: A kind of "comfort zone"* 29
- *Perceiving "old" and "new" as one homogenous entity* 32
- *Complicated challenge: Setting boundaries for borrowing from the West* 39
- *In search of a middle ground between East and West* 49
- *Is it really possible to only pick the fruits?* 52

CHAPTER THREE
Women's rights: Between traditionalism and reformism 55
- *Calls for women's rights and early feminist discourse* 55
- *Wandering between tradition and change* 61
- *Challenging women's seclusion* 65
  - *On women's veiling* 65
  - *On women's incorporation into the public sphere* 68
- *Education and employment of women* 74

CHAPTER FOUR
Tradition and change: Debate on linguistic reform 83
Arabic language moves to the center stage of public discourse 83
- *Strong aspirations for linguistic reform* 87
- *Literary and colloquial Arabic — A cautious approach* 91
- *Rejection of the radical idea to use Latin script for Arabic* 98
- *The lexical challenge in the modern era* 100
- *Teaching Arabic: Another target for reform* 105

CHAPTER FIVE

Egyptian intellectual discourse as a nerve center for globalization of ideas: The case of the Malay-Indonesian world 113
- *Early globalization: Preliminary notes* 113
- *Egypt as a focal point for the Islamic circle of early globalization* 114
- *Islamic modernism in the Malay-Indonesian world: Highlighting the process of the globalization of ideas, originated in Egypt* 121

CHAPTER SIX

Epilogue: Distinctive intellectual chapter in the modern history of Egypt 131

Notes 137

Bibliography 170

Index 196

Acknowledgments

This book represents a sort of milestone in a long academic journey. For me, two academic paths converged: Middle Eastern Studies and Malay-Indonesian Studies. As often happens in a truly challenging expedition, the best thing is the people you meet along the way.

I owe particular thanks to the following Israeli academic scholars: Prof. Emeritus Emmanuel Sivan; Prof. Emeritus Menahem Milson; Prof. Emeritus Aharon Layish and Prof. Emeritus Israel Gershoni. I also wish to thank the dear friends and colleagues I met within the Australian academia for opening the gates to the fascinating garden of Indonesian Studies: Dr. George Quinn; Prof. Emeritus Virginia Hooker; Honorary Associate Professor Dr. Jean Gelman Taylor; Dr. Wendy Mukherjee; and Dr. Christine Campbell. I extend my thanks to Prof. Henk Schulte Nordholt and Prof. Gerry van Klinken, who introduced me to the richness of research on Indonesia in Leiden. In addition, I wish to express my gratitude to both Prof. Laurie Sears and Prof. Celia Lowe for opening a door into the American academia.

CHAPTER ONE
Introduction

Considerable swaths of the Arab world suffer nowadays from increasing political instability, insecurity, deep religious, sectarian conflicts and brutal violence, in which zealous actors play a significant role. Hopes for a better future in the Middle East at the outset of the Arab Spring of late 2010-early 2011, soon abated and have been replaced by despair and agony. Hisham Melhem, a Lebanese journalist, columnist and analyst wrote in August 2014:

> Arab civilization, such as we knew it, is all but gone. The Arab world today is more violent, unstable, fragmented and driven by extremism — the extremism of the rulers and those in opposition — than at any time since the collapse of the Ottoman Empire a century ago.[1]

Even Egypt, that has written very significant chapters in the modern history of the Arab world, as a hub of pioneering political activism and thought and as inspiring intellectual center, has not been left untouched by the current stormy turbulences in the region; still finding it difficult to navigate onto solid ground in the post-Arab Spring era. After decades of dictatorship, Egypt remains far from being a democracy. The public sphere in Egypt does not enable diverse, let alone opposing voices, and the public debate appears to project a sort of monolithic perspective and a mindset of conformity. In addition, inspiring intellectual discourse that also addresses deep philosophical, political and sociological themes goes almost unnoticed. The continued struggle of the state for political, social and economic survival does not leave much space for dreams, visions, and abstract philosophical thinking.

Given the current milieu, there is a great temptation, from a point of view of intellectual history, to go back in time on a refreshing journey to Egypt of the interwar period. In truth, that period, like most chapters in the modern history of Egypt, strongly experienced stormy political winds, conflicts and violence, as well. So, perhaps one might say: "nothing has changed; Egypt of today is the same as it was." However, it is an entirely faulty statement, if only because "no man ever steps in the same river twice," to cite the immortal utterance of the Greek pre-Socratic philosopher, Heraclitus (535–475BC). Hence, a journey back in time to Egypt of the turn of twentieth century and in its early decades, actually brings us to a period in which this country functioned as a significantly motivated, creative nerve-center for pioneering, enriching political activism and thought. It essentially served as a productive political laboratory that inspired other regions of the Arab world and even diverse Muslim regions outside of the Middle East. Moreover, such an excursion would also lead us to a rich intellectual discourse that deeply addressed varied themes, including supra-cultural and supra-historical themes. Moreover, interwar Egypt was also a period of flourishing literary production, while many belle trists were deeply involved in the public intellectual discourse.

However, for a better understating of the entire historical context that has an immediate association to our discussion, there is a need to take several steps back through the history pages, to catch a brief glance and pick up some insights that should serve us in our intellectual journey. Napoleon's 1798 invasion of Egypt actually signaled the dawn of its modern encounter with the rising European power in diverse fields. Similarly, it opened the gates of modernization and Western influence for Egypt, though the French occupation of Egypt was very short and ended in 1801. It was Muhammad 'Ali Pasha (1769–1849) whose name was cemented as the founder of modern Egypt. Indeed, Muhammad 'Ali, who ruled Egypt between 1805 and 1849, opened a new era by initiating comprehensive ambitious reforms, largely inspired by Western-style models and aimed to match Western powers. These reforms touched on a broad spectrum of diverse spheres, such as the military organization and training, weapons production, political institutions, administrative structure of government, economic and trade systems, education, industry, agriculture and irrigation system. Muhammad 'Ali's reforms even enabled certain educated circles in Egypt direct contact, not just with the practical tangible achievements of Europe, but also with its cultural assets, such as its literary, historical and philosophical texts. Direct cultural contact was achieved through educational missions of young Egyptians to Europe, translations, and learning foreign languages in institutions of higher education in Egypt's new European-style schools.[2] In fact, the significant reformist projects of Muhammad 'Ali, along with some of the reforms made by his successors, planted the necessary seeds for placing Egypt, and Cairo in particular, as a hub of the Arab cultural Renaissance. Known as al-Nahda, this renaissance started in mid-nineteenth century in the Arab-speaking land of the Ottoman Empire, on the backdrop of its evident decline and consequently growing European intervention, coupled with the process of Westernization.[3] Al-Nahda provided the fertile ground on which the intellectual discourse that is discussed in this book flourished. Interestingly, even during the second half of nineteenth century, Egypt attracted increasing numbers of Christians from the Ottoman Syria (it also included what is now Lebanon) who had fled from violent religious and sectarian conflicts. Many of these Christians were well-educated and French-speaking emigrants, who were encouraged to migrate to Egypt and were also attracted by freedom of expression there, enabled by the British rule since 1882 that sharply contrasted restrictions imposed throughout the rest of the Ottoman Empire.[4] These Christians from Syria constituted an influential cosmopolitan community, known as the Shawam.[5] Members of this community were strongly drawn into the intellectual, literary renaissance in Egypt and even boosted its growth by their significant contribution to developing of the journalism and printing industry and by their engagement in literary and journalist writing. Thus, Christian Syrian–Lebanese were salient in the intellectual discourse of the interwar period in Egypt, including authors and thinkers such as: Farah Antun (1874–1922), Yaqub Sarruf (1852–1927), and Faris Nimr (1856–1951).[6] They were largely motivated in their journalistic-intellectual activity to open new horizons of the scientific, technological progress and thought for Arab readers — including Darwinism's theory of evolution (*al-tatawwur*), a project they already started in the Ottoman Syria during late nineteenth century.[7] It is hard to avoid a comparative glance at Syria of today that is severely torn by political and religious bigotry, conflicts, let alone by a massive killing; and while millions of displaced Syrians now dwell in refugee camps across the nearby region or knock on the gates of Europe, in hopes of building their new homes there, more than a century after many Syrian-Lebanese people fled to Egypt to escape from the persecution they endured under Ottoman rule. There, in Egypt, many of these refugees played an important role as initiators and promoters of European-oriented reform and change.

Hence, the processes of modernization and Westernization, advanced in Egypt since nineteenth century, almost entirely in parallel tracks, constitute a significant pivot from the narrative of Egypt of the interwar period. Both modernization and Westernization further accelerated in Egypt of post-First World War, which was a period of an extensive urbanization and institutional reforms. The growing feminist voices of this period, largely discussed in this book, also clearly point to these developments. Consequently, the tension, conflict and clash between centuries-old traditional conventions, values, ideas and modes of behavior, on one hand, and modern, secular perceptions and modes of behavior of the West, on the other hand, became more intensive and challenging, causing confusion and feelings of crisis among the contemporary cultural and social elites of that time.

The processes of Westernization and modernization are not the sole narrative axes that tell the story of the interwar period. Highly significant was the real political and ideological drama that has to be viewed within the direct context of shaping national identity and building state institutions. Preliminary signs of nationalist aspirations and anti-colonialist struggle in Egypt lead back to 1870s. However, it was the revolution of 1919 against the British occupation of Egypt in 1882 that constituted a profound peak in the growth of nationalism in Egypt. This formative event can be considered as the watershed and the opening shot that triggered the political and ideological drama of the interwar period. The 1919 revolution was soon succeeded by the constitution of 1923 that enabled a sort of parliamentary life, more freedom of expression and other institutional reforms. These developments also sustained growing exposure of educated elites in Egypt to the Western civilization and increasing understanding within them that Egypt should move further towards modernization. As a result, statesmen, thinkers and literary figures clamored for comprehensive radical reforms that would endow Egyptian society with a new set of secular liberal values and concepts originated in the West, such as gender equality, democracy and separation of religion and state, based on rational thinking. They hoped in this way to replace the entire complex of ideas, customs and norms, traditionally believed to be rooted in the sacred religious revelation of Islam, by new set of cultural values, social norms and political perceptions and institutions.

This approach was also encouraged by the accelerated decline of the Ottoman Empire, in particular the abolishment of the Caliphate in 1924. For many educated Egyptians, this sea of change and the succeeding establishment of the Western-oriented modern Turkey, led by Mustafa Kemal Ataturk, on the ruins of the Ottoman Empire, indicated an end of the traditional, Ottoman, Islamic order, including institutions, images, symbols and ideals. For Egyptian nationalist intellectuals, the Kemalist Turkish model also proved that in order to be progressive and to belong to the modern world: "it was necessary to be culturally Western-oriented and to be willing to borrow extensively from Western civilization."[8]

Obviously, political matters took center stage of public debate. However, in addition, substantial, heated, intense intellectual discourse, colored by academic contours, on diverse themes also stood out. The political backdrop largely supported this conversation at that time. Though being far from perfect, the political system introduced by the constitution of 1923, enabled a multi-party constitutional monarchy. Hence, Egypt of 1920s enjoyed parliamentary government and life, including a semi-political pluralism that also supported the diverse public and intellectual discourse.

However, the rapid process of modernization, growing foreign influence and increasing Westernization instigated Islamic, traditionalist reaction against perceived Western "cultural attack," as a backlash perpetrated by the "guardians" of the traditional world. Salient among them were the *'ulama'* of al-Azhar, the top Sunni Muslim authority. Actually, the *'ulama'*, the religious scholars, failed to present a viable alternative to growing Western influence. Instead, since late 1920s, and subsequent to the global Great Depression, many people turned to the salafiyya movements for answers, and in particular to the Muslim Brotherhood, established in Cairo in 1928. These movements advocated a return to the perceived pure Islamic values of the early generations (*al-salaf*) of Islam and creation an Islamic Order. They strongly propagandized against the West, focusing among other things on its "materialism," "greed and tyranny," international "political immorality," "crusading" and "imperialism" and warned of "retreat of Muslim civilization before Western civilization".[9] In fact, the rising *salafi*-oriented circles strongly pointed to an alleged Western "cultural attack,"[10] as a red warning flag. Hence, these movements, whose popularity was on the rise, strengthened anti-Western and anti-colonial sentiments in the Egyptian society. Furthermore, the defects of the political system had largely increased during 1930s and the power of the parliament was noticeably undermined, while the power of the King increased and the pluralistic public sphere was limited.[11] In such a political climate, secular Western-oriented trends were increasingly defied. Eventually, the traditionalist movements delivered a serious blow to liberal efforts during the 1930s. Nevertheless, even liberal ideas about both politics and society — including calls for democratic-oriented reforms — continued to be expressed in the public sphere with considerable vigor in the years preceding World War II.[12] Therefore, it can be said that even the period of the 1930s enjoyed fairly interesting intellectual discourse that presented a broad spectrum of ideas.

Consequently, the intense political landscape of interwar Egypt sustained highly political conceptual tension. But the conceptual tension was not limited to the political sphere alone. The distinctive, comprehensive, intensive encounter of the Egyptian traditional society and modernity also created a fertile ground for creative thought; a sort of response that clearly indicated shaking generational experiences. Indeed, intensive conflicting political activism and debates took the center stage. Nevertheless, substantial, diverse, apparently "non-political" intellectual discourse was not sidelined during the interwar period. Similarly, the period under discussion was marked by rich literary production, as well. In fact, this intellectual discourse was not isolated and shared significant common ground with the political debates of the time. Yet, the intellectual discourse still had its own motivations, outlines and contours. Hence, it is possible to look at some of its components independently and judge it on its own merits. The interwar period was also supported by increasing production and consumption of written texts and rapid development of print and press. For this reason, the primary resource of this research is the Egyptian press, which served as the main platform for intellectual discussion and polemics at that time, combined with the fact that Egypt of the interwar period established a journalistic center of gravity for the entire Arab world.

The intellectual discourse in interwar Egypt is not alien to Middle Eastern Studies. The research on this subject is largely aimed at featuring the great names, the luminaries thinkers and writers, such as: Ahmad Lutfi al-Sayyid (1872-1963), 'Ali 'Abd al-Raziq (1888-1961), Taha Husayn (1889-1973), Muhammad Husayn Haykal (1888-1958), 'Abbas Mahmud al-'Aqad (1889-1964), Tawfiq al-Hakim (1898-1987) and Ahmad Amin (1886–1954). Consequently, "secondary intellectuals," a notion introduced by S.N. Eisenstadt,[13] have received much less attention. For that reason, this book, addresses a wider circle of "secondary intellectuals"; some of whom were clearly noticeable, others who were much less known, and a few who were practically unknown. The examined sample, or cross-section, is dominated by belletrists, publicists, journalists, scholars, and teachers. By using the classification of intellectuals made by Edward Shils, it can be said that a view into an intellectual sample that includes both "productive intellectuals" — i.e., those who produce intellectual works; and "reproductive intellectuals" — i.e., those who focus on interpretation and transmission of intellectual work,[14] might offer some additional interesting insights into the narrative of Egyptian society of the interbellum period. Furthermore, the majority of the intellectuals who are discussed in this book were engaged in intensive interaction with wider educated circles throughout their prolific writing and teaching careers — what may even have made them agents of conceptual and social change and mediators of knowledge production, both local and universal; certainly, also transmission of knowledge and ideas has its own distinctive effects. No less important, the intellectual sample highlighted here also includes women, representatives of the then rising feminist voice, and of the earlier female circles that were granted access to higher education and public sphere. Defiantly, the women's intellectual voice further makes the examined sample a representative one, a sort of a mirror of contemporaneous Egyptian society. Through this entire methodological approach of exploring the less studied intellectuals, this book actually aims to expose what Zachary Lockman defined as the "lost voices".[15]

Israel Gershoni also systematically proved the methodological flaws caused by focusing on the selected works of very few luminary intellectuals for understanding the intellectual discourse in Egypt of the period of 1920s-1940s.[16] Moreover, Gershoni interestingly illustrated the significant role played by "secondary intellectuals" in Egypt, since late nineteenth century, in molding Egypt's national self-image and its dissemination throughout the public.[17]

Sociologically, the majority of the intellectuals who are included in the studied sample seem to fit, by education and profession, into the category of new *effendiyya*, the contemporaneous new emerging urban stratum, which was one of the most striking social outcomes in Egypt of 1930s and 1940s. This new social category emerged from students of local Western style secondary schools and institutions of higher education. It can be roughly described as new middle class. Many members of this new stratum were largely characterized as modern professionals, and marked by an increasing differentiation of professions. Hence, they were largely made up of white-collar employees and constituted the hard-core civil servants of the emerging modern bureaucracy. Many others of them served in the growing commercial companies, or were teachers and lecturers in Western-style educational institutions, physicians, lawyers, engineers, journalists in expending press and technicians in growing industry. As such, many of these individuals were proficient in foreign languages and familiar with the European society, culture, sciences and literature. In fact, they were also significant actors in modern Egypt, during the formative era of the rise of nationalism.[18]

Perhaps the core of intellectuals who are examined here can also be considered, by definition, as representatives of the conceptual "mainstream"; most of them have been published in journals that were "painted" neither by strict Islamic colors, nor by strict secular ones. More importantly, as will be illustrated, most of the intellectuals featured here are positioned in a conceptual "grey area," in-between the two extreme poles — i.e. zealous adherence to Islam and traditional stances, interwoven with determent opposition to

Western-style modernity, on one hand, and the struggle for uncompromising secular, rationalist-inclined change and reform rooted in the modern Western civilization, on the other hand. It is likely that those intellectuals of the "grey area" were particularly vulnerable to cultural uncertainty and confusion. For this same reason, examining a wider sample of such intellectuals may suggest intriguing insights concerning the conceptual and socio-cultural climate among wider contemptuous educated circles, who were strongly fluctuating between contradicting worlds and sets of values.

In order to make the examined "group" of intellectuals sufficiently cohesive, this book focuses on Muslim intellectuals, believers of the predominant religion in Egypt. Christian Coptic intellectuals, who belong to the largest religious minority in Egypt, are not included; Coptic Christian intellectuals obviously experienced the modern encounter with Western civilization, whose roots date back also to Christian context, in certain different way. However, views of a very few non-Muslim intellectuals will be discussed, in particular those of the well-known writer and journalist, Salama Musa (1887-1958), a Christian Copt by birth, turned convicted socialist. His extreme, uncompromising Western-oriented views will serve to clarify and set the borders of the "mainstream" intellectual discourse.

Three major themes of the intellectual discourse in interwar Egypt are studied in this book. The first theme examines the varied conceptual questions raised by the intensive contact with the Western civilization, such as: tradition versus change, or as it was commonly defined by contemporaneous intellectuals, "old" versus "new". Also discussed in this context is the critical question of cultural borrowing from the West, in particular the challenge of setting borders for foreign cultural influence and Westernization. The second major theme explored is women's emancipation, or women's status and rights — or in more modern terms, the issue of gender equality. The rise of feminism in Egypt is also connected to this theme. The increasing educational opportunity for women in the interwar period and the growing number of women who entered to the public sphere, also enabled highly educated women to participate in the then intellectual discourse, by incorporating their voices through written texts, as well. The third major theme analyzed in this book is linguistic reform; the discussion on this issue offers another insightful mirror into the conflict between traditionalism and modernism — not to mention the fact that this issue strongly challenged the intellectuals as People of the Pen. The combined discussion on these three major themes provides a window into a period in which large sectors of the Egyptian society were strongly challenged by the expansion of modernity and the influence of Western civilization.

The term *globalization* is considered one of the most significant defining buzzwords of the recent few decades. However, scholars identify earlier manifestations of globalization in the nineteenth century. James L. Gelvin and Nile Green argued, for example, that the technologies of steam and print were the two most fundamental enablers of the earlier globalization, during much of the nineteenth century and early twentieth century.[19] This book illustrates, to certain degree, the transformational power of print that further enabled intellectuals of interwar Egypt to be exposed to diverse Western-oriented ideas and concepts.

Indeed, Egypt functioned then, and even since late nineteenth century, as an interesting "peripheral actor" within the orbit of the Western-oriented globalization of ideas. To enlarge the scope of discussion and enrich the perspective of the function of Egypt as an intellectual nerve-center during the interwar period, this book also delves into the intriguing case of transmission of ideas and knowledge, in the Islamic context mainly — from Egypt of the early decades of the twentieth century, to the Malay-Indonesian world. It is an insightful case, almost unknown to the majority of Middle Eastern Studies scholars that teaches us about the distinctive function played by Egypt, and Cairo in particular, in the early globalization of ideas in an Islamic context, which also affected far peripheries of the Islamic world. Certainly, it was largely facilitated by technological developments, in particular, advances in the field of print, and more specifically in the field of journalism. .

CHAPTER TWO
Facing Westernization: Navigating between "old" and "new"

Cultural confusion and fear amidst a fast- changing world
The intensive meeting between the lands of Islam and the West of the modern era, marked by a rapid process of Westernization, is a significant chapter in long history of cultural contacts between the Islamic civilization and foreign cultures and civilizations. From its outset, the Islamic civilization has not avoided borrowing from non-Muslim societies and cultures in varied fields and assimilating elements from foreign cultures. This adaptive approach contributed to strengthening the Islamic civilization in its earlier stages. Indeed, borrowing from non-Arab and non-Islamic civilizations and societies was a relatively less complicated issue then, at the time when the Islamic civilization was a victorious rising power. It is argued, for example, that the intelligentsia of the early Abbasid period borrowed from foreign traditions in varied fields, being "delighted in widening its horizon and gratifying its curiosity about the world without feeling any (but occasional religious) hesitations about taking over elements of non-Arab or non-Muslim origin."[20] At the same time, while taking into account curiosity and practical considerations, it seems through a wider historical perspective that Muslim societies were careful to avoid elements that endangered their religious foundations and significant traditional social norms. Therefore, side-by-side with cultural openness to foreign influence, Muslim societies tried to obscure and disguise the foreign character of borrowed practices, institutions and ideas. Indeed, it was this approach that facilitated acceptance of the new elements.[21]

Naturally, the issue of cultural borrowing has become much more complicated in the modern era, due in large part to the rising power of Europe and the decline of the Ottoman Empire. This time, the encounter between East and West was neither from a point of superiority, nor even on equal footing; as Non-European countries, including the Ottoman Empire, "were assigned places at the bottom of the hierarchy."[22] Thus, the significant need to borrow from the Western Christian civilization that enjoyed scientific, technical and military superiority, caused Muslim societies to be more vulnerable to feelings of humiliation. But at the same time, it was precisely strong feeling of inferiority that urged elites in Muslim societies to borrow from the West, in order to "acquire" its power and become equal to it. Consequently, a constructive approach of relatively selective borrowing from foreign cultures in earlier history was replaced in the modern era by undiscriminating rapid Westernization. Inevitably, this unsystematic, haphazard approach sprouted fears and caused social-cultural uncertainty, confusion and crisis among wider segments of the society.

The complex dilemmas related to the challenge of adoption of the "new" was manifested in the duel image of the West, or Europe, within the intellectual discourse in Egypt, since the second half of the nineteenth century. On one hand, the West was perceived as an external threat to the Islamic civilization that should be resisted. On the other hand, Western civilization was deemed as being highly advanced technologically and scientifically — and as such, Muslims should imitate it for the sake of restoring the power and greatness enjoyed by the Islamic civilization in the Golden Era. The roots of the dilemma that originated from this duel image, lead to the intellectual legacy of significant Islamic thinker, Jamal al-Din al-Afghani (1839–97), and his Egyptian disciple and colleague, Muhammad 'Abduh (1849–1905). Both al-Afghani and 'Abduh were pioneering forefathers of the Islamic modernist, or reformist, stream of thought that emerged in Egypt of late nineteenth century. Through their analytical examination into contemporaneous Islamic societies they also noticed "backwardness" (*ta'akhur*) and "decline" (*inhitat*).

Their reasoned approach led them to some reformist conclusions, based on strong conviction that the answers to the contemporary ills and weakness of Muslim society can be found in Islam itself. Consequently, there is an urgent need for religious reform that would enable Islam to offer a strong basis for a modern society. Thus, Muhammad 'Abduh, who largely formulated the conceptual basis of the Islamic modernist stream of thought, actually sought to advance a rational-humanist interpretations of Islamic doctrines. Hence, he called for comprehensive reforms, mainly related to the religious aspects of Islam. However, being inspired to some degree by Western innovations, his reformist agenda also addressed educational, social, and legal aspects, as well as political institutions. 'Abduh believed that such reforms would not harm Islam, since it is capable of absorbing the fruits of science and reason.[23]

It appears that strong feelings of cultural crisis and distress, while being trapped in conflicting encounters between tradition and modernity, including an uncontrolled, rapid process of Westernization, did not leave the wider educated circles of interwar Egypt untouched. Many intellectuals of that period actually testified about that matter. Being themselves enmeshed between "old" and "new," they often talked about the *fauda* (chaos), *idtirab* (confusion, muddle) and *haira* (bewilderment) suffered by Egyptian society. Perhaps the fact that the majority of Egyptian intellectuals from the referenced group were located in a "grey area" — i.e. in-between two strong-willed poles, zealous guardians of tradition on one hand, and committed advocates of Westernization, on the other hand — made them more sensitive to the cultural changes. Actually, they were particularly affected by the storms of change, often wandering between the "old" and "new" worlds. Thus, for example, Egyptian intellectual argued that the Egyptian nation existed in confusion; while al-Azhar, on one hand, was looking down at it from the Middle Ages, and the Egyptian University,[24] founded in 1908 on a strong belief in Western-style higher education, was asking to reflect the present era, on the other hand. From al-Azhar perspective it would be better if the Egyptian nation could create for itself "one sail only, instead of two for preventing us from being thrown back and forth by two opposing winds."[25] This illustration seems to echo a widely shared mood among intellectuals within Egypt during the interwar period — i.e. being tossed between tradition and change, Eastern or Islamic civilization and Western civilization. In fact, more than a few intellectuals moved between the two extremes, both as scholars and teachers; al-Azhar University, the millennium-old leading seat of Sunni Islamic learning and the Egyptian University, an icon of modern Egypt. To a certain degree, the movement of intellectuals between al-Azhar University and the Egyptian University indicates a wider phenomenon within educated circles during the interwar period. Indeed, many acquired higher education in the West and were largely exposed to Western culture through varied channels. As a result, their modern profession and their engagement in intellectual, literary thought and production placed them on the front line of the encounter with the modern world. Most of them were men of letters; writers, belletrists, journalists, academic scholars and teachers. The process of Westernization and modernization confronted them precisely in their own wheelhouse of writing and literature. They were required to tackle questions of language, style, content, literary aesthetics, sources of inspiration, etc. Similarly, they were obliged to face supra-culture themes, such as traditional classical texts and models versus modern texts and trends; classical language and style versus modern communicative modes of writing. Obviously, such themes were sensitive for Muslim intellectuals, raised and educated in traditional society that placed the remote past, perceived to be the "Golden Age" of the Sunni Islamic civilization, as a benchmark to be followed and a model to be emulated. Virtue, according to the Sunnah, means observing tradition and walking in the accepted true path, by following the words and deeds of Prophet Muhammad. A departure from that recognized truth was strongly rejected and denounced as a *bid'a* ("innovation"), a deviation and even heresy.[26]

Still, the intellectuals clearly understood the need to enjoy the fruits of modernity and progress. Moreover, they seemed to deeply acknowledge the predicament suffered by Egyptian society and other societies in the Muslim world. Thus, likely to be inspired by the heralds of Islamic modernism, al-Afghani and 'Abduh, they also used terms such as: *inhitat* (decline) and *ta'akhur* (backwardness) for portraying the crisis of contemporary Muslim societies. Yet, the majority of them seemed to still possess strong bonds to Islamic values and local cultural traditions. Again, the same as Muhammad 'Abduh, many within the examined intellectual group clearly declared their confidence in Islam as an ultimate, eternal truth, and held strong to their belief in the potential ability of Islam to offer answers for the modern world. They really were caught between two worlds, knowing they belong to a generation in transition. This understanding of their reality was integrated into their rhetoric, and was expressed by using terms such as, *'asr* or *daur intiqal* (period/epoch of transition). Given that they maintained the dual image of the West, as a threat and potential source for moral evil on one hand, and at the same time, a necessary source for borrowing breakthrough ideas, mainly in science, technology, on the other hand, their dilemmas were significantly greater than both extremes; those who were deeply immersed in the centuries-old beliefs and traditions, and who considered Western civilization to be the source of all evil, and those who were at the opposite pole, calling for a total denial of the past and the rapid, unlimited adoption of Westernization. For the latter group, there was only one path for getting out of the current chaos, as the secular, positivist, Islma'il Mazhar (1891-1962)[27] implicitly suggested:

> The chaos whose causes we see surrounding us is a result of our avoidance to go along with the spirit of evolution (*nush'*) and progress [that orders] the destruction of the old methods (*asalib*) and building the new.[28]

Obviously, the dilemmas of finding balance between old and new were more serious for those who were really challenged by the "duel image" of the West, and much less so for those who very strongly inclined to tradition. Mustafa Sadiq al-Rafi'i (1880-1937) who represents the traditionalist, conservative edge of the discussed intellectual sample in this research clearly illustrates it. In fact, he is also the standard bearer of the somewhat delicate border between the "mainstream" intellectual discourse and the Islamist-inclined approach. An examination into his writings further elaborates the deep abyss between the traditional-conservative approach and the stance of radical adherences to Westernization, as was expressed, for example, by Islma'il Mazhar. Al-Rafi'i the thinker, writer, poet, literary critic, publicist, linguist and theologian, zealously defended Islamic and traditional values.[29] According to al-Rafi'i, the term "Western civilization" (*hadara gharbiyya*) is merely a metaphorical, short-lived phenomenon devoid of any truth; i.e., to his thinking, there is no connection between this current Western civilization and superior spiritual values of Europe in the distant past. Moreover, al-Rafi'i contends that it is the European village, where religious feelings and closeness to nature still exist unharmed by the new civilization that prevents the fall of the West.[30] Western civilization is diametrically opposed to the image of the humanitarian society, which Islam strives to build. Al-Rafi'i also argued that Western civilization is deprived of religious faith, and as such, it wrongly tries to find solutions to problems by earthly legal systems and partial conceptions. Consequently, Western civilization is only concerned with the exterior (*zahir*) and is unable to penetrate the inner depths of the soul. Moreover, it is involved in a continuous struggle for existence, in which the laws of power, lust and instinct prevail.[31] Reason and instinct that should be applied with caution are uncontrolled in this civilization. The feminine and masculine traits have both been lost in the "deviant" (*zaigha*) Western civilization. What was known in Europe as women's emancipation was actually an enslavement to instincts, which eventually leads to anarchy. Therefore, the World War (namely the First World War) was a kind of godly correction (*tanqih ilahi*) designed to restore the lost masculinity and femininity. Al-Rafi'i also argued that even compassion — considered by him to be one of the basic tenets of Islam — had been lost in Western civilization, which created a "mechanical man," whose character and personality were both inherited from machines, rather than from the human soul. The freedom and equality, for which Western civilization professed to stand, serves only the few, the oppressors and enslavers of the majority.[32] Neither communism nor socialism are able to offer solutions to social problems, setting aside the fact that communism is destructive, as it professes violence and heresy.[33] Similarly, al-Rafi'i considered the rising new civilization as an "infidel" civilization, estranged from human feelings, being ruled by science, reason and machines.[34]

Dr. 'Abd al-Wahhab 'Azzam (1894-1959), who acquired his higher education in Europe and was a lecturer at the Egyptian University in 1930s, argued that the foundations of the European civilization were based on minerals and stones and that its heart was shaped by gold and iron. The emotionless machines had imprinted themselves on humankind, and as a result, the contemporaneous generation turned to war and destruction, more so than past generations. Nations had transformed to build armies and weapons factories and it was felt by 'Azzam that "the European is the same as a wolf that covered himself with lamb skin and then took it off."[35]

Al-Rafi'i, a fervent advocate of conservative, traditional perceptions and having Islamic inclinations, and 'Azzam, were not alone in the "mainstream" discourse launching criticism against the Western civilization.[36] In fact, criticism of Western or European culture flowed from varied springs. A helpful illustration of these ideas is presented in the following words of Dr. Mansur Fahmi (1886-1959):

> ...I, whom you put the title of 'Dr.' before his name, as a reminder to the academic degree that I received from the Sorbonne, call out to throw away the European culture and to return, with our thinking mind and feeling heart, to ourselves, to the environment and history from which we derive the origins of our culture...[37]

Fahmi, who did receive his PhD in Philosophy from the Sorbonne, was considered to hold a secular modernist outlook. Within the intensive endeavor of nation building and varied efforts to reshape new identities in post-1919 Egypt, Fahmi was known for his Eastern-oriented stance. Fahmi strongly advocated the idea of an Eastern identification, known as Easternism (*al-sharqiyya*), namely the seeking of closer cooperation among Eastern countries, based on the assumption that Eastern peoples share particular similarities. During the 1930s, in particular, this trend further sharpened the conceptual dichotomy between the East, namely Asia and Africa, and the West, namely Europe, as both civilization and colonial power.[38] Essentially, criticism and even denial of Western civilization among intellectuals in interwar Egypt, also reflected a feeling of a crisis of the modern civilization, which started in Europe itself in late nineteenth century and was largely intensified by the suffering and brutality of the First World War. This perception was framed intellectually by the German historian, Oswald Spengler, in his formative book, *Decline of the West* (1918) that was translated into many languages and stirred intellectuals worldwide. This perspective also had some imprint on the state of mind of Egyptian intellectuals during 1920s and 1930s. Spengler's work had a particular impact on those who searched East-oriented identity; they were encouraged by his book's prediction of a historical shift that would lead to the victory of the East over West.[39] Obviously, the influence of Spengler's book was also evident in the discussed group of interwar intellectuals in Egypt.[40]

Apologetic approach as a kind of "comfort zone"

Though critical varied aspects of Western civilization, the dominant majority of the intellectuals who belong to the category that stands in the focus of this book distinctly could not avoid the diverse dilemmas caused by rapid Westernization; as intellectuals of the delicate "grey area" that stretched between two polarized positions, zealous guardians of past values, on one hand, and fervent advocates of Westernization, on the other hand, they were strongly affected by the stormy changes. They were well aware that their society was in urgent need of comprehensive reforms; i.e., that their nation should enjoy the fruits of modernization and that modernizing Egypt was necessary for improving its position — including in the East-West equation. Not to mention, many of these intellectuals had received higher education in the West. Thus, they were really involved in the delicate mission of navigating between centuries-old traditional values and the Western civilization. Hence, the challenge of setting limits for cultural borrowing from the West was considered by them as very significant and urgent.

It appears that while facing this mission, Egyptian intellectuals implicitly found the apologetic approach to be one of the significant outlets from dilemmas related to cultural borrowing from the West. They were not the first to adopt such a "strategy". For decades, Muslim thinkers in the Arab world had widely adopted an apologetic approach. Thus, modern Western-oriented ideas and modes of government were painted with Islamic colour, in order to justify acceptance of varied foreign elements and to avoid recognition of Western civilization's superiority. The essence of such reasoning and argumentation was as follows — Islam was the first to teach what the West now seeks to teach the Muslims,[41] or as Gustav E. von Grunebaum praises it: "The borrowed element is envisaged as something bestowed on the West many a century ago and now come home, as it were, modified perhaps, yet of Muslim origin."[42] Actually, attributing Western-origin innovations to Islamic origin and traditions facilitated change and reform, by reducing prevailing objection within Islamic traditional societies to new ideas, doctrines, mode of behavior and institutions.[43]

Thus, such apologetic arguments did not leave intellectuals in interwar Egypt untouched; perhaps in this case direct roots lead the earlier Islamic reformist polemic of late nineteenth century, in which modern European science was argued to be the direct outcome of Arab discoveries during the Middle Ages. Similarly, it was argued by Egyptian intellectuals during 1920s and 1930s that what Europe had borrowed from the Arab, while it was still mired in ignorance, eventually paved the road for its Renaissance.[44] Counter-arguments that great Arab philosophers were mere translators and transmitters of the heritage of the Greek philosophy were strongly denied, by saying that Arab philosophers contributed both original scientific and spiritual heritage to mankind, by giving the former, i.e., Greek philosophy, a new shape and content colored by Islam. The Historian Muhammad 'Abdallah 'Inan argued that the magnificent heritage of the Renaissance belongs to the entire mankind and is not the historical chapter of particular nations or peoples; "the fruits of the human thought are a wealth of mankind in every period of time and place…."[45] It is hard to avoid comparing this assertion to a poem by Turkish poet, Mehmet Akif Ersoy (1873 - 1936), who shared wider understanding about the need in Turkey to import science from the West. Thus, in a poem written by him, he said: "Import the science of the West, import its arts; And carry out your task with utmost pace. For no longer is it possible to live without them; For art and science alone belong to no nation."[46] Ersoy, who, at the same time, espoused a conservative stance, arguing that despite the need to imitate Europe, local moral values should be kept intact, criticized the speed and the form of the secular, Western-oriented reforms implemented by Kemal Ataturk. In mid-1920s he took refuge in Egypt; for about ten years he worked as a professor of Turkish language and literature at the Egyptian University.

Sayyid Qutb (1906-1966) entered into the pages of history as the zealous ideologue of the Muslim Brotherhood. He was even executed, along with some leaders of the Muslim Brotherhood, in a charge of plotting against the Egyptian regime. Qutb's radical legacy has strongly influenced contemporary radical and militant Muslims worldwide. Yet, by his background, activity and fields of interests, Qutb of 1920s and 1930s very closely fits the profile of the examined intellectual circle; as he received a modern education at the Dar al-'Ulum, the Western-style academy in Cairo where 'Abduh had taught years before. During 1930s, Qutb made his career as a teacher and was even a functionary in Egypt's Ministry of Education. It was only in late 1949 that Qutb's first book on Islam, *al-'Adala al-Ijtim'iyya fi al-Islam* ("Social Justice in Islam"), appeared. It was not before the 1950s that Qutb joined the Muslim Brotherhood. In the preceding years, Qutb was also engaged in writing novels, poems, and critical literary essays.[47] According to his earlier view, borrowing from European culture was to be considered unavoidable, merely a temporary need, since Europe now enjoyed an advantage of progress over the East. Similarly, Europe had been required to borrow from the Eastern world in the past, when it was ahead of the former in progress; the world civilizations are following on another, meaning, "one takes from the other according to the circumstances."[48] Dr. Zaki Mubarak (1895-1952), a graduate of al-Azhar University who obtained his doctoral degree from both the Egyptian University and the Sorbonne University, in addition to serving as the head of the Department of Arabic Language at the American University in Cairo, argued that only weak nations have an independent culture; strong nations, in contrast, are able to borrow inventions in varied fields and to remold them to fit their own distinctive nature. Therefore, Mubarak states that the East should not hesitate to borrow from the West in assorted areas of thought, the same as the West formerly borrowed from the East in varied fields, including religion, science literature and philosophy. Great ancient civilizations behaved in this manner. Hence, being included among the stronger nations, the East should unapologetically take from Western civilization. Furthermore, the East can consider the borrowed elements as it own possessions.[49]

Perceiving "old" and "new" as one homogenous entity

As has already been said, one of the most significant themes that highlighted the intellectual discourse between the two World Wars was the conflicting meeting between tradition and change, or modernity. This clash was also often portrayed, in the context of literary debate in particular, as a conflict between the "old" and the "new." Even prominent tradition-inclined intellectuals seemed to feel uneasy with this dichotomist categorization, perhaps also wanting to avoid label of anachronism. Mustafa Sadiq al-Rafi'i, who was strongly identified in the fervent literary debate as a zealous advocate of the "old," asked to blur the distinction between "old" and "new". He criticized a common division made mainly by Western-oriented writers between the "old school" (*al-Madhhab al-Qadim*) and the "new school" (*al-Madhhab al-Jadid*). According to al-Rafi'i, these two terms are alien to the Arab literature; Arab intellectuals had always been open enough to skillfully absorb foreign influences, though no one pretended to be dubbed as a "new school." Moreover, according to al-Rafi'i, the Qura'n itself can be considered as a "new school" in every sense, though no one deemed it necessary to say. Ergo, the current controversy between the two schools is not really a conflict between the "old' and the "new," but a battle between talent, purity of the language (*fasaha*), loyalty to heritage, history, and Islamic belief on one hand, and incapability, wrongness, zealous adherence to foreign literature, people and even heresy, on the other hand.[50] Dr. 'Abd al-Wahhab 'Azzam also argued that the history of Arab literature is full of innovations, but the innovators never tried to ignite a literary struggle over the issue of the "old" and the "new." 'Azzam who did not principally reject modern literary manifestations, feared that a call for renewal (*tajdid*) was liable to lead to abandoning of the old (*qadim*). Consequently, he explained: "...We are in a greater need in this era, the era of temptations (*fitan*) of holding fast the old, of loyalty [to it] without rushing into a blind emulation (*taqlid*) and going astray between the old and the new."⁵¹ In a somewhat similar way, Dr. Muhammad Ahmad al-Ghamrawi wrote that what is actually at stake in the literary debate regarding the "old" and "new" was a choice between Islam and adherence to the novelty of the West and renunciation of Islam.⁵²

Moreover, concepts of renewal, (*tajdid*) change, (*taghyir*) and reform (*islah*) per se, are even accepted within the examined intellectual discourse as necessary for responding to contemporary needs, even though it might undermine tradition and expose people to error. The arguments used to sustain this opinion were drawn from diverse worlds of content. For example, a graduate of Dar al-'Ulum in Cairo, a significant pioneering institution of higher education for the training teachers, founded in early 1870s to offer both Islamic and secular, Western subjects to its students, argued in respect to the idea of reforming matrimony, that such a move was not only required by contemporary civilized needs, but was also ordered by the godly laws that dictate human perfection and survival.⁵³ Sheikh Amin al-Khuli (1895-1966), a graduate of Madrasat al-Qada' al-Shar'i (School of Islamic canonical law), philologist, literary critic and scholar of Islamic Studies, who had a career in the Faculty of Letters at Cairo University, argued that the concept of renewal (*tajdid*) is clearly embedded in Islam, and is as well a cosmic rule and constant social law.⁵⁴ Dr. Ahmad Dayf, who received his PhD from the University of Paris and taught at Cairo University and Dar al-'Ulum, called for renewal and reform, including of language and literature. Dayf explained that the world is in permanent motion; both science and literature are an outcome of this motion and are moving and changing simultaneously.⁵⁵ Another scholar asserted that renewal (*tajdid*) is necessary intellectually and socially, since life, by definition, is a change (*tahawwul*) and transformation (*intiqal*) and "the alteration (*taghayyur*) is part of the laws of the nature (*sunan al-tabi'a*) and the revival (*ihya'*)."[56] However, it seems that he rejected cutting off links to Arab culture and the past through process of culture borrowing from the West.[57] Sheikh 'Abd al-'Aziz al-Bishri (1866-1943), a graduate of al-Azhar University, also considered renewal (*tajdid*) as essential, since renewal and development (*tatawwur*) indicate signs of life. At the same time, and in the context of literary renewal, al-Bishri warned of the possibility that such renewal would be distorted and deformed.[58]

Indeed, though wider approval by "mainstream intellectuals" for the idea of renewal and change, they often criticized strong avowed advocates of modernization of ignoring the heritage, traditions and the past, by focusing on the future alone. Thus, it was argued that in this way, the future, or the "new" (*jadid*), is cut off the past, or the "old" (*qadim*), and that while the "new" is admired blindly, the "old" is abrogated indiscriminately.[59] According to the rather prevailing view among intellectuals from the discussed category, the "old" and the "new" should be tied together, since the latter emerges from the former; a new entity that is cut off from its previous stages is rejected. Even Mustafa Sadiq al-Rafi'i, who fervently championed the defense of old traditions, yearns for an "Imam" who would bind together the past and the future in contemporary literature and settle the conflict between these two time dimensions.[60] However, at the same time, al-Rafi'i bitterly criticizes innovators or reformists (*mujaddidun*) who wrongly claim that the "new" (*jadid*) could only be established on the ruins of the "old" (*qadim*). He turned to them by saying:

> Don't you know that definitely the old cannot be destroyed since it creates the new and gives rise to it, and once the old of a nation is distracted the new also vanishes…according to the law of the cosmos, the new is a restoration (*tarmim*) of some aspects of the old, and refinement (*tahdhib*) of part of it….[61]

Dr. Mansur Fahmi is also afraid of a process of renewal that tramples over the past and causes the legacy of the ancestors to be lost. Instead, Fahmi hoped for a revival (*nahda*) that enabled unification of the "old" and the "new." For this same reason, in a speech he made in Jerusalem in 1924, he called upon Arab youth to lead an Eastern revival based on both "old" together with "new" — i.e., the Eastern civilization and the Western civilization. Hence, he asked them not to abandon and neglect the Arabs' distinguished traditions and glorious history, while not sticking fanatically to the past, either. Fahmi went as far as to ask the youth not to discard the "worthy new" (*al-jadid al-salih*), but warned of becoming fanatically attached to the "new".[62] Dr. 'Ali Mustafa Musharrafa (1898-1950), who obtained higher education in Europe and served as the first dean of the Faculty of Sciences at Cairo University, contributed a scientific perspective to the cultural literary debate, by stating that science does not reject the "old" merely on the ground of its being old, the same as it does not accept the "new" just on the ground of its novelty. According to Musharrafa, literature — the same as science — is like a skeleton, for which cutting off its upper part from the lower part inevitably causes its destruction.[63] Dr. Zaki Mubarak argued that an educated person should not be content either solely with the "old,' or only with the "new," since both old and new literature include good and bad — considering that the human mind is enamored with engaging in the world of interpretation and meaning. The derivation of meaning, according to him, produces rational fruits that are not exclusive to any specific nation or particular generation.[64] In addition, Mubarak looked at this issue through utilitarian perspective; considerations involved in a decision about what is worthwhile learning are connected neither to the term of old, nor to the term of new; they are based on the benefits (*manafi'*) and interests (*masalih*) of the human beings, since the knowledge should serve them. The Egyptians should not be afraid of accepting contemporary traditions, as long as they do not contradict true and good manners (*al-adab al-haq*) and the right religion (*al-din al-sahih*).⁶⁵ Adherence to traditions is not an end in itself; traditions should be judged by their own benefit (*naf'*). At the same time, the Egyptians should be careful of fomenting violent revolution against transmitted traditions. Mubarak even suggested a sort of compass for the somewhat perplexed Egyptian society: "… hence, make the national benefit (*al-manfa'a al-qaumiya*) your guiding rule (*ra'id*)…"⁶⁶ Indeed, a cautious utilitarian approach that dictates both acceptance of beneficial or useful (*nafi'*) aspects of the Western civilization and of the "new," while avoiding the harmful aspects, appears as a leitmotif in the discussed intellectual discourse. Such a benchmark was sometimes suggested as the guideline for a decision about what elements of old traditions should be preserved or abandoned.

Dr. Ibrahim Bayumi Madkur, a graduate of Dar al-'Ulum in Cairo, who earned his doctoral degree in Philosophy at the University of Paris and taught at the Egyptian University, argued that the "old" shouldn't be separated from the present and that the renaissance (*nahda*) should be built on a firm foundation made up of the "vibrant old" (*al-qadim al-hayy*) and of the "beneficial new" (*al-jadid al-nafi'*)."⁶⁷ Shaykh Ahmad al-Iskandari (1875-1938) was a linguist who graduated from al-Azhar University and Dar al-'Ulum. Al-Iskandari taught at both institutions, as well as at the Egyptian University, and was among the founders of the Arabic Language Academy. He considered as true innovators or reformists (*mujaddidun*) those who knew how to gather beneficial elements from the "new" and to discard its harmful ones.⁶⁸ Another intellectual, who seemed to be influenced by theories on cultural and social evolution, praised a balanced approach concerning the "old" and the "new" as the right way to be followed. According to him, the proper measure of progress (*ruqiy*) for rising nations is to take the mid-way (*wasat*) between two edges, "attachment to old and transition (*intiqal*) to the new, since the jump is harmful the same as the stagnation (*jumu*d)…"⁶⁹ He considered England as a good model for balancing (*i'tidal*) between preserving old traditions and adoption of the new.⁷⁰ According to another scholar, both a call for comprehensive destruction of old traditions and a call for total denial of the new are faulty; adherents of the former stance should act moderately, and those who support the latter stance should move on.⁷¹ 'Abd al-Rahman Shukri (1886-1958), poet, writer and literary critic, who learned literature in England, taught in high schools and served in Ministry of Education, saw cooperation between young and old people as necessary; a sort of a mutuality between the hammer and the anvil, respectively.⁷² He considered giving respect to the boundaries of the "right" (*haqq*) and the duty (*wajib*) as highly important, let alone during periods of social revolution (*inqilab ijtima'i*) or social change (*taghyir ijtima'i*) when people tend to increasingly challenge these boundaries. What is really essential in such periods is just the opposite; maintaining the equilibrium (*tawazun*) on which life is based. Shukri criticized reformists who seek to weaken these boundaries in order to set new principles, the same way that "a wrecker strikes his pickax at the old to destroy it and create a new building instead..."⁷³ The fault of those who behave in this way is ignoring basic fact that human society, the same as the human body, is a growing organism, not a building made of hard and solid stones.⁷⁴ In such considerable consensus among "mainstream intellectuals" that the "old" and the "new" should be tied together, a statement made by Ibrahim 'Abd al-Qadir al-Mazini (1889–1949) attracts attention. It was made in the context of the hot literary debate between the adherents of the "old school" (*al-madhab al-qadim*) and those of the "new school" (*al-madhab al-hadith* or *al-madhab al-jadid*). Referring to complaints that the "new school" destroys, but builds nothing to fill the void it has created, al-Mazini, a novelist, poet, journalist and translator, wondered whether a man could build, before "he removes the debris and reclaims the land and prepares it for building."⁷⁵

Indeed, this statement was said by al-Mazini in a particular context, the literary one. However, strict denial of the "old" and the past was an exception within the discussed intellectual category. In fact, a comprehensive and systematic rejection of the past was mainly expressed outside of the boundaries of mainstream discourse by zealous adherents of Westernization, who sought to see a total devotion to the "new". Thus, for example, Ibrahim al-Misri, a Christian by birth,[76] a writer, publicist and literary critic, extolled the image of the modern young man who is committed to the Western life, first and foremost, and therefore, he perceives everything as new. According to al-Misri, who by definition is not included in the discussed "mainstream" intellectual category, this modern young man is:

> A free, winged human being who does not sink to the ground under the burden of the past, does not float in the paradise of the ancestors and does not let his soul to be rotten in the clay [land] of the righteous forefathers (*al-salaf al-salih*)…[77]

Isma'il Mazhar, the secular, positivist intellectual, radical Westernizer, and sharp critic of the tradition, also delivered a strong message calling for detachment from the past and worship of the present:

> …we should erase from our minds an idea of being influenced by the past [and at the same time] strengthen in our mental worlds, as much as possible, the idea of worship of the present, in order to be able to cut a way for helping us through the darkened gloom around us.[78]

But such calls to entirely abandon the ancestral legacy and aged tradition and to unconditionally adopt Western culture were denied by "mainstream" intellectuals; who tended to espouse a middle-of-the road stance that coalesced around an understanding that the new layers should be built on the old ones. Consequently, they seemed to show a cautious, selective approach on the issue of Westernization and cultural borrowing. Indeed, the majority of them were substantially exposed to the modern world and the Western civilization.

Yet, their conceptual framework, generally speaking, clearly indicates Islamic belief, an attachment to tradition and to collective historical conscience. Therefore, careful consideration of the "new" was recommended.

Such prevailing opinion within the discussed intellectual discourse seems to be influenced by both traditionalist world view that basically considers the "old" as a foundational pillar and basic Islamic perception that sets the past as a pillar value for the believers and glorifies earlier generations as models to be followed. Therefore, it appears that cultural classism imprinted itself on the common stance among "mainstream" intellectual during the discussed period.[79] But at the same time, this stance is not anchored in the strict Orthodox approach that largely blocks renewal. This moderate stance, relatively speaking, resembles to a certain degree Muhammad 'Abduh's perception of binding new elements together with the principles of Islam. In this way the "old" that is already valued and respected actually allows for, or legitimizes acceptance of the "new". Perhaps such positions can also be explained as a type of tactic taken by creative intellectuals and reformists in traditional society in order to reduce opposition to renewal, by grounding the new borrowed elements in the past that is respected as a source of authority.[80] As such, this stance "joins" the apologetic approach that portrays the elements borrowed from the West as having originated in the Islamic civilization and the East. In other words, a form of historical justice has been carried out by returning these elements to their original home.

Complicated challenge: Setting boundaries for cultural borrowing from the West

A prominent motif within the intellectual discourse on Westernization, in general, and cultural borrowing in particular, is the urgent need for setting boundaries, lest blind and uncritical emulation of the West might rise to threaten Egyptian society. Obviously, such understanding is expected to take hold among intellectuals who incline to middle-of-the road stance in the discussion on the "old" and the "new". Ahmad Hassan al-Zayyat (1885-1968), founder and editor of *al-Risala*, a significant journal at that time, which sought to popularize Islamic heritage and varied cultural themes, and to bridge between East and West,[81] complained about the cutting-off of the Islamic East from its early period, including by saying:

> [The entire Islamic East] has not returned to look through its eyes and to walk on its own feet…it eradicated itself by vanishing into the West…as if it was not enough to its people to become slaves in body to Europe by force and coercion, so they readily and obediently agreed to become slaves in soul… [82]

Dr. 'Abd al-Wahhab 'Azzam complained that many contemporary Muslims have been afflicted with blind imitation (*taqlid*) and feeling as if they were slaves; they felt inferior to the Europeans in the field of science, technology and systems and considered whatever they had as bad, and whatever Europe possessed as good. As a result, they discarded their distinctive character, religion and culture.[83] Dr. Mansur Fahmi complained that Egyptian society had gone too far in the process of modernization; the call for religious reform had developed into an abandonment of religion, rather than into reforms, and a call for women's unveiling had been transformed into cries for libertinism. Fahmi explained the problem as exaggerated worship of Europe by Egyptian society, indicative of losing it way and being oblivious to its original goals:

> …we resemble the crow that attempted to walk like a peacock, but failed and even forgot its original manner of walking, over the course of time, and started to be an object of ridicule for all the crows and the peacock.[84]

Nabawiyya Musa (1886–1951) a very significant figure in the early narrative of the feminist movement in Egypt, argued that subjugated nations tend to indiscriminately accept customs, regardless of whether they are good or bad, "believing that this way will bring them to perfection..."[85] It seems that insights offered by the famous influential Muslim historian, Ibn Khaldun (1332-1406), echo into Nabawiyya Musa's argument; according to Ibn Khaldun defeated or subjugated nations desires to emulate the victorious, dominant nation, in custom, dress and emblems, assuming that the victorious nation is gifted by perfection and the secret of its victory is embodied in its customs and way of life.[86]

In fact, Ibn Khaldun's "voice" on this matter seems to be particularly manifested in the debate in Egypt of 1920s and 1930s, on the issue of the tarbush, which was triggered by the banning the fez in Turkey of 1925 by its leader, Mustafa Kemal Ataturk. This move, a demonstrative act of removal of oriental relics of dress, had been integrated into a wider process of modernization conducted by the Turkish leader, aimed at achieving radical reorientation towards Europe, met with substantial mixed reactions in Egypt. The debate in Egypt on the tarbush[87] (common Egyptian term for the fez) and to some extent, along with the controversy on another reformist move initiated by Ataturk in 1928, Latinization of the Turkish Alphabet, yielded colorful deliberations. Obviously, avowed advocates of secularism and sweeping Westernization, prominent among them Christian Copts, encouraged a removal of the tarbush and supported Latinization of the language in Turkey. Thus, Salama Musa,[88] a strong advocate of modernization, a radical Westernizer and opponent of the Eastern identity for Egypt, argued:

> ...when we make use of a hat, we feel, without being aware of, that we cut off Asia and Africa, that the imprint of 'East' has been removed from us and that our spirit will not come across hindrances to adoption of the industrial civilization. Furthermore, we will

embrace it and try to get ahead of Europe in it. The value of the hat is its allowing us to share in the European mentality. Similar is the case of the Latin script…[89]

Dr. Mahmud 'Azmi (1889-1954), European-educated Egyptian intellectual and outspoken proponent of Westernization during 1920s, who was also known as an ardent advocate of Arab nationalism, explained his decision to wear a hat rather than a tarbush, at length. Among other things, 'Azmi argued that a dominant civilization exists in every epoch; to whose culture and norms other civilizations were entirely subjected. Therefore, it is necessary to borrow from the dominant civilization in order to achieve rapid progress and development.[90]

But strong calls for Westernization did not win an agreement within the discussed intellectual category, certainly not since late 1920s—beginning of 1930s. Ahmad Hassan al-Zayyat who generally tended toward a traditional-oriented approach, seemed to consider the discussion regarding the hat and the tarbush as an insignificant issue that evades the essence of things; the style of head covering is insignificant, since it does not generate a change. Al-Zayyat implicitly argued that the question of the tarbush should not be considered the root cause of the weakness suffered by the East; if the East was powerful and in a better position in varied fields, the tarbush would be a non-issue: "you cannot find a more worthless man than one who feels inferior and deceives himself to believe that mightiness is achieved by wearing the dress of the mighty."[91] Similarly, another writer wonders about banning the fez in Turkey, "as if wearing a hat [brings] all virtues of the West and encompasses its entire power and science and as if the tarbush or the turban signify misfortune and are the cause of backwardness and reason of decline."[92] Another intellectual argued that real civilizations are concerned with essential issues that enable nations to achieve progress, such as sciences and industries, rather than about superficialities. Therefore, dress reforms aimed at adoption of European fashion are insignificant issues that are related to the externals only.[93] He also noted that when he wakes up in the morning and sees an example of a peasant wearing a European dress, he could not refrain from mockery and laughter, since that peasant "plays a comical role by imitating the foreigner — without reason and consideration — the same as monkeys do."[94] Unsurprisingly, Mustafa Sadiq al-Rafi'i, the devout defender of Islamic and traditional values, categorically rejected replacing of the tarbush by the European style hat. According to al-Rafi'i, advocates of the hat do not have any limits; they renounce the morals, the religion and the Eastern character of the society. They are engaged in cutting off and tearing up the valuable Eastern texture. Actually, al-Rafi'i concurred with the basic assumption underneath the banning of the fez in post-Ottoman Turkey, i.e., that headwear is not a mere marginal, external manifestation, however, his conclusion was entirely the opposite:

> I stick to the tarbush, as I want an accurate expression of my soul when it declares my kinship and nationality…the Eastern and Islamic thoughts [that reside] beneath the hat differ from those beneath the tarbush, since by replacement of the symbol, its inspiration is also changed…[95]

Nevertheless, as has already been shown, there was a widespread understanding within the examined "group" of the inevitable need to borrow from the Western civilization. At the same time, they considered as highly important the defining of the "permitted spheres" and the "forbidden spheres" for borrowing for setting up boundaries between them. This issue became one of the most significant themes in the intellectual discourse in Egypt in the discussed period on the issue of Westernization. Since many intellectuals were engaged in diverse literary and journalist pursuits, quite often side-by-side with their formal positions in the academia and other institutions of education, varied questions related to Westernization in the context of literature and journalism were largely discussed.

The challenge of drawing a type of guideline for an alleged proper emulation of the West was illustrated, for example, through Dr. Mansur Fahmi's approach. The guideline, set by Dr. Fahmi, suggests benchmarks, which are anchored in the roots of modern intellectual debate in the Muslim world; making a distinction between the spirituality of the East and the materialism of the West. According to Fahmi, nations that imitate other nations to achieve progress should not belittle themselves. Similarly, nations that represent civilization and progress should not be haughty and arrogant. Therefore, the East can take whatever is suitable for it from Western civilization. Moreover, the East "has rightful possession of it thanks to its historical action and its being part of the humankind that recognizes human rights and equality…"[96]

However, likely due largely to his Easternist perception, Fahmi called for a selective approach with regard to cultural borrowing. Fahmi explained that there are two tendencies in every human personality. The first tendency connects him with the personalities of all human beings, regardless of place, time, ethnicity, etc. The second tendency prompts and encourages a person to retain his distinctive character (*mumayyizat*), in order to strengthen the distinctions of the different people and emphasize their unique nature (*mushakhkhisat*). Similarly, every nation has its own distinctive character. Therefore, the people of the East should consider various factors while seeking to adopt aspects of the Western civilization, such as: race (*jins*), geography, history and believes (*'aqa'id*). For this reason, Fahmi argued that the East should be guided in the process of borrowing from the West by both the criterion of usefulness (*salahiya*) and need to preserve its distinctive character. According to Fahmi, the East would find it useful to borrow materialist aspects of the Western civilization, i.e., technical and scientific achievements, as well as political and economic structures, which are not in conflict with the people of the East. Following that path, the East can turn away from many aspects of Western civilization that are not inevitable outcome of its science and innovations, such as, greed, hostility, controversy, selfishness, and outburst of passions. Employing such a cautious disposition will not harm the ability of the East to enjoy the fruits of a true progress.[97]

Making a distinction between the materialist achievements of the West, namely science and technology, as the allowed sphere for borrowing, and the Western culture as a complex of perceptions, beliefs, values and customs to be the forbidden sphere, was widely accepted among Egyptian intellectuals in the interwar period. Thus, Ahmad Hassan al-Zayyat denounced those in the East who are entirely enslaved to the Western civilization by speaking its languages, emulating its morals and tastes, and changing their own temperament and personality to suit its character, "as if the distance between the East and the West does not make a difference, nor change its character nor alter its nature."[98] Science, noted al-Zayyat, lacks a homeland, since it is supposed to be used for the welfare of the entire humankind, whereas morals (*akhlaq*), taste and tradition are foundations for nations.[99] Similarly, Dr. 'Abd al-Wahhab 'Azzam differentiated between the moral and religious civilization (*madaniyya khulqiyya wa-diniyya*) and industrial civilization (*madaniyya sina'iyya*). According to him, in contrast to the former that differs from one nation to another, in the latter, that is based on the natural sciences, there is no distinction between nations, including between East and West. A nation can acquire varied sciences and industries without converting religion and changing morals.[100] Dr. Muhammad Ahmad al-Ghamrawi, a medical scholar, a graduate of the Teachers' College in Cairo (Madrasat al-Mu'alimin al-'Ulya) and of London University, agreed that the science, the sphere of the reason, has neither national identity nor homeland; as such it is shared by the entire human race. Ergo, acquiring of scientific knowledge from foreigners does not mean taking something that is special to a specific segment of the human race. However, imitation in the field of literature is different. Since in contrast to sciences, it is the spirit of a nation that gives birth to its literature. Thus, imitation of foreign literature means subjection and weakening of the spirit of the nation. Therefore, it should be done in discretion and only to a certain extent, without exaggeration.[101] The writer and journalist Ahmad Hassan al-Zayyat, who was engaged in translation of modern European literature, thought that in order to enrich contemporary Arab literature the same as had been done in the past, it was necessary to augment it using foreign literature; more precisely, by grafting genres of the European arts onto Arab literature and connecting it to modern trends of thought.[102] Despite his outright opposition to Western civilization and strong belief in the tremendous richness of the Islamic heritage, even Mustafa Sadiq al-Rafi'i didn't completely oppose cultural borrowing from the West. Al-Rafi'i explained that he opposed a blind imitation (*taqlid*) of the West, but not selective, controlled cultural borrowing.[103] Such borrowing should be confined to the good (*salih*) in the West to replace inferior elements in the East. Even in this case, the borrowed elements should be deeply anchored in Islam and its moral values.[104] For example, borrowing from foreign systems of government should be limited to those institutions, which conform to the principle of *shari'a* and social freedom as determined in the Islamic heritage, while great care must be taken to avoid harming the character of the *umma*.[105] For al-Rafi'i, the question that should guide the East in cultural borrowing from Western civilization is the extent to which the borrowed elements contribute to expanding the personality (*dhatiyya*) of the East in terms of the sciences and techniques.[106] Al-Rafi'i, whose writings and in particular his poetry, reveal a sort of admiration of Western scientific inventions,[107] considered Europe's personality as the source of its strength in the world struggle. However, he thought that there is no room whatsoever for cultural borrowing of social customs (*'adat ijtima'iyya*), since that matter relates to heritage (*mirath*), temperament (*mizaj*) and character (*taba'*) — i.e. three elements that are entirely different in the East from those in the West, not to mention the fact that Western social customs led to social decay. Europe's attempt to transmit its social customs to the East is one of its means to attempt to dominate the East. Moreover, Eastern social customs are an inseparable part of Islam itself.[108] Al-Rafi'i's stubborn battle against the new literary style of his contemporaneous writers can be also understood in this context. He considered attempts to find new literary paths as a threat to Islam and to the Qur'an as an ideal model, both spiritually and aesthetically.[109] Nevertheless, he examined new genres to a certain degree, while seeking to set selective rules for cultural borrowing in prose and poetry.[110]

Another intellectual suggested a distinction between good and evil as a guideline for emulation of the West, i.e., useful vs. harmful, or manifestations of power and progress vs. those of decay and rottenness.[111] The journalist Mohammad Tawfik Diab complained that the women's revival in Egypt walked partly in the footsteps of Western women. He explained that "there are Western species of trees and plants that we cannot raise in Eastern lands", and vice versa.[112] It was also argued that Easterners should know that East and the West do not share the same mentality (*'aqaliya*) and moreover: "the fear is that we will eat blindly both suitable and unsuitable food and our Eastern stomach will not be able to digest it or be upset by bad blends. The law of nature has no compassion…"[113]

'Abd al-'Aziz al-Bishri pointed to an existing interaction between the true literature of a nation and the sentiments, feelings, sensations, and tastes of its people. Likewise, there are some other significant elements that shape the personality (*shakhsiyya*) of each nation and distinguish it from other nations such as: history, a particular piece of land, landscape and sky sceneries, inherited customs, deep imprinted morals (*akhlaq*).[114] Similarly, talking about literary borrowing from the West, al-Bishri stated that the sentiments of a nation cannot be borrowed and passed on as sciences and industries.¹¹⁵ At the same time, he strongly recognized that for the sake of the revival of the Egyptian literature, Egyptians should read and study Western literatures and translate what can be adopted into Arabic. However, to make Western literature useful for the Egyptians, they would need to refine its character (*khulq*), its colour and shape, in order to harmonize it with the characteristics of the Egyptians, to suit it to their customs and align it with their tastes.¹¹⁶ As such, artists who are moved by foreign works of art are required to cultivate and fine-tune them to suit the art of their own people, their characteristics, tastes and sentiments. Therefore, one who "seizes quickly" works of art done by others, which he himself is unable to thoroughly stomach, the same as his own people, actually distorts and defaces his art in the name of renewal.¹¹⁷ A similar perception that indicates a kind of organic connection between a nation and its literature was expressed by Ahmad Hassan al-Zayyat. He complained about a type of contemporary Egyptian writer who ignores Arabic and Arabic literature, and chooses to learn European languages and read foreign literature. Whereas such a writer is blind to the landscapes of the Egyptian land, its beauties and the glorious deeds of its people, he tries to gain inspiration from the foreign scenery that unfolds in the texts written by European authors and poets. Modern Egyptian literature, the same as modern Egyptian society, was argued by al-Zayyat to be based on the death of personality (*shakhsiyya*), a vanishing of the self (*al-dhat*), *obliviousness* of the history and alienation of its origin (*asl*). Art, in contrast to science, does not submit to an idea of collective mind, but to the regional dispositions (*taba'i' al-iqlim*), the unique characteristics of the milieu (*khasa'is al-bi'a*) and the purposes of the individual (*manazi' al-shakhs*).¹¹⁸

This perception of the Egyptian nation as an organic living entity, that maintains and nurtures a distinctive nature (*tabi'a*), i.e. personality, namely, "the Egyptian personality" (*al-shakhsiyya al-Misriyya*), morals (*akhlaq*) and milieu (*bi'a*), has to be largely seen in the context of the then contemporary discussion on the Egyptian territorial identity, as well as in Eastern identity.¹¹⁹

It is salient that these terms and concepts, as well as other related notions run through the discourse on cultural borrowing from the West as a leitmotif, in particular in the context of the debate on literature. Elements of this leitmotif also trace to the legacy of French philosopher, literary historian and critic, Hippolyte Adolphe Taine (1828–1893). Taine was known for his deterministic view that "la race, le milieu, et le moment" are the three great forces that shape culture, literature, art, social norms, etc. His naturalist philosophy was largely diffused into the intellectual discourse in Egypt between the two World Wars, through Egyptian thinker, novelist and journalist, Muhammad Husayn Haykal. Thus, Taine's concepts were also evident on efforts to shape the Egyptian territorial-nationalist approach, including on the distinctive character of the Egyptian society, as well as regarding Egyptian literature.[120]

Obviously, it was not only Taine's literary historicism that was interjected from Western philosophy into the intellectual debate in Egypt, starting in the late nineteenth century, regarding Westernization in general, and cultural borrowing, in particular. Thus, for example, the influence of liberal European thinkers is also evident, including British utilitarian philosopher, John Stuart Mill (1806–1873), whose writings influenced likewise, to some extent, Muhammad 'Abduh's thought.[121] Perhaps, it was a utilitarian approach that encouraged many intellectuals to establish the degree of potential harm, on one hand, relative to the degree of potential benefit, on the other hand, as the criterion for cultural borrowing.

In Search of a Middle Ground between East and West

Dr. Zaki Mubarak wished to see a conciliation (*taufiq*) between the adherents of Western civilization and those who clung to Eastern civilization. Mubarak believed that it would enable the formulation of new traditions that tie together the sharpness (*hidda*) of the West and the gentleness (*rifq*) of the East.[122] 'Abd al-'Aziz al-Bishri thought that for the sake of acquiring science, art and power and keeping pace with the world and its civilization, the people of East should adjust between the old (*qadim*) of the East and the new (*jadid*) of the West, and work to achieve harmony (*mula'ama*) between them.[123] Another intellectual argued that while Egypt wandered between East and West, it should walk on the middle (*wasat*) path — which could be done through acquisition of Western sciences, industries and means of wealth and power, while, at the same time retaining its distinctive Eastern character (*mumayyizat*), spirituality (*ruhaniya*), generosity (*samaha*) and virtue. This approach would enable Egypt to complete what was missing in Eastern civilization and to cure the ills of Western civilization.[124] Referring to an article written by the prominent Egyptian scholar and thinker, Ahmad Amin (1886-1954), under the title, "Halqa Mafquda" ("missing link"),[125] Dr. Muhammad Mahdi 'Alam argued that the famous educational institution, Dar al-'Ulum, actually constituted the "missing link", that should connect between Islamic culture and Western science; this institution offered its students a mix of Islamic and secular subjects and trained them to teach modern subjects. Thus, 'Alam, who himself graduated Dar al-'Ulum and was a teacher in that institution – he also acquired his PhD in England — supported his arguments by stating that a portion of the graduates of Dar al-'Ulum had also graduated from universities in Europe and taught in both the religious al-Azhar University and the Egyptian University (known now as Cairo University), the European-inspired institution for higher education.[126] Even Dr. Mansur Fahmi who sometimes expressed skepticism about the ability to emulate the Western civilization without harming the distinctive spirit of the East, hypothesized that close contact between Easterners and the Western civilization would create a future civilization that contained the best qualities of East and West and would be free of the defects shown by both Eastern and Western civilization. In this way, the future civilization would show both reason (*'aql*) and emotional life (*wijdan*) in their purest manifestations.[127]

Obviously, arrows of criticism were directed at such a middle of the road position on Westernization by strong ideological opponents, in particular, devotees of strict orthodoxy who sought to ward off Western-oriented modernization, and the new Salafiyya movements and groups — the Muslim Brotherhood in particular — who were very assertive in their rejection of European civilization and decried European/Western influence on the Egyptian society. On the other extreme pole of the conceptual spectrum was positioned a relatively small circle of secular intellectuals who, in a sharp contrast, were fervent advocates of modern Western worldview. They sought to establish Egyptian society on a secular, rationalist set of values. As such, they did not hesitate to strongly defy traditional values. Not surprisingly, Christian Copts were significant among the spokesmen for this circle. Indeed, they are not included in the intellectual discourse examined here. However, a review of their arguments on cultural borrowing from the West helps to further illustrate the borders of the discussed intellectual discourse.

The Christian Coptic, Salama Musa, a devout advocate of Westernization, rejected what he described as the indecisive position (*mauqif al-taraddud*) of the Egyptians, who wander between the East and the West. Musa considered Egypt's connection to the West as natural from many reasons, and called for unlimited connection with Europe, including borderless, comprehensive cultural borrowing that would enable Egyptians to look at life the same way Europeans do.[128] Dr. Isma'il Ahmad Adham (1911-1940), a declared atheist,[129] who definitively denied the midway position, aspired to see the inclusion of the Arabs, Egypt in particular, in the "universal civilized family."[130] Adham thought there was no other way for Egypt, but to gravitate toward Western culture and logic, which constituted the contemporary "center for the social gravitation" (*markaz al-jadhb al-ijtima'i*). The mentality (*'aqliya*) of the West aims to guide human beings to know the laws that rule life. Therefore, Western logic (*mantiq*) that is based on mind and knowledge, will lead Egyptians to the essence of human life. The Eastern mentality, in sharp contrast, turns to mysticism and belief in fate and divine decree (*al-qada' wa- al-qadar*).

Moreover, the spirit of the East, which is based on the sentiment (*'atifa*), is liable to guide the Egyptians to the hereafter (*al-akhira*), but in this life.[131] Ibrahim al-Misri denied the common "middle-ground solution" (*al-hal al-wasat*) as a fitting response for Egyptian society, arguing that enacting such a compromise would cause Egypt to become an odd blend of Eastern traditions and Western reforms. Instead of alleged harmful, faulty "middle-of-road solution", al-Misri suggested that Egypt follow the ideal (*mathal a'la*), in the sense of embracing a new feeling (*ihsas*) and belief (*'aqida*) of being an active part of Europe.[132] Al-Misri considered Kemalist Turkey to provide a good example of how to guide a nation toward Europe.[133] For the same reason, and in contrast to the appreciation garnered by the Japanese model from intellectuals in the examined discourse,[134] al-Misri deemed Japan's model as faulty, since it helped generate Japanese achievements in the industrial field, but neglected to promote progress of thought, which in turn, has left Japan with improper, obsolete ideas, beliefs and traditions.[135]

Is it really possible to only pick the fruits?

A hidden thread extends between the sort of midway position on the issue of borrowing from the West held the among mainstream of Egyptian intellectuals of interwar Egypt and preceding generations of Muslim intellectuals of late nineteenth and early twentieth century. Both generations deemed mainly "materialist" aspects of the West as appropriate for borrowing or emulation. In this way, scientific and technological achievements, as well as political and economic institutions were prone to be stripped of modern ideas and concepts, along with the cultural values and perceptions that enabled them, such as freedom of thought, rationality, and human rights. Common apologetic arguments by Muslim intellectuals that aimed to justify use of Western achievements have facilitated such attitudes by claiming that scientific-technological achievements lack any distinctive cultural character, namely that they are not culturally dependent, not to mention that their sources lead back to the Islamic civilization of the Golden Age, which gave scientific methods, philosophy and arts to the world.[136]

A clear criticism of the logic of such midway positions was launched from within the circle of devout Westernizing intellectuals in Egypt. Thus, Isma'il Ahmad Adham denied such positions that consider Western science and technology, either explicitly or implicitly, as a mere product, able to be imported or consumed, without internalizing the modern values and concepts which created them. He argued that it is impossible to use the material outcomes of European Civilization without acquiring the logic of the positivist science that generated them; a society that avoids this logic would turn to be a burden on the humankind.[137] For this same reason, Adham implicitly negated the Japanese model, since it focused on adoption of the machines produced in Europe and avoided the logic of European thought.[138] On the other hand, the same as Ibrahim al-Misri, Adham praised the modernist Kamalist model of Turkey for liberating the "Turkish mind" from the connection between state and religion, which allegedly caused stagnation of the "Turkish mentality". Once this implicitly destructive bond was severed, the "Turkish mentality" succeeded to advance in great strides.[139] Such a position is clearly at odds with dominant view among intellectuals who make up the discourse stands at the center of this book. Therefore an exceptional voice of Egyptian poet, novelist and literary critic, Ibrahim 'Abd al-Qadir al-Mazini, is rather striking. Al-Mazini warned that though the Egyptians could acquire Western education and manners, they would continue to hopelessly drag their feet behind the West. Al-Mazini explained his position by arguing that what is of importance is the spirit that gave birth to Western education, manners and strong character. He further illustrated his point metaphorically: "you can stretch out your hand and pick ripe fruit from the treetop, however, in order to do so, you do not need to move the tree to your garden..."[140] He continued: "if we take fruits from the West, without the tree roots (*usul*), we will not profit, since we take the external manifestation...and pay no attention to the truths behind them."[141]

In fact, the rough distinction made between the allowed sphere for borrowing, mainly scientific and technical achievements, and the forbidden sphere of cultural and social values, is very problematic by definition — it is a case of walking on a thin ice. This rationalization, originated as the result of an attempt to find a balance, or a middle path, between the urgent need for modernization and obligation to preserve traditional values, has been challenged by the reality that advanced technology and scientific innovations of the West and its complex of ideas and values are tightly interwoven. Hamilton A.R. Gibb phrased it as follows:

> Even for ourselves, it is sometimes hard to distinguish between the idea and its manifestation, so closely are they linked together. In the same way, it is quite impossible to dissect Western influences in the Middle East with precision, and to make a distinction between those which are material and those which are cultural.[142]

Actually, substantial efforts to thoroughly explore the root of the success of the Western civilizations are hardly found in the examined intellectual discourse in Egypt. Even Mansur Fahmi, who sought to offer a set of guidelines for cultural borrowing, while sharing the common opinion that essential differences exist between the Western civilization and the Egyptian context, seems to be skeptical about the ability of doing it.[143] Thus, Fahmi argued that those who seek to follow the middle path regarding the question of East and West, believing that they can embrace together a portion of Eastern life and a portion of Western life, would be wrong; manifestations of civilizations are not selected the same way as a person selects his wardrobe of clothes. Adherents of the middle-of-the-road approach ignore the fact that forcible laws, which are not subjected to human will, lead nations into the stream of civilizational development, such as the law of imitation (*muhakah*) and adjustment (*takayyuf*) into the "unity of resemblance" (*wahdat al-tashabuh*).[144]

CHAPTER THREE
Women's Rights:
Between traditionalism and reformism

Calls for women's rights and early feminist discourse
Muhammad 'Abduh's reformist agenda did not leave the matter of reforming the status of women in the Muslim world untouched, including the idea of advancement of their rights and improving their education. However, it was his disciple, Qasim Amin (1865–1908), who was the first Egyptian intellectual to clearly bring to the fore the question of advancing the status of women in society. His two books, *Tahrir al-Mar'a* (1899) and *al-Mar'a al-Jadida* (1900) succeeded to make the enhancement of women's rights a theme for intellectual and public discussion. Hence, Amin is largely deemed to be a pioneer for women's rights in Egypt. Amin fought against polygamy in Islamic, patriarchal society, in which men had superior status, including the right to marry as many as four women, and also the enjoyment of much freedom in terms of divorce. According to Amin, the ruler possesses the right to forbid polygamy, and ought to do so out of concern for the public interest. Furthermore, Amin strove to limit the rights of men to divorce their wives.[145] He also stressed the need to expand educational opportunities for women and fought against the wearing of the *hijab* (veil) as a barrier raised before women, whose life was largely confined to home, and the world outside. Along with his call for the unveiling of women, Amin, who asserted that the *shari'a* does not mandate covering the face with a veil, also asked for a gradual reduction of the social seclusion suffered by women. In his book, *Tahrir al-Mar'a*, Amin placed his demands for reformation within the context of the Islamic reform approach promoted by 'Abduh and the framework of the Qur'an and the *shari'a*. In those matters for which Amin found no clear Islamic directives, he followed the practice of

'Abduh and acted according to the principle of *maslaha* (public interest), which had been emphasized by the latter, in order to harmonize Islamic principles with the spirit and exigencies of the modern period. In *al-Mar'a al-Jadida*, Amin was guided by the principles of social progress advocated by nineteenth century European thought. Though Amin had taken pains to avoid departure from the Qur'an and the *shari'a*, nevertheless, his book evoked a wave of criticism and opposition;[146] Egyptian society of his time seemed averse to the focus of intellectual attention on the question of the status of women.

In fact, earlier calls to improve women's rights were not exclusive at all to some pioneering male voices. Earlier seeds of feminist awareness had been evident in Egypt since the late nineteenth century. Feminist awareness was basically sustained by the earlier process of modernization, including new, but yet very limited, educational opportunities for women. The appearance of modern journalism, in conjunction with the founding of journals for women, also supported very early feminist voices, by providing a certain stage for very small circle of Egyptian women who had benefited from the improvement of school and formal education.[147] A significant feminist voice, during the period leading up to the First World War, was that of Malak Hifni Nasif (1886-1918), better known by her *nom de plume*, Bahithat al-Badiyya. As early as 1909, Malak Hufni Nasif published *al-Nisa'iyyat*, a collection of many of her speeches and essays, including her lectures at universities, at the Umma Party headquarters, and a series of her columns written in *al-Jarida*, the major newspaper of that party.[148] Nasif believed in gender-equality in diverse fields. For example, she disapproved of polygamy and men's abuse of their right to divorce. Nasif asked to see limitations placed on the marriageable age for women. However, Nasif hoped to achieve reforms through a gradual process, thinking that women, let alone the entire Egyptian society, were not yet prepared for radical changes. Therefore, she deemed the expansion of educational opportunities for women as having great significance.[149]

An interesting, distinctive contribution to the early feminist voices and activism was evident through the role played by Mayy Ziyada (1886 -1941). Her impact can be associated with the narrative of the al-Nahda, the cultural, intellectual and literary renaissance, or awakening of late nineteenth, early twentieth century in the Middle East, in which Cairo played a very significant role. Mayy Ziyada's role can also be viewed through the substantial and important contribution made to al-Nahda by Syrian-Lebanese emigrants. Mayy Ziyada was a prolific Christian Lebanese-Palestinian poet, essayist and translator who immigrated to Egypt with her parents in earlier years of the twentieth century. The famous literary salon she established in 1912 functioned as a center for intellectual life, for both male and female writers and intellectuals. She also advocated ideas for promoting women's equality and presented a living model of a highly educated woman. Ziyada's knowledge of languages was very impressive and she was an exceptionally productive thinker. Moreover, her salon was a courageous model of a cross-gender public forum. Hence, Ziyada is considered a notable figure in al-Nahda and her salon is regarded as a microcosm for the al-Nahda, the cultural, literary renaissance.[150]

But it was only the national revolution of 1919 against British colonial rule that brought about a turning point in the struggle for the reform of the status of women. The participation of women in these rebellious demonstrations, framed a formative event that entered into the Egyptian collective national memory as the "Ladies Demonstrations". These rallies, which were led mainly by urban upper class and middle class women, were considered to set the foundation for women's movement. The "Ladies Demonstrations" garnered participation in the streets from women alongside men, as active partners in the national struggle, which was seen as a move that strongly expressed women's desire to break with subservience, seclusion and debasement. Consequently, the formative narratives of Egyptian feminism and Egyptian nationalism are closely bound together. There is no wonder that calls for reforming the status of women and women's rights, by both women and men during the interwar period, were also sustained by nationalist-inclined argumentation.[151]

The period between the two World Wars was also a stage for early feminist discourse that went hand-in-hand with the development of a feminist movement, working for the advancement of a wider reformist agenda. The establishment of the first explicitly feminist association al-Ittihad al-Nisa'i al-Misri (the Egyptian Feminist Union) by Huda Sha'rawi (1879-1947) in 1923, constituted a momentous milestone. The Arab term, *Nisa'i* can signify anything pertaining to women, in a sense of either "feminist" or "feminine". Thus, the concept of feminism, originally coined in France of 1880s, has long been strongly connected to the struggle in modern Egypt for women's rights.[152] In light of her accomplishments, the name Huda Sha'rawi was written in the collective memory of the entire Arab world as a central pioneering feminist figure.[153]

Due much to the growing of active, determined feminist voices, organized into a movement, the post-First World War period experienced a variety of gender reforms. Notable among the varied reforms were changes in the field of women's education, which became a primary goal for the Egyptian feminist movement. Women across the entire Muslim world had suffered significant discrimination in this field. Actually, limited and initial reformist steps were taken during nineteenth century, but a true breakthrough seemed to be achieved in the 1920s. It should be noted that the constitution of 1923, an outcome of 1919 revolution, preceded by British recognition of Egyptian independence in 1922, stipulated elementary education as compulsory for boys and girls alike. Consequently, the educational system for girls was expanded considerably. In 1925, the institution of a high-school system for girls was officially established. Towards the end of the 1920s, for the first time, women were admitted to the Egyptian University. Women's claim for implementing reform in the field of education was based, among other things, on Islamic-historical grounds, arguing that Islam ordains the equality of the two sexes.[154]

Side-by-side with progress in and the improvement of women's educational opportunities, many more women, from the upper-middle class in particular, succeeded to enter into the public sphere; a masculine arena by its nature, and one from which women were traditionally excluded. In addition to the fact that women had traditionally been kept confined to their duties as mothers and wives, the entrance of women into the public sphere further triggered the debate on social intercourse between men and women. Certainly, the role of women had been a sensitive issue in traditional Muslim societies, in which a strict code very strongly limited social interaction between women and men. Moreover, the respectability of Muslim family members was largely defined by the moral conduct of its daughters and sisters, let alone its wives.[155]

The emerging feminist reformist movement, led by the activism of al-Ittihad al-Nisa'i al-Misri, also took actions on the political stage to demand political rights for women. Indeed, Egyptian women had not won substantial formal gains before 1950s, when the 1956 Constitution recognized the political rights of women. But the feminist struggle for women's political rights in the interwar period that was largely accomplished through cooperation with the Wafd party (more precisely, through Wafdist Women's Central Committee) cannot be ignored.[156] Significant, as well, were efforts to address the personal status code, or family laws, in Egypt of that time, which Margot Badran defined as the "last bastion" of the patriarchal society with control over women.[157] Feminist pleas to reform the personal status code covered diverse issues, such as, restriction of polygamy, regulation of divorce, reformation of inheritance laws, and the establishment of a minimum for marriage age.[158] These combined efforts also generated certain profound reforms in the legal status of women. Thus, in 1920 and 1929, Egypt adopted rules that provided women with greater opportunities for divorce. In 1923, the minimum age for marriage was set at sixteen for women and eighteen for men. In 1929 a mother's legal rights to custody for her children were also extended. Yet, advocates of reforming the legal status of women faced significant opposition and their objectives were only partly realized. Thus, other important feminist demands, including substantial regulation of men's ability to divorce and restriction of men's practice of polygamy were not realized during the discussed period.[159]

However, the changing reality, women's growing access to education and to the public sphere, as well as the emerging of women's press since late nineteenth century, both enabled women and encouraged them to articulate ideas through written texts and speeches, which facilitated the circulation of their ideas among wider audiences. Thus, more women can be categorized as intellectuals in the discussed period. Moreover, women were not confined to their own gender discourse; their texts were also published in leading journals and magazines alongside those of male writers. Malak Hifni Nasif and Huda Sha'rawi were prominent among these pioneering women intellectuals. Another renowned female intellectual was Nabawiyya Musa, an educator, and prominent figure among the leading, founding circle of the feminist movement in Egypt, who came from modest middle-class and expressed a clear demand for gender equality.[160]

Women's status and rights issues were not solely of interest for women reformers during the interwar period. Male intellectuals also discussed these issues and concerns, though it is hard to identify a substantial, strong full-fledged perception of gender equality among male intellectuals. Indeed a blunt, direct male-chauvinist approach appeared to be a rarity. However, it did still exist side-by-side with a call for reforming the women's status, and sort of patronage stance, steeped in traditional patriarchal themes and ideas can be identified as a motif, either overtly or covertly. Sometimes such stance was slightly camouflaged by mobilizing diverse scientific arguments to validate and support the existing social structure, the traditional gender-division of labor, and even male dominance, which was done, for example, by talking about physical and psychological differences between the two sexes and of their complementary roles.[161] Obviously, attempts to sustain argumentation by sciences also could testify to the impact of Westernization on the intellectual discourse in Egypt at that time, through the globalization of ideas, as well as the fact that many Egyptian intellectuals graduated from universities in the West and Western-type educational institutions in Egypt.

Wandering between tradition and change

Qasim Amin looked upon the oppression of women as a deviation from the principles and spirit of Islam and emphasized that reform of the status of women conformed to the Islamic way of thinking and was in fact, mandated by its teachings. According to Amin, about twelve hundred years ago, the *shari'a* had endowed women with rights acquired by Western women only at the beginning of the twentieth century, and that Islam drew a distinction between the genders only regarding the matter of polygamy.[162] In his argumentation Amin followed the steps of the forefathers of Islamic reformist movement, Gamal al-Din al-Afghani and Muhammad 'Abduh, who believed that the remedy to the "inner decay" and "backwardness" suffered by contemporary Islamic societies was found in the Islam itself. To that end, its truths should be revealed through a reformist process focused on purifying Islam from later corrupted ideas and practices, and manifesting a return to its original teachings, to the true Islam. It was believed that such a process would enable a harmony between Islam, human reason, and science, since the roots of Islam contain potential for the modern era.[163] Certain initial footprints of the conceptual heritage of Islamic reformist thought can also be found in the polemical and apologetic arguments used by Egyptian intellectuals in the context of discussions on women's status and rights during the interwar period. Thus, for example, early Islamic history was glorified as an alleged reformist model in the context of the discussion on women's status. Dr. Husayn al-Harawi (d. 1954), a physician by occupation, argued that Islam was the first to enhance women's worth and to give them equal rights. According to him, the Islamic view on polygamy and divorce even contains a social and ethical message. Al-Harawi sustained his argument also by saying that before the advent of Islam, during the *jahiliyya* period, women's status had been clearly inferior.[164] Interestingly, in contrast to the traditional Islamic perception of the *jahiliyya*, the pre-Islamic period of Arabia, as a period of barbarity, ignorance and godlessness, some intellectuals argued that women had enjoyed a remarkably high status, even during the *jahiliyya*. Women were said to have been entrusted then, as well as entrusted during the first centuries of Islam, with positions of influence and were said to have enjoyed freedoms that were only given centuries later to Western women.[165]

Nabawiyya Musa shared a common traditional view that the female nature is essentially distinct from male nature. Nevertheless, she argued that men and women are equally capable, since women equal men in knowledge and intelligence. She pointed out that women's equality had been amply demonstrated during national struggle. According to Musa, every woman is an independent person, and as such, no one has a right to ask her to nullify herself and be subservient in the company of men; women should behave as equals.[166] Huda Sha'rawi, who in contrast to Musa came from the land-owning class, also collaborated on efforts to lay down foundations for a clear feminist voice. Sha'rawi stressed the great importance of education for women that would enable them to achieve legal, political, civic and moral equality and to fully participate in the public sphere, through social and cultural reform. She even directly targeted sensitive issues that strongly pointed out gender inequality in the traditional society, i.e., marriage, polygamy, and divorce.[167]

Standing out strikingly, in contrast to reformist feminist voices, were the ideas expressed by Mustafa Sadiq al-Rafi'i, whose viewpoints are positioned on the traditionalist, conservative edge of the examined discourse. Al-Rafi'i rejected outright rising voice for gender equality. He argued that the "secret of life" is incompatible with the idea of granting equal status to women; it had been decreed that women would always be inferior to men and remain dedicated to serving them. He asked to implore young women of the East to avoid following the frivolous pattern of European women, in their attempt to achieve equality.[168] Some other Egyptian intellectuals also appear to reject the Western-oriented idea of gender equality, though they avoided direct, blunt expressions of their ideas, as those used by al-Rafi'i. In an article published in late 1920s, Sayyid Qutb lashed out against those who maintained that women were actually repelled by their state of subservience and that women should enter the field of general employment to compete with men. In Qutb's view, if a woman were to candidly express what disturbed her, she would say, "I want the man so that I can be absorbed within him."[169] Women have been endowed with meekness, tenderness and a delicate nature, which complements the strength, violence and pride of men. All of these are vital characteristics in the relations between the sexes. Qutb was equally vociferous in his criticism of the young Egyptian males, who emulate women in their excessive use of perfume and make up, a conduct, which he considered to be a violation of the laws of nature.[170] Similarly, another intellectual argued, given that men and women had been created differently, women's domination over men, as exemplified in the West, contradicts the "law of creation".[171] The Journalist Fikri Abaza (1895–1979) described women as dependent beings whose character is determined by men. Women possess a dual-personality of both angel and Satan. The responsibility lies upon the husband and father, as to which of these two aspects would dominate a woman's character. According to Abaza, the rising social revolution was determined by chaos and restlessness, while fathers had lost control over their daughters, and husbands failed to set rules of constraint for their wives. Consequently, the satanic force predominated.[172] Another intellectual shared a description of women's personality as being determined by men. According to this view, the extent to which a man would derive benefit from or be hurt by his wife's behavior depends entirely upon himself — since women are not equipped with the ability to determine their own character and are completely dependent upon their social environment. Hence, they could be molded without difficulty. Women are as easily influenced by high moral ideals and by examples of excellence, as they were liable to be corrupted by detrimental behavior. This writer, who seems to reflect a traditional perception of women as weaker than men in mind, body and even morally weaker, thought that it was of utmost importance which kind of education women are given.[173] Ibrahim 'Abd al-Qadir al-Mazini stated that despite assertions regarding the equality of men and women, and the need to grant women the same rights as men, one can not ignore the undeniable differences between them. Man's superiority is shown by his capacity for abstract reasoning, which explains, according to al-Mazini, why for example, women increasingly come to accept men's criteria for the judgment of beauty.[174]

A different male stance was expressed by Mustafa Lutfi al-Manfaluti (1876-1924), novelist and poet, who was also engaged in translation from European languages. Al-Manfaluti leveled sharp criticism against the "oriental" attitude of men towards women. While wondering whether a woman ever received a word of thanks from her husband for the happiness she brought him and the suffering she endured on his account, he wrote:

> We love her and have compassion for her, but this attitude is similar to a master's compassion for his slave. It is not the compassion of one friend for another ... Moreover, we entrust her with the duties of a governess, a woman-servant or a nursemaid, and in that we regard her as we regard our domestic animals ...[175]

In al-Manfaluti's view, when a woman equaled a man in knowledge and intelligence, he ought to treat her as an equal. On the other hand, he should act as a teacher to a pupil, or a father to his son, when her knowledge and intelligence did not match his, in order to help her reach his level.¹⁷⁶ Another intellectual argued that men, who by nature follow the course of knowledge and logic, find it difficult to understand women whose behavior is determined by emotion and instinct — which therefore causes women to appear to be enigmatic and mysterious creatures in the eyes of men. However, the same writer emphasized that the differences between men and women do not imply that women were inferior. According to him, it would be an unhealthy state of affairs if women were not to be equal to men, since it would mean a return to the barbaric period.¹⁷⁷ Dr. Mansur Fahmi said that psychological studies prove there to be differences between the natural characteristics of men and women. Notwithstanding, Fahmi evidently thought that none of these differences justify either superior rights for men, or an abuse of one sex by the other.¹⁷⁸ In fact, Fahmi views indicate a sort of modern perception; men and women are different, but yet equal.

Challenging women's seclusion
On women's veiling

Qasim Amin's revolutionary remonstration against the *hijab*, the veil, was more than defying of the use of cloth which masks women completely, and favoring instead a return to modest dress as ordained by Islam. His protest against the *hijab* actually also referred to its meaning as a barrier; so he also asked to gradually end the social seclusion suffered by women, established by the barrier created between the woman and the world beyond her home. As to the *hijab*, Amin maintained that *shari'a* did not oblige women to cover their face and hands. In his opinion, women who had to hide themselves from the eyes of men encountered difficulties in fulfilling their functions in society and safeguarding their rights. Wearing a veil would not in fact forestall temptation. On the contrary, the fact that a woman's face was covered and unidentifiable might encourage her to conduct herself in such manner as to rouse temptation. Furthermore, Amin protested against the notion that women were to be confined to their homes and prevented from social interactions with men. He did urge, however, that the removal of barriers between the two sexes be implemented in a gradual and controlled manner, accompanied by appropriate educational training of women, which would prepare them for the change. In this way, it would be possible to prepare young women to associate safely with men. Amin believed that the social seclusion imposed on Muslim women was akin to life imprisonment, which caused considerable harm to their intellect and health, and was responsible, in part, for their decline. The claim that this seclusion enabled a Muslim woman to preserve her chastity was totally rejected by Amin. He asserted that education alone constituted a guarantee for her moral behavior.[179] Indeed, Amin laid down a pioneering vision for liberating women; and unveiling women was a very significant pillar of that vision.

For the emerging feminist voice and movement of the turn of the twentieth century, the unveiling of women (*sufur*) soon became one of the significant standards that should be largely seen in a wider context of the feminist endeavor to undermine traditional seclusion of women, in particular, women of the upper class. The custom of veiling, which did not originate in Islamic law, was much more common among urban women, particularly among upper-class women, than among village women[180] — since poorer women in the cities, and most those in the villages, were required to work outside of home. It was therefore impossible to enforce face veiling on them. Surely, the idea of women's unveiling was also associated with the primary feminist agenda of advancing equality and rights. It is also likely that the protests against viewing a woman's image as an object of temptation were connected. Actually, it was Christian women from elite families who were the first to reveal their faces at the end of the nineteenth century. However, it seems that at this stage, the push for unveiling was not really an act of feminist protest, but an emulation of European fashion, through a process of Westernization.

But when Nabawiyya Musa and Huda Sha'rawi first unveiled their faces in public in 1923, it was a feminist statement. It was only during the 1920s and 1930s that many more Muslim women were encouraged to do it. Nabawiyya Musa and Huda Sha'rawi conceptually rejected women's veiling and denied attempts to justify this custom on moral and religious grounds. Still, Sha'rawi appeared to prefer gradual process of unveiling in the society, in preparation for this change.[181] Malak Hifni Nasif, on the other hand, did not call for unveiling and even rejected the notion. However, she clearly gave priority to carrying out a gradual reduction of women's social segregation, believing that there was a need to first strengthen women's self-confidence, through increasing education opportunities, while preparing the Egyptian society for such radical change. Nasif thought Egyptian society was not yet sufficiently enlightened to accept unveiling, since the *hijab* was a deeply rooted custom. It was also suggested that Nasif's rejection of unveiling could be explained by her nationalistic refusal to favor Westernized ideals and mere emulation of Western practices, styles, and modes of behavior, over what she considered as indigenous Egyptian priorities.[182]

The issue of the unveiling didn't remain untouched by the dominant male voices in the intellectual discourse. Ahmad Hassan al-Zayyat, who generally upheld traditional attitudes, opposed the view that veiling of the woman's face was a religious obligation and guarantees her chastity. In his opinion, veiling actually displayed a lack of religious faith and represented a sort of educational bankruptcy. Like Qasim Amin, al-Zayyat thought that education, rather than the *hijab*, assures that women would behave chastely.[183] Husayn al-Harawi, who also generally showed heightened respect to traditional values, supported the notion that Islam does not prohibit women to bare their face and hands. In his view, this demand pertained only to the wives of the Prophet Muhammad, and the question had been resolved, once and for all, by Amin's study *Tahrīr al Mar'a*.[184] Mubammad Zaki 'Abd al-Qadir, a lawyer, viewed the question of unveiling as belonging to the past Dark Ages. Despite removing her veil, a woman should be able to conduct herself in society with respect. However, al-Qadir was concerned about the growing emancipation of women, lest it lead to a decline in morality.[185]

Opposition to unveiling was also expressed. It was also argued, among other things, that unveiling by women indicated moral decline in the Egyptian society, and resulted in the weakening of faith.[186] Mustafa Sadiq al-Rafi'i, like Qasim Amin, considered the *hijab* as having dual meaning — i.e. a woman's veil and a barrier between men and women. However, in a sharp contrast, al-Rafi'i criticized unveiling. It seems that al-Rafi'i's opposition was largely motivated by defending traditional customs, mode of behavior and order. For him, the *hijab* constituted a symbol of good manners, balance, stability and religious spirit. Al-Rafi'i maintained that by the very nature of their birth, women were endowed with the traits embodied by the *hijab*, for example, their sensibilities. The *hijab* also safeguarded women's spirituality, increased their worth within society and, in fact, assured their genuine liberation. Women's abandonment of *hijab* constituted a surrender of their natural inclinations.[187]

On women's incorporation into the public sphere

Women in the Arab East were traditionally confined to the domestic sphere and their duties focused on taking care of the family and home. However, actually, it was by custom, not by Islamic law that a woman was prevented from coming into social contact with men who were not members of her family. The segregation of women from the company of men was considered to have great importance. Women were also prohibited from joining in communal activity, assuming public position, or appearing in the company of men.[188] Thus, along with the reformist call for unveiling, raised a demand for the entrance of women into the public sphere, and voicing against the taboos on social intercourse between the sexes (*ikhtilat*). This call was very closely connected with the emerging feminist voice and can be largely understood by the cluster of political, social, and economic developments that emerged during the interwar period. The changing reality succeeded in bringing more women, from both the upper and lower classes, to enter into the public sphere. The demand for the removal of the barriers between the sexes — among other things, by enabling mixed-gender social interactions — seemed to win substantial support within the intellectual discourse in Egypt during the interwar period. At the same time, it is evident that controlled, gradual reforms were preferred, either explicitly or implicitly, in order to prevent social, cultural and moral shock and upheavals. Indeed, the varied developments initiated during the interwar period that worked toward opening of the public sphere were relatively moderate, incremental and cautious. It seems that these advances were guided, to a certain degree, by prevailing traditionalist perceptions — such as the image of the distinctive role of women as wives and mothers. For example, women's entrance into educational institutions was largely justified by the interest to improve their morals and develop their functioning as mothers. In this context, the biological differences between men and women were also emphasized.[189]

Ahmad Hassan al-Zayyat strongly criticized the absence of women from Muslim society. He argued that this phenomenon produced a sense of monotony, an attitude of loathing towards work, introduced an aura of sadness into the home, as well as, vulgarity and anarchy within society as a whole.[190] Another intellectual put forward the argument that man-made restriction of women to their homes denied them of their right to enjoy God's wonders, which He had bestowed even on the lowliest insects.[191] The journalist Hafiz Mahmud expressed a clear desire to break down walls that isolate women. In a discussion on "erotic literature" (*al-adab al-makshuf*) and "chastity literature," (*al-adab al-mastur*) he wrote that the social changes that were taking place prevented a return to the self-deception that the woman represents the mystery of life, by possessing certain secrets. He added that there is no justification in continuing to deceive the woman by telling her that "her world by creation is placed far away from ours."[192] Dr. Ibrahim Naji (1898-1953) strove to eradicate the traditional concept that upheld distance and boundaries between the sexes. Thus, he opposed the imposing of "suppression" (*kabt*) by the traditional society on relationships between educated young men and women.[193]

The discussion on the status of women also reveals a concern over a crisis in the institution of family in Egypt. The following indicators were mentioned: poor relationships between husband and wife; an increasing rate of divorce, a growing phenomenon of bachelorhood and late marriages, and the increasing number of marriages to foreign women. In fact, Qasim Amin highlighted earlier indications of a crisis related to the Egyptian family. He complained about the absence of social contact between the sexes and the lack of opportunities for early acquaintances between them. Amin emphasized that marriage between young people should be based on their freedom of choice and mutual love, and not on an arrangement decided for them by others.[194] Malak Hifni Nasif, an early feminist voice, criticized the traditional Egyptian marriage system, maintaining that it was responsible for many instances of marital incompatibility and subsequent suffering. Hence, she stressed the importance of marriage based on love, and went even further, by arguing that it was preferable for young people to remain unmarried, than to enter into the bond of marriage without love, which might cause subsequent misery. However, Nasif rejected the possibility of free and continuous meetings between man and woman who were engaged to be married, and favored the presence of a chaperone in such cases.[195]

The understanding that the family structure and the institution of marriage in Egypt were undergoing a serious crisis also encouraged a discussion on social intercourse between men and women. Nazla al-Hakim Sa'id, who held degrees in philosophy and psychology from the University of London, rejected the widely accepted approach, which allowed social contact only out of utilitarian considerations, namely, finding a suitable partner for marriage. Perceived deterioration of family life, including growing hostility between husbands and wives, encouraged her to urge the introduction into Egyptian society of what she termed as "logical social intercourse" (*ikhtilat ma'qul*). In order to avoid shocking people with practices to which they were as yet unaccustomed, she insisted that the new ideas and concepts involved would be introduced gradually. Namely, both the state and the parents would carry the responsibility for paving the way through this education. Sa'id deemed it mandatory for the state to reinvigorate and modernize the educational system, in order to achieve this aim, including by the establishment of a co-educational system to replace the existing separate school system. Parents, for their part, should make efforts to transform the Egyptian home into a social meeting place. The husband was asked to transfer part of his outside activities into his home, in order to be involved with all his family's members. Children from different families would be brought together to spend their free time with one another, under parental guidance, in an atmosphere of mutual respect and with the modeling of good manners.[196] Another intellectual put forward a similar proposal to prepare children for married life — one involving the entire family — as an alternative to having them grow up in separate worlds, surrounded only by either men or women. He argued that modern co-educational schools had already proven successful in this direction, and moreover, that the extent to which co-education had brought about a decrease in existing sexual tension between pupils would serve to enhance morality on the whole.[197] He considered the traditional role played by the woman matchmaker (*khatiba*) in Egyptian society as another possible reason for the deterioration of family life. He also rejected a traditional practice, in which a young male who wished to get married would request the women of his family to engage the services of a professional "intermediary" (*wasfta*). According to him, women suffer more than men from these practices. While this arena had greatly improved for a lot of young men in Egypt, young Egyptian women had two courses open to them for expressing their emotions: reckless endangerment to the point of prostitution, or total restraint, which would rob them of the glow of youth. With an aim to better this situation and nullify the role of the "intermediary" in matchmaking, Hafiz Mahmud proposed that a special day be set aside for meetings between prospective couples, under parental supervision. Though such a procedure was contrary to tradition, it was preferable to the immorality and outrage involved in the use of an "intermediary," not to mention that it would enable the prospective mates to gain insights into each other and would help create ties of love between them.[198] Another intellectual saw the increasing number of divorces as a result of the selection of grooms for young women by their mothers or by matchmakers. Although he did not favor a circumstance in which an Egyptian young woman would enjoy the same social freedom in her relationships with young men as her European counterpart, he maintained that the possibility of the young Egyptian man to learn about the character of his chosen future wife prior to marriage formed a basic condition for their chances for marital success. Their relationship was to start within the circle of relatives and friends, whose morality was beyond doubt, and only later was this circle to be broadened gradually, since "a sudden change would undoubtedly cause a social upheaval with unavoidable risks and dangers."[199] Muhammad Zaki 'Abd al-Qadir, though not principally in opposition to social interactions between men and women, also insisted that its implementation be gradual and cautious. He argued that Egyptian maidens lacked the strong character of Western women and expressed concern, lest young Egyptian women "fall into sin" because of a premature involvement with men.[200] Another intellectual stated that no freedom of social intercourse should be allowed until "our state of mind undergoes a change. Furthermore, inherited jealousy and haughtiness amongst us should be avoided, so that when, for example, a man might see his wife dancing with another, he would not become furious."[201] This writer believed that the success of increasing social interaction was by no means certain and depended on the social environment. To test whether such social interactions would be suitable within Egyptian society, he advised gradual integration of educated women within the company of men. He added that in order to minimize the dangers for those liable to become victims of the greater freedom offered, it would be preferable for interaction between the two genders to be introduced during childhood.[202]

Alongside with the encouragement of removal of the traditional barrier between men and women, also opposite views are unfolded. [203] There is no wonder that Mustafa Sadiq al-Rafi'i, who was a prominent and decisive defender of tradition, was one of those who spoke out against the attempt to remove the barrier dividing between the sexes. In his view, a woman keeping company with men would naturally be courting temptation and lust.[204] Another intellectual emphasized that social intercourse between the sexes was not a new invention at all, but, was in fact, an ancient error: it cultivated a plague that produced many victims, and therefore, should be eradicated before it spread any further.[205] Sayyid Qutb was of the opinion that the freedom of social intercourse between men and women was responsible for the "marital crisis" in modern society. Qutb did not deny that social intercourse between men and women facilitated the chances to come to mutual understanding and love, but maintained that love encouraged in this manner was both weak and shallow. Social intercourse, in his view, also diminished the excitement and anticipation preceding marriage, thereby causing a loss of interest in forming a permanent union. Moreover, social intercourse between the sexes went accompanied by moral corruption, especially in Egypt, where this social process had only just begun.[206] In answer to the argument that moral corruption did not spread in the Egyptian villages, where women were not forbidden to mix with men and were required to cover their faces, Qutb stressed the socio-moral differences between village and city life. In his opinion, such arguments ignored the fact that the society outside of the urban areas was naturally immune to moral corruption; whereas the unnatural turbulence and chaos that characterized urban life made such immunity impossible.[207] Another intellectual sought to support his opposition to the removal of barriers between the sexes by putting forward the differences existing between East and West. He argued that if indeed morality and ethics in the West permitted social intercourse between the sexes, this did not mean that the same would apply in the East, since its people breathed different air and were nourished on different food.[208] Very rare female voices joined the opposition to free social intercourse between the sexes. Amina Ahmad Taha was among these very exceptional female voices; she advocated for a termination of the demand for social intercourse in Egypt, while it was still possible to nip the problem in the bud. Taha maintained that the integration of men and women "would bring back to the primeval period when humans lived like animals among trees in the jungle."[209]

Education and employment of women

From the outset of the feminist movement in the West it was widely understood that providing women with equal opportunity in education and employment was a primary precondition for reforming the status of women and their rights. This assessment was also strongly shared by advocates of women's rights in Egypt. The ignorance of Egyptian women was conceived as a primary reason for their age-old inferiority. Hence, from the very outset of public discourse on this issue, calls to expand educational and employment opportunities for women were clearly evident. These calls were largely associated with expectations to enlarge women's circle of activity, beyond the confines of the home, and to enable all women, family, society and the country, to benefit from the abilities of women. Along with his reformist vision, Qasim Amin had raised arguments demonstrating both the damage, which resulted from women's ignorance and the benefits that would be derived from their education. Women's ignorance actually led to a loss of one half of the country's production capacity, which damaged the Egyptian economy. The education of women, while providing them with an ethical basis to guarantee their chastity, would also insure that the single woman, the divorcee or the widow, could support themselves, instead of becoming a dependent on others, liable to succumb to unethical, immoral practices. Although Amin did not demand equality of opportunity, other than in the field of education, he did insist that women be trained in the arts and sciences, as well as in subjects, which would prepare them for their roles as good wives and mothers.[210]

Malak Hifni Nasif, whose breakthrough writing inspired many female thinkers, scholars and activists, went further than Amin by proposing that elementary education be made compulsory and that high-school education be made available for all women. She wanted opportunities for women to study the sciences and even proposed the establishment of a medical school for women, whose standards would be equal to the schools training male doctors. With respect to those who contended that women did not require a wider education, she answered that knowledge in itself paves the way towards wisdom, and was important as such, irrespective of the question of whether or not the knowledge gained was later put to practical use.[211] Nabawiyya Musa, a pioneer of women's education in Egypt, and a very dedicated educator, stated that the needs of women for study, education and knowledge were not different from those of men, and moreover, the means for enhancing their knowledge is identical — a fact ignored by those who advocated separate educational systems for men and women. Furthermore, elementary and high schools basically aim to provide general education. Since motherhood is a professional specialization, no different from that of medicine or law, it is inconceivable that the primary stage of providing general education would be neglected in a woman's education. Hence, viewing women as independent individuals,

Musa maintained that they should be given the same opportunities as men to prepare themselves for life, in general, and to select professions which suited their capabilities, in specific. Granting Egyptian women advanced education would prevent a situation in which the riches of Egyptian society would fall into the hands of foreign women who occupied positions as yet unattainable for Egyptian women. Musa looked upon society as a body, the limbs and organs of which were made up equally of men and women: for proper functioning of the whole body these all needed to be equally strong. The ignorance of Egyptian women was, therefore, harmful to the nation as a whole. It also encouraged young Egyptian men to marry foreign women who, unfamiliar with Egyptian society, instilled in their offspring an attitude of hatred towards Egypt, which caused them to feel alienation and contempt for their native land. Through equal education, unmarried Egyptian women should be given an opportunity to earn an honorable living, be accorded with respect, and attain a status that would not involve moral vulnerability.[212] Asma Fahmi, who shared the feminist perception of gender equality, argued that there was no difference between the intelligence of men and women, and it was therefore essential for Egyptian women to benefit equally from the advantages of higher education. She expressed sorrow regarding the reluctance of Egyptian leaders to accept the notion of equal education for both genders as a basic principle for genuine progress. According to Fahmi, women's need for advanced education was even more acute than that of men, since the women had the added disadvantage of their initial deficit in educational development, as a result of the deprivation they suffered within the confines of their homes, in the absence of social intercourse between the genders. Those who feared the threat of competition by women as a consequence of improving their education proffered a purely selfish argument, i.e. considering only a man's viewpoint. Fahmi conceded that granting women advanced education would cause a decrease in the birth rate, but the benefit of educated mothers would provide a cultural advantage, which outweighed this danger.[213]

A more mild reformist approach that demonstrates a less egalitarian stance unfolds through the male voices. Muhammad Shafiq Ghurbal (1894-1961) argued that since the social system underwent continuous change, it was erroneous to think that the current division of labor would remain static. The number of women obliged to seek work increased with each passing year. Although Ghurbal based his views on educational and psychological studies conducted in the West, he saw no contradiction in maintaining equal, but separate, educational systems that suit the natural social needs of each sex. However, Ghurbal thought that the differences between the two systems should find expression only in the proportion of hours devoted to vocational training and methodology.[214] According to another writer, the sole aim of educating women was to provide them with the means, whereby, they could fulfill their tasks as mothers — including taking care of their children's education; as in this way Egypt's prestige would be elevated. This writer further asserted that education should provide women with a sense of their "feminine obligations" and knowledge of their household functions.[215] Another intellectual, who taught at Dar al-'Ulum, claimed that for quite objective reasons, it was foolish to foist a uniform program of education on both sexes, since they differed physically and intellectually. To his thinking, co-education was invalid, since education was meant to prepare young people to fulfill their natural functions and improve their inborn abilities.[216] Sayyid Qutb, who welcomed the improvement in women's education, expressed the view that the objective of such education was not mere learning, but to forge an adjustment toward women's "natural" functions, those for which she had been created. Qutb clearly sought to base his position on practical and social considerations. Though he was not opposed to uniform education for all within a co-educational system in principle, he thought that Egyptian society was not yet ripe to assimilate such innovations. Comparing the limited labor market in Egypt with the European one, Qutb explained that since Egypt was already unable to provide sufficient work opportunities for its educated men, the entry of women into men's jobs would only increase unemployment. Qutb noted that the market of "female" occupations was open to Egyptian women, but that currently only foreign women were employed in these positions. If the labor market were to expand to provide work for all men seeking jobs, and, if at the same time, fewer jobs would be made available to women, Qutb would have no objection to the unification of study programs for both sexes.[217]

Also very limited, exceptional female support for traditional perceptions about gender roles could be found in the discussion on education. Thus, a woman wrote that education should prepare young people for functions determined by society. Hence, the young woman whose function differed from a man's, required a different education, and her curriculum should include child psychology, economics and home-making rather than mechanics, trigonometry and stereometry. This woman insisted it was not her intention to thwart those women who desired to pursue advanced studies, but that it was necessary to draw a clear distinction between those preparing themselves for careers in medicine or law, and the vast majority of Egyptian women who were expected to be "soldiers" in the service of society, working to elevate the level of the Egyptian family and home.[218]

The call to reform women's education, including perceptions regarding gender equality in education, went hand-in-hand with another feminist demand — i.e. the call for advancing women's opportunities in employment. The increasing involvement of European women during the First World War, in what were until then considered exclusively male occupations, also stimulated demands to encourage a similar socio-economic development in Egypt. The historian Muhammad 'Abdallah 'Inan noted with approval, how European women had entered a variety of fields, which had previously been closed to them, as a consequence of the war. Nevertheless, he thought that they still had a long way to go.[219] Nabawiyya Musa maintained that the integration of women into fields of general employment was mandatory for the nation. She contended that women possessed the same capacity for work as men and, as Malak Hifni Nasif had already argued before the First World War, she stressed the need to train female doctors. According to Musa, the war had changed women's image. Young Egyptian women could not ignore the reality realized by their European peers — i.e. that the modern woman was no longer a mere plaything, but a serious-minded and hard-working individual, capable of competing with men in the sphere of public professions. Her emphasis on the need to provide Egyptian women with advanced education was meant also to enable them to fulfill functions, which so far, had been executed only by foreign women.[220]

At the same time, both women and men adopted a cautious approach, lest changes in women's employment have a negative impact on the family. Some strove to find compromises, and also suggested that in the field of general employment, meaning, outside the home, women could find "appropriate" employment. Even Nabawiyya Musa, though being committed advocate of women's rights, insisted that after marriage women should cease to work outside their home, in order to dedicate themselves to the tasks of family life. In her view, it was unnatural and harmful for her children if the responsibility for financially supporting the family rested on the woman; while it was similarly inconceivable that the husband should be entrusted with the supervision over their children's education.[221] Nazla al-Hakim Sa'id remonstrated against the view that general employment was the exclusive domain of men. She stated that just as — apart from pregnancy and childbearing — women could not claim any form of monopoly over their children, men had no right to monopolize the field of general employment.[222] However, she sought to lend greater attraction and depth to the instruction of "feminine' subjects" in girls' school. In her opinion, the poor manner in which such courses were taught had a negative effect, causing the Egyptian girl to neglect her feminine tendencies and characteristics. She also proposed the establishment of institutions to advance learning beyond high school, in which the emphasis would be on the more "feminine" sciences.[223] Even Dr. Suheir al-Qalamawi (1911-1997), a significant feminist activist, who was among the first women to attend the Egyptian University, and who later became a prominent novelist and scholar of Arabic literature, glorified women's chief functions as wife and mother, companion and homemaker. Al-Qalamawi stressed the great importance of these functions for the Egyptian society and the Egyptian nation and strove to have them considered areas of specialization, which required extensive preparation. Women who did not bear the burden of motherhood should, in her view, become an important component in the "peace-time corps", contributing to the revival of Egypt in the various areas open to them, whereby she primarily suggested the fields of education, health and charity.[224]

Some intellectuals, mostly men, even expressed suspicions and were critical of the approach calling for substantial gender equality in the field of employment. Opposition toward women entering the field of general employment away from home had also been observed. This opposition reflected certain conservative motives and even patriarchal, as well as male chauvinist attitudes. Sayyid Qutb held motherhood as the Egyptian woman's primary function. Nevertheless, if a woman had to leave the family home in order to work, he insisted that she be involved in "feminine" occupations, such as education or nursing. However, Qutb did not reject the integration of the Egyptian woman of the future into the various fields of general employment, provided that changed conditions made that integration possible.[225] In discussions on the revolution caused by the First World War regarding the general employment of women, Qutb maintained that the main cause of it lay not in women's desire for competition with men, or their craving for independence, but was primarily motivated by their natural instinct to arouse the admiration of men and to be at their side. Since modern times required more mental than physical work and since employment in modern society often meant that men would be away from home for the greater part of the day. Thus, according to Qutb, women find their entry into employment field, outside home, as a way, adapted to the modern circumstances, for staying within hearing and vision range of menfolk.[226] Concern for the traditional family system and the wife's central role in it echoed strongly in the views of Mustafa Sadiq al-Rafi'i, who basically insisted that the barriers between women and the outside world be preserved. It appears that according to al-Rafi'i these barriers largely contribute to women's excellence as mothers.[227] Husayn al-Harawi argued that the entry of women into the general workforce, and the propagation of their image as equal to men in every occupation, constituted an injustice — i.e., when a woman would come to fulfill a man's position, the family fortress would crumble and leave the husband without his responsibility towards the survival of his family.[228] Another intellectual expressed a wish that an "insurmountable dam" be erected between women and work outside their homes, since they could find sufficient occupation by managing the household. According to him, for those women left without financial support, the Ministry of Education should take responsibility and train them in professions within the field of "feminine" tasks, e.g. medical care for women, caring sick and disabled people, educational or domestic work.[229] Ahmad Hassan al-Zayyat argued that it was not his intention to see young Egyptian women wield an axe, carry a hammer, busy herself with trading, or even sit in judgment. Rather, than having her pushed into the flames of life's furnace, "I wish that she be granted her natural freedom within the confines of her natural work..."[230] Muhammad Lutfi Jum'a (1886–1953) conditioned women's emancipation upon limiting their partnership with men in the world of trade and profession to cases where there was an urgent necessity to ensure the family's survival.[231]

From a wider historical perspective on the achievements of the women's emancipation process in Arab lands, including in Egypt, it is evident that the changes in the position of urban women in economic life has been incomparably slower and met with many more obstacles than the spread of education among these women.[232] Indeed, reforms in the area of education were a "flagship" of the feminist struggle of earlier decades of the twentieth century. Interestingly, the asymmetry between significant, growing educational opportunities for women in the modern era and the hurdles they met with in the field of employment is also raised within the discussed intellectual discourse. Basically, the need to reform education for women was not in dispute; the debate chiefly revolved around the nature of the education that women should receive. On the other hand, reforms of women's employment met concern and reservations, even by women. A fear of undermining the traditional division of gender roles and the negative implications on the family life was clearly evident. Consequently, the common understanding about the significance of women's functions as mothers and home makers encouraged demands for expanding their functional educational opportunities, and less so for their full integration in the general employment market.

CHAPTER FOUR
Tradition and Change: Debate on linguistic reform

Arabic language moves to the center stage of public discourse

Since the nineteenth century, questions related with the Arabic language started to move to the center of the public discourse in general, and of the intellectual sphere, in particular. The root causes for this process were diversified and often overlapped with each other. The modern encounter and increased contact between Muslim societies in the Middle East and Western civilization since the turn of the nineteenth century, also seriously challenged the former on the linguistic level. Arabic has been deeply considered as a sacred language by Muslim societies and the Qura'n has been believed to have been revealed to the Prophet Muhammad in Arabic. In addition, the Arabic language has remained in the Muslim collective memory as significant cultural vehicle that enabled Muslims in the "Golden Era" of the Islamic civilization to provide the world with philosophy, sciences, including mathematics, astronomy, medicine, as well as prolific literature. However, in sharp contrast, since the nineteenth century, Muslim societies in the Middle East found themselves in a strikingly inferior position; as they faced the victorious armies of Europe, with its superiority in the sciences and technology, along with challenging modern institutions, values, concepts and modes of behavior. Ayman A. El-Desouky clearly portrayed this new challenging reality, referring to the entire project of al-Nahda:

> The encounter was also with a new epistemological horizon that demands new modes of expression, a different relation to language and to the self, and grounds the struggle for acquiring a new voice.[233]

Local elites were eager to acquire the "tempting" novelties of the Western civilization and to emulate them. But soon they found that their own language, or more precisely the language of literary Arabic (*fusha*), which was highly esteemed by them as rich and productive, was rendered dysfunctional under conditions of the modern civilization commencing rapidly across their lands. In other words, Arabic was found to be incapable of transmitting modern terms, concepts, and ideas in diversified fields from the European languages, and to properly incorporate and internalize them. Hence, since the second half of the nineteenth century, growing efforts to make literary Arabic more suitable and effective to address the needs of the modern world can be observed. The substantial developments in the field of printing, the expansion of the printed media, together with the increased number of consumers of such media, as a result of the broadening of educational institutions, further sharpened the understanding of the need to simplify literary Arabic, and to do away with linguistic prerogatives held by a small group of educated people. Rising nationalism, known as the "national revival," that was largely triggered by the British colonial occupation of Egypt in 1882, also played a very significant role in bringing the Arabic language to the center of attention within educated elites. In addition, since the turn of the twentieth century, the idea of reforming or modernizing the Arabic language was also strongly linked to efforts in Egypt to form territorial national identity, including the creating of Egyptian national literature. Hence, there was strong motivation to make Arabic a national language that could both serve effectively to form and articulate national identity, and be instrumental for communication and expression in modern life. It was also believed that through linguistic reform, the Arabic language would also compete successfully with "linguistic colonialism" — namely, the success of European languages, as part of the growing Westernization, to strengthen their foothold, particularly amongst elites. Efforts to strengthen the status of the Arabic language, including through linguistic reform, can also be seen in the context of the decline of the Ottoman Empire; its disintegration triggered clashes between emerging Arab nationalism and Ottoman identity — including linguistic tension in Arab-speaking lands within the Empire — notwithstanding the fact that it was the Ottoman Turkish language, rather than Arabic, that was the official language of Egypt until the early 1870s.[234] Other historical threads lead to al-Nahda, the cultural Renaissance in the Arab-speaking lands of the Ottoman Empire, in which Egypt, and Cairo in particular, played highly significant role. Naturally, al-Nahda, which began in mid-nineteenth century, was largely marked by the flourishing of literary and journalist production, a development that also triggered debates regarding language. The significant role played during this era by Syrian-Lebanese emigrants, who were well educated and French-speaking, also sustained the linguistic debate in Egypt.

It was not only literary Arabic (*al-fusha*) that was largely discussed then; it was also spoken Egyptian colloquial Arabic (*al-'ammiyya*), along with the relationship between those languages and literary Arabic and linguistic reform also became a theme for intellectual debate at the turn of the twentieth century. Again, these debates can partly be seen in a wider Middle Eastern context, related to the disintegration of the Ottoman Empire.[235] In fact, difficulties posed by literary Arabic, which had remained unchanged and static for so many centuries, were among the main reasons for directing attention to the colloquial language in Egypt. Being a "living" language, there were those who expected the spoken Egyptian dialect to offer some solutions. Additionally, diverse, even controversial, ideas were expressed about the need to bridge the gap between the literary Arabic used by a small circle of learned people and the colloquial Arabic, which served the masses. Particularly strong motivations to discuss the colloquial language seems to emerge in the context of the already mentioned intensive efforts in Egypt to shape national identity, more precisely to form Egyptian territorial nationalism, at the turn of the twentieth century and during the interwar period. Significant efforts were involved in the development of a distinctive Egyptian literature, or national literature, to be distinguished from Arabic literature, a much wider category of literature that was produced in the entire Arabic-speaking regions. Thus, through their literary texts, contemporaneous Egyptian writers sought to express the local particularity of Egypt, including its milieu, in particular the Nile Valley, as well as the "personality" and "spirit" of the country. Their writing also involved ideas about the Egyptianization of the language (*tamsir al-lughah*), including a blending of the colloquial spoken dialect of Egypt with formal Arabic language. Ideas of adopting the colloquial language as a medium for literature were also raised. Even certain radical ideas of replacement, or partial replacement, of the written literary Arabic with the spoken colloquial language were discussed. Such suggestions, that were very controversial in the intellectual, literary discourse of that time, also triggered calls to reform the colloquial language, including through standardization of it. Prominent in this search for achieving rapprochement between the standard literary language and the colloquial one was Ahmad Lutfi al-Sayyid, a leading advocate of both liberal political ideas and the Egyptian territorial identity, during the early decades of the twentieth century.[236]

Obviously, the debate on linguistic reform, the same as the major conceptual, social and cultural themes of that time, had not been left untouched by the tension between tradition and modernity. In this case, it was a conflict between two opposing paradigms that loomed, either explicitly or implicitly, through the arguments brought into the discussion on linguistic reform or modernization; a religious-traditionalist paradigm versus a modern rationalist, functional one. The rigid religious-traditionalist approach was based on a strong belief in Arabic as a divinely inspired, sacred language, given by God in a perfect form; i.e., Arabic is God's creation. Hence, since Arabic is perceived as being very tightly connected with Islam, it is believed to be a holy, uniform, immutable language and its purity, based on the Qur'an and classical Arabic literature, should be strictly preserved.[237] Obviously, zealous advocates of such a view in Egypt of the turn of twentieth century and interwar period rejected calls for linguistic reform, believing in the perfectness and sacredness of the Arabic language, and fearing, lest reforms impair its purity. In sharp contrast, the modern, rationalist-functionalist paradigm, or approach, indicated a motivation to adapt literary Arabic to the needs of the modern world, with little regard for tradition. Advocates of this approach were largely inspired by the secular Darwinian notion of evolution, in contrast to the religious-traditionalist perception of creation. For them, the language was a living organism, a social artifact, and a medium of communication for human needs. As such, Arabic, the same as other languages, should be capable of continuous changes and adaption the modern era; in other words, language is a sociological, rather than historical phenomenon.[238]

Strong aspirations for linguistic reform

Tension between the religious-traditionalist perspective and the rationalist-functionalist approach echoed also into the intellectual discourse of interwar Egypt. However, though the dominant voice showed strong commitment to literary Arabic as a pivotal traditional, cultural asset, the majority also shared a strong understanding of the challenges faced by literary Arabic in the modern era. Consequently, they gathered around a consensus over the need for linguistic reforms of a balanced and cautious nature; as a 'People of the Pen' they were equipped with a very sensitive linguistic seismograph, let alone that they were well aware of the particular difficulties concerning the ability of Arabic to keep pace with the modern civilization, as compared to European languages. At the same time, intellectuals expressed their confidence in the ability of literary Arabic to transform into an efficient, capable linguistic medium of the modern era. Hassan al-Sharif argued that Arabic was a rich, robust language, capable of conveying any thought, feeling and emotion, reliably and accurately and that its current inability to provide words for modem technological terminology is not an inherent limitation in it. Rather, Arabic users had "halted its growth at the point reached by the forefathers…and made no advances to keep pace with modern thought as it developed and progressed."[239] However, this shortcoming was only temporary and would disappear when Arabic would free itself from the current stultifying, reactionary trend inhibiting it.[240] Mansur Fahmi thought that Arabic contained elements of weakness and exhaustion (*inhilal*) [241] 'Abd al-Qadir Hamza (1878–1941) emphasized that the development of Arabic had ceased about 600 years earlier, at the time when Arab civilization entered its stage of "demise" (*ihtidar*) and that this lack of movement forward had transformed the Arabic language "into a relic of the past, incapable of keeping pace with a period marked by airplanes and electricity…"[242] Dr. 'Ali Mustafa Musharrafa proudly pointed out the contemporary rebirth of literary Arabic, after a period of hundreds of years during which, in his view, it had been remote from any contact with realms of literature, philosophy and science. Musharrafa praised the ability of literary Arabic to serve as a medium for writing and teaching in a modern civilization. However, he argued that the gulf between literary Arabic and its environment had still not been bridged. Literary Arabic was incapable of expressing many meanings. People sensed this weakness, particularly when dealing with technical and scientific material.[243] Sheikh 'Abd al-'Aziz al-Bishri held that despite a process of revival, Arabic was still incapable of fulfilling the demands of the modern sciences.[244] Ahmad Khaki, who graduated from Dar al-'Ulum in Cairo, studied in the University of Exeter, served in Ministry of Education, and wrote books for teaching English, argued that Arabic was a traditional language that had turned its back on foreign expressions and lacked the flexibility to absorb novel concepts.[245] Similarly, the physician and philologist Dr. Ahmad 'Isa (1878-1946) asserted that what had been stated about the backwardness of Arabic and its alleged lack of growth was just not correct. According to 'Isa, what had languished and lagged behind were the Arabic speakers: "They have stagnated in science, declined in their capacity to understand, fallen behind in industry and it was this which caused the lack of progress in their language."²⁴⁶ To provide clear, decisive proof of the capacity of the Arabic to also be used for modern scientific purposes, the Golden Age of the Islamic civilization was mentioned. It was argued that during that flourishing period, the Arabic language served as a stable and widely used scientific language. Thus, Dr. Muhammad Sharaf (1890–1949), a physician and philologist, spoke of the richness of Arabic, and its proven ability to serve scholars in philosophy, science, history and law. Sharaf regarded the historical precedent as testimony for the ability of the Arabic language to serve scientific needs in modern times, as well.²⁴⁷ Similarly, another intellectual rejected allegations of the weaknesses in literary Arabic, emphasizing that the Arabic language could keep pace with any development, whatever form it might take. To him, it was inconceivable that a language, which had previously absorbed Greek, Roman, Syrian, Indian and Chinese civilizations, could not also absorb modern civilization.²⁴⁸

Interestingly, the rationalist, functionalist, communicative paradigm was clearly insinuated into the debate on linguistic reform; it was one of insightful signs of the time that should obviously be seen in the context of Westernization. Thus, this modernist perception of language, largely inspired by the Darwinian-oriented concept of the language as a living organism, had a clear imprint on contemporaneous Egyptian intellectuals. Muhammad Amin Wasif maintained that language was a "living creature" (*ka'in hayy*), subject to the laws of evolution.²⁴⁹ 'Ali Mustafa Musharrafa agreed and asserted: "Where harmony exists, the creature becomes stronger, increases and grows. Where incongruity exists, it stagnates and diminishes."²⁵⁰ In opposition to those who maintained conservative linguistic postures (whom he labeled the "*hanbali group*") and bowed to the alleged supremacy of the earlier generations (*al-*

salaf), Muḥammad Sharaf asserted that language had not been created in one instant, but had developed gradually, in accordance with the changing circumstance. Consequently, there was no turning away from acceptance of the growth and expansion generated in a language, since it bears the responsibility for clarifying every new thought or sensation. Language, he added, was like any other living organism that could grow.[251] In this spirit, Sharaf censured those who sought to bring the Arabic language back to the past, thereby accepting its alleged stultification, locking the gates of *ijtihad* (individual and independent theological reasoning), and linguistic creativity.[252] Hafiz Mahmud complained about the unsuitability of the fundamental principles of Arabic to the "law of motion" (*namus al-haraka*) that controls the universe. Similarly, Mahmud sought to emphasize the communicative aspect of the language. In his view, language was a means for the understanding and exchanging of ideas; and as such, it should not exhibit any deficiencies in the expression of notions and concepts.[253] The evolutionary and communicative aspects of the Arabic language are also salient in the thinking of Ibrahim 'Abd al-Qadir al-Mazini. In his view, the Arabic language — any language — is no more than an instrument for transmitting meanings, pictures, feelings, or needs from one mind to another, and from one soul to another.[254] Therefore, those living in modern times, but writing in ancient patterns, without any alteration to show the influence of those times, resemble monuments, rather than living people. Even if everything belonging to the past were worthy of praise, it would still be inconceivable that language should be incapable of rendering descriptions of new life styles and thoughts.[255] Ahmad Khaki argued that language serves as evidence of advancement in thought, since it is the means by which ideas and understanding crystallize. It is evident that Khaki regarded the utility of the communicative function of language as the criterion by which its value is assessed. Furthermore, a language's capacity to express even the subtlest ideas and to describe all possible thoughts is a form of proof of the way it keeps pace with intellectual progress.²⁵⁶ 'Abd al-Qadir Hamza also shared the opinion that language was a means, rather than an end. For Hamza, the transfer of thoughts and knowledge was one of the important functions of language; and the simpler the language, the easier it would be for that to be accomplished.²⁵⁷ Similarly, Hassan al-Sharif considered language to be, first and foremost, an instrument. Therefore, it was imperative for language to be simple and convenient to use. The main objective of language, continued Sharif, was to make mutual understanding possible; this could be accomplished by introducing simple means for comprehension and memorization.²⁵⁸

Literary and colloquial Arabic – A cautious approach

Between the two World Wars, the Christian Coptic intellectual, Salama Musa, stood out among advocates of radical modernism in Egypt. He too questioned the capacity of literary Arabic to serve as the sole writing medium, largely due to that difficulty involved in its study and its inability to satisfy literary and scientific needs. Musa even stated that Arabic was a Bedouin language, which could hardly function in an advanced civilization, such as the contemporary society. Consequently, Musa urged a narrowing of the gap between literary and colloquial Arabic, by having the latter influence the former. In his view, colloquial Arabic was preferable to literary Arabic, and even surpassed it in for use in fulfilling literary objectives. Nevertheless, Musa asserted that the stage at which the colloquial language could be used exclusively as a literary medium had not yet arrived. Therefore, he favored a "compromise" (*taswiya*) between literary Arabic and colloquial Arabic, which he sought to achieve through the broad use of expressions drawn from colloquial Arabic for writing purposes, and through the abolition of the desinential inflection (*i'rab*). As a substitute for the inflectional system, one of the most striking characteristics of literary Arabic, Musa was prepared to accept one involving vocalization of word-endings by the *sukun*, a diacritic that marks the absence of a vowel after the consonant.²⁵⁹ Another prominent radical modernist, Dr. Isma'il Ahmad Adham, appealed to the Egyptian people on grounds of distinctive national Egyptian identity, imploring them to abandon literary Arabic:

> "Leave literary Arabic, for in your colloquial language you possess a national language. Improve it and determine rules for its use. Liberate yourselves from the yoke of literary Arabic and its control over you."²⁶⁰

The attempt by radical Egyptian reformists to undermine the traditional status of literary Arabic or, alternatively, to imprint colloquial Arabic on to it, met with strong opposition from intellectuals belonging to the group under study. Intellectual opposition to incorporating colloquial Arabic into literary Arabic was chiefly motivated by the following positions: adherence to a traditional perception that the language of the Qur'an formed the ideal model for Arabic; belief in linguistic purity and insistence upon an unbroken link between Islam and literary Arabic; rejection of the idea of a distinctive Egyptian nationalism and consequently a fear, lest the mark left by colloquial Arabic on the literary language might impair the unity of Arabic, a pre-condition for shaping a national Arabic identity; and finally, a questioning of the suitability of colloquial Arabic to address the needs of modern writing, since as a language rich in dialects, Arabic lacked unity and fixed linguistic patterns. Mustafa Sadiq al-Rafi'i, who adhered to the traditional concept concerning the *i'jaz* inherent in the Qur'an, namely its inimitable uniqueness in both content and form,²⁶¹ totally rejected the attempt to Egyptianize literary Arabic. Al-Rafi'i insisted that the language of the Qur'an had shaken off all dialects by selecting the dialect of the Quraysh. He argued that Islam opposes "native tribalism" (*'asabiyya wataniyya*), and that Egyptianization represented one of its manifestations. In his view, anyone advocating for the Egyptianization of Arabic was equally obliged to advocate the absurd idea of an Egyptianization of Islam. In addition, he also rejected Egyptianizing literary Arabic on purely linguistic grounds: the colloquial language was unsuitable for writing, since it was devoid of definite structure and meter. Furthermore, colloquial Egyptian is an undefined linguistic phenomenon, which includes a large number of dialects subject to quick changes and unclear influences.[262] Al-Rafi'i also complained about the domination of the colloquial language in writing in Egypt, particularly in journalism, while he regretted the neglect of Arabic rhetoric (*balagha*). In his view, the source of colloquial Arabic was to be found in the reckless, irresponsible spirit sweeping through modern civilization.[263] 'Abd al-Qadir Hamza held that literary Arabic, rather than colloquial Arabic, should serve as the language for the Egyptian novel, since education, study and the acquisition of knowledge were its primary objectives. He argued that these aims contradicted the nature of colloquial language, which was in effect "street language," rather than book language. The function of writers was to elevate the public to a genuine literary level, rather than descend to the level of colloquial language.[264] Muhammad Lutfi Jum'a emphasized literary Arabic as one of the cornerstones of Arabic civilization. Jum'a asserted that the obligation to keep this language sacrosanct and protect it stemmed from its religious foundation. The view that the colloquial language simplified writing was totally rejected by Jum'a, as was the claim that the colloquial language was easier to understand, on the grounds that the large number of dialects gave rise to misunderstandings even between people of different regions within Egypt. A person speaking literary Arabic can travel from one Arab country to another and understand its inhabitants, "but if he makes use of the colloquial dialect, he will, perforce, be enmeshed in difficulty."[265] In the view of another intellectual, the expressive capacity of literary Arabic surpassed that of colloquial Arabic. Those attempting to transform colloquial Arabic into a medium for the arts and sciences are in error. Literary Arabic is a sufficiently rich language for the purposes required by science and provides prolific means for expressing

Western culture.[266] The way to bridge the gap between the spoken-language used by students and their written language involved the inclusion of literary expressions learned at school into their spoken language, which came to replace colloquial expressions.[267]

Novelist and playwright, Muhmud Taymur (1894-1973), who in the 1920s, at the very outset of his literary career, stood out among the pioneers using colloquial Egyptian in their writings,[268] also joined the ranks of defenders of literary Arabic. In an article published in 1933, Taymur assessed the benefits to be gained by employing the colloquial language for everyday needs. In his opinion, the colloquial language was a natural language, subject to the "law of progress," undergoing changes each day and keeping pace with life, which included discoveries and inventions. Attempts to employ colloquial language in writing raised difficulties. Nevertheless, Taymur asserted that over the course of time, colloquial Arabic would become a worthy vehicle for writing. While citing the virtues of colloquial Arabic, Taymur attempted to defend the status of literary Arabic, including expressing faith in its religious and national worth. In his view, literary Arabic was indispensable for understanding the Qur'an and its directives. The Qur'an, asserted Taymur, was the miracle (*mu'jiza*) of Arabic. Preserving literary Arabic was a national obligation, since it formed the strong link, which united the Arab countries. It was also a historic obligation, since the abandonment of the language of the forefathers was similar to forgetting history and constituted a denial of the power of the past. Abandoning literary Arabic was, in effect, a defilement of something sacred (*hurma*). Faithful to his anxiety to ensure the continuation of literary Arabic on the one hand, and conscious of the advantages inherent in the use of colloquial Arabic of the other, Taymur stated that it was necessary to strengthen both — i.e. the literary language for spiritual needs and the colloquial language for material ones. In Taymur's opinion the "modern colloquial language" (*lugha 'ammiyya hadidtha*) would become the language of the future — meaning, colloquial Arabic would become the official language for daily correspondence (*mukatabat*) and conversation, whereas the literary language would remain the language of writing.[269]

Loyalty to literary Arabic was also advocated by Dr. Ahmad Dayf (1880-1945), who is deemed to be among the pioneers of Egyptian national literature.[270] Differing from radical modernists, who strove to abandon literary Arabic in its current form, Ahmad Dayf asserted the following: "All we ask is that we maintain an Egyptian-Arabic literature; Egyptian in its subjects and knowledge, Arabic in its language, rhetoric and styles."[271] In Dayf's view, it was necessary to be zealous regarding Arabic and its literature, just as the Europeans demonstrated zeal for Latin and Greek, which constituted the basis of their knowledge and the treasure house that constitutes the secret of their civilization. He argued that no one should be admonished for manifesting such zeal toward Arabic, since no one could deny the imprint of Arabic civilization on the Muslim world.[272] Ibrahim 'Abd al-Qadir al-Mazini, who made limited use of colloquial Arabic in his literary writing,[273] rejected the possibility of it becoming the written language. In his view, a colloquial language could become a language of writing, only if it lent itself to correction and improvement — i.e. if it could be structured with permanent rules and if it could be removed from the state of disorder, which normally characterized colloquial languages. Colloquial Arabic, in its current state could, in his view, serve only as a medium of expression for everyday matters. It could not become the language of writing, because it lacked a uniform structure and also because it included an unwieldy mixture of dialects. In contrast to literary Arabic, the colloquial language was unstable. At the same time, al-Mazini supported the idea of a gradual and controlled absorption of vocabulary from colloquial Arabic into literary Arabic. This notion, which had started to gain supporters before the First World War, differs from that of Egyptianizing literary Arabic; as it did not wish to impose the stamp of the Egyptian dialect on literary Arabic, but to strive toward enriching the literary language, without impairing its character — through an attempt, for example, to return colloquial Arabic words, which had been termed corrupt, to their Arabic source. Al-Mazini argued that those guarding themselves against the use of colloquial words were amiss. The colloquial language is not a foreign language, but a corrupt form of Arabic. Writers who were revolted by words in colloquial Arabic created a gap between the author and reader. Those who accepted colloquial Arabic as an offshoot of the Arabic language would find "treasures" and "gems" within it. Good use could be made of many words within the colloquial language of Arabic origin, even if they were somewhat corrupted. Suitable words from colloquial Arabic should be found and where necessary, restored to their source. In this manner it would be possible, in his view, to cease the futile effort to seek replacements for words that have ceased to exist in literary Arabic.[274]

Dr. Ahmad Zaki Abu Shadi (1892-1955), the poet, critic, physician and scientist, presented a view, which deviated, to a certain degree, from the "mainstream". In the introduction to his *diwan, al-Shu'la* (1933), Abu Shadi wrote:

> Readers know that I am not a supporter of the colloquial dialect, but I do agree with the Egyptianization of Arabic, or with the Arabization of Egyptian in such a way that our Egyptian literature be marked with the distinctive spirit of our homeland (*watan*).[275]

In an earlier essay, dated 1926, Abu Shadi expanded on his view concerning the Egyptianization of Arabic, saying that every genuine poet was a messenger (*rasul*) to his people. He argued that, as such, the poet's rhetoric (*bayan*) should be the rhetoric of his people and his voice should not rise above their hearing range and comprehension level, lest he become a stranger to them. Abu Shadi emphasized that despite its virtues, he did not advocate the use of colloquial language. According to him what he favored was the use of a flexible form of literary Arabic, which would absorb only selected and polished expressions from the colloquial language. Shadi explained by saying that every one of the European nations possessed both a literary and a colloquial language. Nevertheless, none of them considered the abandonment of the literary language as a cultural device. They turned to the colloquial language only when the need arose to support the literary language. There is a considerable difference between abandoning the literary language altogether and employing colloquial language, at times, for support. In the first instance, there is a complete break with the legacy of the past; whereas, the second process strengthens the link between the present and its cultural legacy, which benefits the future. The possibility of relying on legacy alone was rejected by Abu Shadi, who felt that any one who buries his thoughts and language in the past causes his own extinction. At the same time Abu Shadi insisted that a national poet carried the obligation of not cutting himself off from the past. Annihilating the genuine Arabic literature would certainly lead to the impairment of Islam. Though, indeed, the poet is not an Imam, he has no right to cause damage to the religion, by an offensive act, which would render no service to literature. Nevertheless, Abu Shadi asserted it was possible to endow the Arabic language with "native color" (*sibgha wataniyya*). In his view, such attitude would in no way harm Arabic, as long as the foundation was preserved, and it would be possible to employ words selected from the colloquial language, while preserving the perfect style in the best possible manner. According to Abu Shadi, this is the course he was willing to accept regarding Egyptianizing Arabic in poetry and prose.[276]

Rejection of the radical idea to use Latin script for Arabic
Another aspect of the debate on reforming of the Arabic language was the push to use Latin script as a replacement for Arab script; suggestions of this nature were not limited to interwar Egypt and raised from time to time during the twentieth century.[277] Promoters of such ideas believed that using of Latin script

would fulfill the goal of simplification, let alone modernization of Arabic, as well as enrich the language with modern terms. Certainly, Turkey's adoption of Latin script in 1928,[278] further sustained the discussion on this issue. Thus, Salama Musa was again encouraged by Turkey's radical linguistic reform to urge to replace Arabic script by Latin script. In this way Musa had hoped to simplify the script and to facilitate Arabization of foreign words. Musa also hoped that such move would also encourage a comprehensive cultural change, including strengthening the European mindset within Egypt.[279]

The question of reforming Arabic script, in general, and the Latinization of Arabic, in particular, was not widely deliberated within mainstream intellectual circles. Nevertheless, one can clearly discern a rejection of replacing the Arabic script by Latin one, lest one promote cultural assimilation with the West, detachment from the past, and strike a blow at Islam.[280] 'Abd al-Qadir Hamza defended the Arabic script, emphasizing that Arabic letters had preserved and maintained the Arabic civilization and the scientific and literary legacies of other past civilizations, transmitting them to the modern European civilization. Those asserting that the Arabic script was unsuitable for scientific needs and incapable of addressing the demands of the times were doing it an injustice, and overlooking facts that had been proven over hundreds of years. In Hamza's view, writing in Arabic was quicker than writing in Latin letters, which lent Arabic a decided advantage. Moreover, employing the Latin script would not facilitate matters in any way, since it would result in the loss of letters present in the Arabic alphabet and lacking in the Latin, which would lead to the loss of a considerable portion of the Arabic vocabulary. Hamza also rejected the less radical notion concerning the replacement of vowels by specific letters. He argued that this would involve a further complication, because of the difficulty of distinguishing the original letters in the word from those, which would be employed as substitutes for the vowels.[281] Dr. Ahmad Zaki Abu Shadi suggested that perhaps it would be more advantageous if mankind enjoyed one universal language, though he had doubts concerning the possibility of creating such a linguistic medium. Writing Arabic in Latin letters would not contribute to realizing this suggested objective and would only harm Arabic, as a result. In his opinion, such action would, first of all eliminate the use of Arabic and would subsequently destroy the social, literary and political values that constituted a source of pride and formed the basis for a cultural renaissance. Writing Arabic in Latin letters would also result in severing the link with the past and its precious legacy. Furthermore, the adoption of the Latin script would also create a hybrid language, lacking a supportive culture.[282] Another intellectual argued that through the use of the Latin script, early literary and scientific works written in Arabic would be lost, as had happened to literatures written in other languages whose scripts were no longer employed. It would produce an insurmountable barrier between the Egyptian people and the legacy of its forefathers — a situation from which future generations would suffer, just as the present generation was suffering over the issue of hieroglyphics.[283] Dr. Zaki Mubarak suggested reforming the Arabic script to overcome the confusion caused as a consequence of not using Arabic vocalization. At the same time, he was well aware of the difficulties in vocalizing words, especially in print, because of the variety of forms Arab letters possessed. Mubarak proposed the use of only one form for each letter, irrespective of where it appeared. Aiming at preventing any difficulties, which might result from vocalization, he suggested the temporary abandonment of the practice of the desinential flection. In his opinion, even if his suggestion might somewhat impair the beauty of Arabic script, the advantages would be considerable, because of the resulting exactitude. Moreover, in his view it was paramount to consider such a reform, in order to prevent the example of the Turkish innovation (*bid'a*) of using the Latin script as an alternative. If no efforts were made in Egypt to forestall this trend, future Egyptian youth would be influenced by notions that justify the practice followed by the Turks.[284]

The lexical challenge in the modern era

Arabic, the same as other living languages, has been required to enrich its lexical inventory along the path of history. In other words, expansion of the language by enriching it with new words is not a new phenomenon in literary Arabic. However, since the beginning of the nineteenth century this challenge has become more serious for Arabic speaking societies: rapid modernization and the process of Westernization demanded more urgent and comprehensive efforts, especially with regard to designating new scientific and technological terms. Moreover, this time, the issue was not limited to language per se, since it touched sensitive political, historical and cultural nerves, on the backdrop of the encounter with the "victorious" Western civilization. In addition, this controversy, that was largely identified with the concept of *ta'rib*, the Arabization of foreign words, became another arena of contest between traditionalists, who sought to preserve the lexical purity of the Arabic by coining native scientific, technical terms for new inventions and concepts, and modernizers who wanted to borrow terms from foreign languages.

In fact, since the outset of the modern encounter between the Muslim world and the Western civilization in early nineteenth century, Arab intellectuals started to turn to philological methods that were recognized in the tradition of the Arab philology of the Middle Ages,[285] in order to enrich lexical inventory of the Arabic. Actually, at this preliminary stage, the method of *ta'rib* for Arabization of foreign words proved adequate in providing a speedy answer to the insufficiencies of literary Arabic in the area of scientific and technological terminology, in particular. However, the employment of this method aroused considerable disagreement, among traditionalists in particular. Traditional Arabic philology perceived derivation of new words from existing Arabic roots (*ishtiqaq*), in accordance with the analogical method (*qiyas*), as the most natural way of developing the Arabic language. The capacity of literary Arabic to grow from within, and the concomitant degree of homogeneity, served as a source of pride for those who were particularly jealous of the Arabic. The purist traditional view undoubtedly contributed to the prime position held by the *ishtiqaq* method. It also supported the insistence that Arabization of foreign words should be accompanied by a strict adherence to the grammatical metrices (*qawalib*) of Arabic, marking these words with the imprint of the Arabic language. This approach was contrasted from the strict modernist view, which enabled acceptance of foreign words into Arabic, without considering the extent to which these words conformed to the linguistic matrices of Arabic.[286]

Obviously, the intensive debate and controversy over making the lexical treasures of the Arabic language compatible with the modern era also had a strong imprint on the intellectual discourse in Egypt of the interwar period. Dr. Zaki Mubarak criticized the dominance of English and French in the faculties of the Egyptian University.[287] In his opinion, such dominance had no logical explanation. Mubarak claimed that it was possible to Arabize modern terms, in a careful way, and in that manner to enlarge the Arabic vocabulary.[288] Hassan al-Sharif argued that, especially in the area of scientific and technological terminology, the inadequacy of the Arabic language stemmed from a reactionary purist approach. Sharif maintained that it is possible to make Arabic one of the richest of all languages. Any attempt to avoid the borrowing of foreign terms was doomed to failure. No language was ever created that could exist without the need to borrow from other languages. Those who insisted upon of deriving new words from Arabic roots (*ishtiqaq*) alone and the formation of compound words (*naht*)[289] were in the wrong. Innovation required the restructuring of foreign words from science, industry and technology into Arabic. Past generations more frequently derived words from Arabic roots and formed compound words. Nevertheless, they had also Arabized foreign words, some of which even entered into the Qur'an. Sharif asserted, therefore, that there was nothing to prevent one from applying the same laws, which had directed early generations, and from using foreign words for the new needs of industry, science and technology. The objective here was to facilitate understanding, and to save time.[290] Similarly, Dr.

Ahmad 'Isa praised Arabic for having borrowed from other languages in the past, without impairing its own beauty. 'Isa also mentioned that foreign words had found their way into the Qur'an and that this process of borrowing had added splendor to the Qur'an's rhetoric (*balagha*) and to its inimitable flowery quality (*i'jaz*).[291] According to Dr. 'Ali Mustafa Musharrafa it was permissible to use foreign terms in Arabic after they had undergone a change, to align with Arabic structure and style. Nevertheless, Musharrafa stressed that a foreign term should only be adopted after it had been found in all, or at least in most, scientific languages. On one hand, since in most cases, such a term had been derived originally from Greek or Latin, there was no harm in employing it in the Arabic language, just as other nations had done. On the other hand, if a given term were to be employed by only one or two languages, it would be preferable to find a parallel Arabic term.[292] Dr. Mansur Fahmi held that Arabic could provide the answer to the requirements of modern civilization by unearthing its linguistic treasures and by expanding it in the traditional manner, e.g., by forming new words based on the metaphorical sense (*majaz*)[293] and by deriving new words from Arabic roots. In his view, the activity of the Royal Academy of the Arabic Language in Cairo, founded in 1923 by King Fu'ad, had aroused optimism over the possibility of relying on Arabic alone as a source for the creation of new terms. Nevertheless, he didn't oppose Arabization of a number of terms for which it was impossible to find parallel terms in Arabic. In such a critical situation, the Royal Academy of the Arabic Language could authorize the Arabization of foreign words.[294] It is evident that Fahmi accepted the traditional cautious position on Arabization (*ta'rib*) adopted by the Academy.[295] Dr. Muḥammad Sharaf was also inclined toward a cautious position. In his view, people of letters and science were divided into three groups concerning this issue. One group concentrated all its energies on the study of European languages, making no attempt at examining the treasure house of Arabic, insisting on using European words and embedding them into Arabic in their

European form without any change. A second group totally rejected the practice of borrowing from foreign languages. A third group adopted a middle of the road position, saying that foreign words should be used only if they constituted new words for which Arabic could provide no equivalents. In such cases, Arabic should provide some form of "vestment" (*hulla*) for these words. Sharaf admitted that he himself belonged to the third group and emphasized that Arabization should be implemented in accordance with the rules governing Arabic language structure. Sharaf also advocated the forming of new words derived from Arabic roots, in accordance with the rules of derivation in the Arabic language.[296]

Al-Shaykh Ahmad al-Iskandari (1875-1938), a linguist and member of the Royal Academy of the Arabic Language, strongly advocated a position of strict purism. Like other advocates of linguistic purism, al-Iskandari asserted that it was imperative to prevent the acceptance of colloquial or any non-Arabic words into the treasure of classical Arabic. The development of the Arabic language, in his view, should take place along the lines of its analogous traditional methods, *majaz*, *ishtiqaq* and *naht*. He argued that modern concepts could be expressed in Arabic using traditional roots and vocabulary, and that the language was capable of expansion, without limitation. Various arguments raised by advocates of Arabization were completely rejected by al-Iskandari. Thus, for example, he rejected the call to accept Arabization for the sake of unifying scientific language and effecting greater cultural proximity between nations. He argued that because of their difference from European nations, the Arabs had been able to preserve their language as a language of religion and race (*jins*). As a pure language, Arabic constituted a requirement for fulfilling their religious duties and the understanding of Islam. Having one common language, served as a link between their nations. The Egyptian use of foreign words suitable to their needs was apt to produce the emergence of a different language for each nation. Moreover, the practice of Arabization could not contribute to unifying the language of science; a Westerner would be unable to understand the Arabized word, since it would be formed in accordance with the rules of Arabic, and would be written in Arabic letters. According to al-Iskandart, concessions concerning the penetration of foreign words into Arabic would very likely doom Arabic to the fate of Maltese[297] and would also presumably lead to the formation of another language.[298]

The aforementioned purist position, as held by Ahmad al-Iskandari, which totally rejected the Arabization of foreign words for achieving the linguistic renaissance of the Arabic, was a view shared only by a minority in the discussed intellectual discourse. Yet, an imprint of traditional limitations on applying the method of linguistic Arabization can be observed in positions taken also by other intellectuals within the discussed group; diametric opposition to al-Iskandari's view can be found just outside of this examined group. Thus, according to Salama Musa, many of the learned people in Egypt were afflicted with a "linguistic complex" (*murakkab al-lugha*); they carried within them "various ambiguous feelings causing them to regard the language in a manner which contradicted logic and interest."[299] He complained that in Egypt, the Arabic language, which represented the history and sacredness of its religion (*hurmat al-din*), was regarded as a place of refuge in the face of foreign pressures and imperialism. This "complex," in his view, had led to a fear of foreign words and new expressions, which were considered part of a conspiracy against Egypt's history and religion. Musa argued that surrounding Arabic with a retaining wall of sanctity had brought about the stagnation of the language and a lack of Arabic writings dealing with modern subjects. It had also turned Arabic into an abstract entity, detached from its speakers. The attempt to fix the rules of *ishtiqaq* and the *ta'rib*, set forth in the Middle Ages as a supreme model, from which there could be no deviation, was regarded by Musa as a further expression of this linguistic stagnation and detachment from life. According to him, contemporary individuals enjoyed no less of a right to fix rules than the people living during the 'Abbasi period. Moreover, there was no harm in some measure of detachment from the 'Abbasi period:

The nation needs useful books on the subject of the *otomobil, talifun* and *radiyofun,* and doesn't need to be told that these are actually called *sayyara, misarra* and *midhya',* and that it was cutting itself off from the 'Abbasi Empire by using *otomobil* rather than *sayyara.*[300]

Musa also argued that during the current period, a total incapacity in Arabizing words was in evidence. Furthermore, he asserted that the Royal Academy of the Arabic Language coined words, which tended to evoke laughter, pointing out the gap between the Academy and the spirit of the times. Since Arabic lacked terms for the sciences developing in Europe, it was necessary to simplify the method of the Arabization of language by using Latin script; Arabization would not be easy if Arabic were written with Arabic letters, since the derivation of loan words would be simplified only within the syllables of the Latin word.[301]

Teaching Arabic: Another target for reform

Up until the outset of nineteenth century, the religious, traditional order had left its exclusive imprint on education in Egypt. Education, like other areas of life, was immune to the cultural changes, which had been taking place in Europe since the Renaissance. The *kuttab* constituted the basis of the traditional educational system, in which memorizing the Qur'an represented the basic component, with the endowment of the moral and religious ideals of the Muslim community its chief objective. At the pinnacle of traditional education were the *madrasas* headed by al-Azhar. Religious studies were very dominant in the curriculum, with linguistic subjects as auxiliary courses that were considered essential for the instruction of religious subjects. A great deal of memorization, lacking independent thinking, characterized this method of study. Similarly, the traditional method of memorization was used for the instruction of language studies, aimed at endowing students with linguistic proficiency and extensive knowledge of Arabic grammar. This expertise was regarded as a basis for the correct reading of the Qur'an, to facilitate the understanding of religious texts.[302]

It was during the long reign of Muhammad 'Ali (1805-1848) that first steps in the direction of educational reform were taken. The object of these reforms was essentially practical in nature — i.e. the training of the enlightened class, especially in the fields of science and technology, was implemented so as to carry out comprehensive reforms in the military and administration. The fact that due to the impact of the encounter with Europe the traditional system could not, in any way, satisfy these needs, called for the establishment of a modern educational institution in Egypt and for sending abroad of groups of trainees. These initial steps opened the doors for increasing efforts to create a comprehensive educational system outside the purview of the traditional methods, incorporating modern concepts and practices.[303]

Nevertheless, the educational system of the interwar period could not free itself completely from certain significant traditional characteristics. H.A.R. Gibb has shown that certain features of the old *madrasa* system were reproduced in modern schools and universities, including the memorization of textbooks and lectures.[304] Abu al-Futuh Ahmad Radwan, an Egyptian researcher and educator, confirmed that the old Islamic education had left its imprint on modern education in Egypt. Radwan asserted that in the twentieth century, the continued emphasis on memorization and subordination of the role of the pupil stood out as remnants of the former social, religious and ethical system.[305] Similar criticism was also voiced during the period between 1919-1939, especially by Egyptian intellectuals with radical views. Thus, Coptic intellectual, Dr. Amir Boktor (1898-1966), a lecturer in education at the American University in Cairo, spoke out against teaching methods, which sanctified the written material, sacrificed independent thought in favor of memorization, and promoted the distance between pupil and teacher and an atmosphere of animosity between them.[306] Voices of criticism also came from the group under study. Ibrahim 'Abd al-Qadir al-Mazini, for example, argued against the Egyptian school and home for their failure to stimulate imagination or independent thought in students, which could arouse their creativity and sense of "adventure". Furthermore, such an environment did not awaken the desire to seek knowledge and to "free the soul from the accepted paths."[307]

In addition, the effectiveness of the traditional method of teaching Arabic was seriously questioned, and concern was expressed regarding the great damage it was causing. This criticism did not leave out those responsible for education in Egypt. The Egyptian Minister of Education, Bahiy al-Din Barakat, pointed out (at the beginning of 1938) that Arabic, in effect, was like a foreign language to those studying it. Students in Egypt found difficulty in reaching the level attained by foreign students in the study of their own language. In his view, the solution to this problem could be found in the simplification (*tashil*) of the instruction of Arabic grammar. Barakat argued that the Arabic language's set of rules, or syntax (*nahw*), morphology (*sarf*) and rhetoric (*balagha*) were still being studied according to the old methods, which had been used for centuries, with no fundamental change in method or form. The complex nature of the rules of syntax and morphology in Arabic were understood by hardly anyone. Barakat stressed that these rules had not been created for themselves, but were merely vehicles for achieving accuracy in language usage. In his opinion, if scholars could simplify these rules, they would render a great educational service to the younger generation, since the time saved could be used to expand their intellectual abilities and increase their store of knowledge.[308] Barakat's position worked to expose certain tensions between the traditional demand for giving an important place to linguistic study within the curriculum and the modern position, which insisted upon expanding science courses at the expense of the native language. Actually, failure of the Egyptian educational system to provide its students with the linguistic tools to acquire expertise in the various spheres of modern knowledge, gave rise to concern among those responsible for this system. To improve the instruction of Arabic within the Egyptian educational system, the Egyptian Ministry of Education set up two committees in 1938. The first committee was established with the objective of examining various ways for advancing the teaching of Arabic and enhancing the students' interest in reading literature written in Arabic. The second committee was assigned to examine means for simplifying (*tabsit*) grammatical, syntactical, and rhetorical stylistic rules.[309]

Obviously, interest in this issue was not limited to senior functionaries in the educational system and successfully caught attention in wider intellectual circles, including intellectuals who belonged to the discussed category. The effectiveness of the methods utilized for teaching Arabic was seriously questioned, including the exacerbated efforts for memorizing complex grammatical rules and the acquisition of ancient linguistic patterns. Some asserted that the objective of education was to acquire scientific knowledge and that the language was only a means toward this end. Therefore, the student should not be burdened with the study of unnecessary grammatical rules. The essence of the proposed solutions for improving the instruction of Arabic were: streamline teaching by eliminating subordinate grammatical matters and simplify grammatical rules for teaching purposes; employing livelier methods in the teaching of grammar; blending the instruction of grammar with that of literature; and shifting priorities from the teaching of grammar to the reading of literature, with an emphasis on modern literature. A more radical position, adopted only by a minority within the studied category, also demanded basic changes in grammatical rules.

'Abd al-Qadir Hamza maintained that the prevailing system of education was creating a gap between Arabic and those studying it. From the earliest stage of his education the Egyptian student was required to study complicated grammatical rules and trite expressions extracted from old dictionaries that were thought to serve as the perfect example of style. As a result, the student became estranged from his own language and literature, which for him, came to represent a source of suffering and hardship. Consequently, he would turn instead to a foreign language, which he could acquire without difficulty and trouble.[310] Language, stressed Hamza, is merely a means, and therefore, it should be simplified, especially in view of the expansion of science.[311] Mustafa Muhammad Salam, a teacher of Arabic, argued that the Egyptian educational system had failed to produce students with adequate reading, writing and speaking abilities. Moreover, he asserted that this situation had been caused by the policy of forcing students to memorize grammatical rules, without distinguishing between that which is necessary and that which is superfluous — i.e. grammatical rules that were supposedly only the means had become ends in and of themselves. In his view, an additional difficulty in teaching Arabic stemmed from deficiencies in the set program of teaching literature. The literature being studied presented the student with linguistic models from the past and was unsuited to the student's intellect. The writer suggested several solutions to the problem, including the following: elimination of unnecessary and little-used grammatical forms, for example the diminutive (*tasghir*); eradication of rhetoric from the high school curriculum; on the other hand, inserting into the curriculum of elementary schools reading simple, and vocalized literary excerpts. High schools ought to offer literature exemplifying the grammatical material under study; and the teaching of literature should be relevant to the students' environment.[312] Ahmad Hassan al-Zayyat favored the omission of seldom-used grammatical rules. In his view, such rules were inherited from obsolete dialects, only of interest to linguistic historians and scholars concerned with investigating the accepted readings of the Qur'an (*qira'at*).[313] Dr. Hafiz 'Afifi, who devoted a special section to criticism of the teaching of Arabic in his book *'Ala Hamish al-Siyasa* (1938), maintained that the teachers' attention to the question of desinential inflection, namely, the syntactical analysis of sentences (*i'rab*) and the many hours devoted to its study, constituted a sterilized approach: "In any case, the student is incapable of using the desinential inflection before comprehending its content and understanding it. What benefit follows from the desinential inflection!".[314] 'Afifi also insisted that various secondary aspects be eliminated from grammatical teaching and that efforts be made to simplify the rules of Arabic, with the objective of making its study pleasant to the student. In addition, ʻAfifi complained that the teachers in Egypt were more concerned with teaching grammatical rules than Arabic literature or influencing their students to develop proper reading habits.[315]

Certain intellectuals even suggested detailed ideas for reform, as did, Ibrahim Mustafa, a lecturer in the Faculty of Arts in the Egyptian University, in his linguistic study, *Ihya' al-Nahw* (1937).[316] In this work, which aroused criticism upon its appearance within intellectual circles, the author attempted to examine classic Arabic grammar using new criteria. Particularly striking was his position concerning *i'rab*. Ibrahim Mustafa included within the category of *i'rab* only the nominative (*rafʻ*) and the genitive (*jarr*), eliminating the accusative (*nasb*), which had received considerable attention by the classical grammarians.[317] Hassan al-Sharif argued against the intention of merely simplifying the methods of teaching Arabic grammar and asserted that it was necessary to simplify the rules themselves and to affect a genuine reform in the grammar. In his view, there were many rules that could be eliminated. He offered several examples to illustrate his point, such as the abolishment of the existing limitations in Arabic grammar concerning the complete inflection of part of the nouns (*al-mamnuʻ min al-sarf*), or in his own words, *mawaniʻ al-sarf*. He also offered to limit the number of plural forms by elimination of the broken (irregular) plural forms of nouns bearing a sound (regular) plural form in the masculine form. A noun for which it was impossible to form a sound plural would be used in only one of its broken plural forms, and the other forms of the broken plural eliminated. Al-Sharif also offered to reform the rules for numbers, which created incompatibility between the number and the gender of the noun, causing unnecessary difficulties for people speaking Arabic. Thus, in the phrase *khams ʻashara imra'a* (fifteen women) the first part of the number is masculine, while the noun is feminine. In the phrase *arbaʻa kutub* (four books) the number possessed a feminine suffix, while the noun was masculine. In *thalatha wa-'ishrun rajul* (twenty three men) the first part of the number bore a feminine suffix, while the noun was masculine. Al-Sharif instead suggested consistency between the gender of the number and the gender of the noun. According to this suggestion, one would say *khamsa 'ashara imra'a, arba' kutub, thalath wa-'ishrun rajul*.³¹⁸ He stated that such changes did not impair the basis of Arabic and its fundamental rules, without which the Qur'an could not be read.³¹⁹ Sharif also made it clear, rather poetically, that his approach toward linguistic reform of Arabic did not involve destruction of its base:

> It is correct that it would be disgraceful were I to destroy my forefathers' home with my own hands. However, it would be no disgrace, but rather, an instance of pride and honor if I were to renew this ancient home by installing pipes to carry running water and wires to transmit electricity…and if I were to cut openings for windows to admit the entrance of refreshing sunlight and crisp invigorating air.³²⁰

As was already shown, one of the ideas suggested for removing the deficiencies in the teaching of Arabic involved changing the methods of teaching literature, e.g. the creation of a strong link between the instruction of grammar and the reading material being studied. Ahmad Ahmad Badawi, a teacher by profession, strongly supported this position. In his view, the causes of the Egyptian student's poor knowledge of Arabic partly stemmed from teaching the grammatical rules independently, namely, without their application in writing or reading. Therefore, he suggested the use of textbooks containing literary passages compatible with the comprehension level of the students; passages from which examples to illustrate grammatical rules could be taken. He also suggested that the knowledge of Arabic could be improved by encouraging students to read interesting Arabic literature, rather than the prevailing material, which obviously diminished the students' desire to read. Badawi asserted that it was necessary to enlarge the poor selection of books in the school libraries, particularly in the area of scientific literature.[321] Muhammad Taha al-Hajiri maintained that the knowledge of Arabic grammar did not guarantee knowledge of the language. The basis for linguistic expertise depended upon extensive reading:

> The foundation of the language depends on an instinct (*saliqa*), which should be nurtured, and a talent which should be molded. This might be accomplished not by means of grammar, which is no more than a collection of dead rules, but by means of rhetoric (*bayan*), and the literature which represents the forefront of the language and the reflection of its vitality.[322]

In a similar way, Ibrahim 'Abd al-Qadir al-Mazini aspired to build an educational system, in which language would be rooted in instinct (*saliqa*), contrary to the current system which hindered the development of any rapport between the language and its students. In his view, compared with periods long past, it was impossible to acquire a knowledge of Arabic without a knowledge of grammar. Nevertheless, he maintained that grammar should not be taught separately, but rather as an auxiliary subject in the course of reading literature.[323] In his opinion, the instruction of literature — in chronological order — in which the period of the *jahiliyya* represented the starting point, also posed difficulties in teaching Arabic. Since the student was transported from the style of his own period, to one quite alien to him, he had to labor considerably in order to understand the text. Therefore, al-Mazini argued that it was better to start by studying the literature of the modern period and then to work back, chronologically, to the literatures of the past. He hoped that the students would be spared cultural shock and unnecessary difficulties by teaching through this method.[324]

CHAPTER FIVE
Egyptian intellectual discourse as a nerve center for globalization of ideas: The case of the Malay-Indonesian world

Early globalization: Preliminary notes

Egypt of the late nineteenth and early twentieth century was a central stage of several formative "scenes" which widely imprinted on Arabic-speaking lands; significant among them was an encounter, and even a clash, between tradition and change or modernity, "old" and "new", religiosity and secularism, or East and West. This encounter occurred while Muslim societies deeply suffered political and military inferiority, which caused fear and confusion that touched sensitive nerves of their historical consciousness. It also triggered fear among contemporaneous Muslims of an "attack upon tradition"[325] and even of a comprehensive "cultural attack" by the West. Strikingly, this distress did not paralyze intellectual creativity. On the contrary, it even encouraged the intellectual formulation of a spectrum of ideas and vigorous discourse that transformed the interwar period into a unique, intellectually prolific, and creative chapter in the modern history of Egypt. This intellectual yield successfully reached front-center stage, though Egypt was largely troubled by many concrete and immediate challenges during the period under discussion. Thus, this scholarly discourse served as a sensitive litmus test facing the diverse whirlwinds of the early decades of the twentieth century and as an intriguing laboratory of thought. The stimulating intellectual discourse of the interwar period made Egypt of the early twentieth century, and to some extent even of late nineteenth century, an intriguing case history in the wider context of the globalization of ideas.

The term *globalization* is widely described as one of the most significant defining buzzwords of the recent few decades. However, traces of the concept of globalization have been identified in the nineteenth century. Thus for example, William Scheuerman wrote that at least since the advent of industrial capitalism, "intellectual discourse has been replete with allusions to phenomena strikingly akin to those that have garnered the attention of recent theorists of globalization."[326] In his book, *The Birth of the Modern World, 1780-1914: Global Connections and Comparisons*, C.A. Bayly asks to show that since the nineteenth century – namely, time before the supposed onset of the contemporary phase of "globalization" after 1945 - worlds events became more interconnected and interdepended. Bayly pointed among other things at the growing economic dominance of Western Europe and North America as a critical factor that account for this entire process. He also associated the shift toward globalization, implicitly, with the decline of the Ottoman Empire; noting that while in 1780, the Ottoman Empire was still a powerful, world-class entity, in 1914, in sharp contrast, it was on the verge of fracture and collapse.[327] Similarly, James L. Gelvin and Nile Green, as has already been mentioned, pointed that our age of globalization did not begin with the fall of the Berlin Wall, or the invention of the microchip. According to Gelvin and Green the era of globalization was made possible and in many ways defined by earlier globalizing events, such as those of "the Age of Steam and Print." Gelvin and Green point out that the technologies of steam and print were the two most fundamental enablers of the earlier globalization, during much of the nineteenth and early twentieth centuries.[328]

Egypt as a focal point for the Islamic circle of early modern globalization

Indeed, the Egyptian case testifies to the advent of this earlier globalization in the Islamic context; since the second half of the nineteenth century Egypt began to stand out as a center of printing technology and of the prolific production of printed matter and literary materials for Arabic-speaking lands. The discussed vibrant intellectual discourse in interwar Egypt needs to be understood, to a large degree, on this backdrop, in which printing technology and its products enabled Egypt to be to be integrated into a web of globalized ideas, dominated by the Western civilization.

Egypt, and Cairo of the interwar period, in particular, played an interesting role in the periphery of Western-oriented web of globalization, by serving as an active, productive regional nerve center for the Arabic-speaking lands that responded to the challenges of growing modernization and Westernization. Actually, during the interwar period, Cairo also functioned as a focal point for educated Muslims worldwide. The attention focused on Cairo by Muslim intellectuals was, in large part, due to the centuries-old al-Azhar University, the leading most prestigious institution for higher education in Islamic studies and Arabic for the Sunni Islam. As such, it has been a pole of attraction to many generations of seekers of knowledge from the entire Islamic world. This centuries-old process has created a sort of global network of Islamic scholars that also functioned as a platform for transmitting Islamic knowledge and ideas.

This unique role of Egypt in Islamic context, and even beyond the religious sphere, was amazingly manifested in the early decades of the twentieth century by the interaction between Egypt and the Malay-Indonesian world, or the Malay-speaking lands, often alleged to be a "periphery" of the Islamic world. Notably, in this case, print and steam were very significant enablers of this earlier globalization, to use Gelvin and Green's formulation. Hence, Egypt functioned as a distinctive center of stimulation for a web of globalization of ideas that was not limited to the religious, theological aspects, and addressed social and political aspects, as well.

Globalization, argued Azyumardi Azra, is a new "pet theme" among scholars today. However, he noted that with respect to the history of Islam in Indonesia, globalization is not a new phenomenon; since relatively early in the history of Islam in Indonesia there has been a continuous "globalization" of Indonesian-Muslim discourse. He added that the Haramayn, the two Protected Cities, Mecca and Medina, were the center of the global system of which Indonesian Islam was a part.[329] Indeed, seekers of knowledge, or pilgrims of learning, from the Malay-Indonesian world who moved to Mecca and Medina, along with returning hajjis, played a significant role in this earlier globalization. As early as the sixteenth century, seekers of knowledge started to move from the Malay-speaking lands to the Arabian Peninsula, the cradle of Islam, mainly for learning in the two Holy Cities, Mecca and Medina. Many of them, known as *muqimin*, residents, stayed there from several months, to a number of years and established their networks of *'ulama'* and distinct community, known collectively as the *Jawa* (this term has been used by Arabic speakers as a synecdoche for Southeast Asia).[330] They were largely engaged in Islamic scholarly creative activity and were exposed to varied Islamic traditions through their mingling with *'ulama'* from different parts of the Islamic world. Pilgrims from the Malay-Indonesian world were also exposed during the Hajj, the annual gathering of Muslims from the worldwide Islamic community, the *umma*, to diverse Islamic streams of thought. Indonesian pilgrims were even exposed to Wahhabi puritanism and militancy, as early as the second half of the eighteenth century, close to the initial emergence of the Wahhabism. In Minangkabau, in West Sumatra, Wahhabi ideas, brought across from Arabia, even developed at the outset of the nineteenth century into a remarkable militant movement, known as the Padri movement. This movement was engaged in *jihad* against the *adat* order, the local traditions or customs, that were either animist or Hindu-Buddhist, and as such, were denounced for their alleged *jahili*, pre-Islamic, nature. Taking control of a vast area, the movement imposed the *shari'a* and Islamic codes of behavior. Only at the end of the 1830s, after long years of war and Dutch military intervention, the movement was finally defeated. Despite its defeat, the

Padri movement's revivalism is regarded, in retrospect, as a significant landmark in the narrative of Islam in Indonesia. [331]

The rich Islamic knowledge of the returning scholars, let alone of those who received *ijazah*, permission that was given by significant *'ulama'* in Mecca and Medina to teach certain traditional texts, and even the prestigious status enjoyed by the returning hajjis, facilitated their function as propagators of Islamic belief and ideas. Many of the returning scholars also established their own circles of followers and mosques. Sufi *tariqat* were also established. In this way, returning scholars and pilgrims functioned as cultural brokers and emissaries of the process of early Islamic globalization. In addition, for centuries, Muslims from the region have turned to *'ulama'* in Mecca and Medina for guidance in religious matters, through their requests for a legal opinion (*fatwa*).[332]

The period of late nineteenth century and the early decades of the twentieth century indicated a new stage in this process of globalization, namely, the transmission of knowledge and ideas in an Islamic context from the Middle East to the Malay-Indonesian world. This new stage was very tightly connected with technological developments, prominent among them were the establishment of steamship lines between the two regions during the second half of the nineteenth century; the opening of the Suez Canal in 1869; and the spread of modern printing technology in Arabic-speaking lands. Steamship, trains, and the Suez Canal wrote Clifford Geertz, "suddenly shrank the world to domestic dimensions."[333] Thus, Geertz gave comparative figures about the substantial growth in number of Indonesians who were reported departing to Mecca for the Hajj — i.e., from two thousands by 1860, to ten thousands by 1880 and fifty thousands by 1926.[334] Certainly this process increased the transfer of ideas in Islamic context to the homeland. The returning hajjis also brought back new winds of pan-Islamism from Arabia that were partly connected with anti-European and anti-colonialist sentiments. The influx of these beliefs caused great concern to the Dutch colonial government in Indonesia, then the Dutch

East Indies (or the Netherlands East Indies), since it viewed the returning hajjis as a source of potential unrest, chief troublemakers and political propagandists. This suspicious attitude was argued to have developed into a "hajjiphobia", namely, seeing every returning Muslim scholar and hajji as a potential enemy. It caused the Dutch to impose restrictions upon the Pilgrimage. Dutch suspicions of political manifestations of Islam even included fears of the Ottoman Empire's involvement in Indonesian affairs. This policy was ceased at the turn of the twentieth century, after a revision that led to limiting control and restrictions, by focusing only on political aspects of Islam.[335]

The establishment of steamship routes between the Middle East and the Malay-Indonesian, as well as the opening of the Suez Canal, further stimulated the emigration of Arabs, in particularly Hadrami Arabs, also known as the Yemeni-Hadramis, to the Malay-Indonesian world. Their earlier Hadrami migration dates back to fifteenth century, but the growing, substantial migration started in earlier nineteenth century. Earliest census figures from 1859 indicate that the number of the Hadrami population in the Dutch East Indies was close to 7,800. In 1930 this population numbered about 71,300. It was estimated that by the mid-1930s around 110,000 people from Hadramaut lived abroad, nearly a third of the population. The majority of emigrant Hadramis lived in the Dutch East Indies.[336] The Hadrami community in the Malay-Indonesian world, the same as their communities in the entire Indian Ocean region, were considered to be both a significant "trade diaspora" and a "religious diaspora."[337] As such, the Hadrami Arabs enjoyed high religious prestige among the native population that looked upon them as models of Islamic pietism. In addition, and also due to its economic success, the Hadrami community was proved to be an energetic and influential one in the Malay-Indonesian world at the turn of the twentieth century and its earlier decades. The Hadramis also actually functioned as effective cross-cultural brokers and as a significant conduit for transmitting Islamic ideas. It can be explained by their strong involvement in the maritime trade between the Malay-Indonesia world and the Middle East, along with the significant connections they maintained with the Middle East, including sending their children to schools in Arabian Peninsula, Cairo, and even Westernized schools of the Ottoman Empire.[338]

This new process of globalization in an Islamic context, started in late nineteenth century, substantially upgraded the position of Egypt as a nerve center for transmitting ideas and knowledge to the Malay-Indonesian world. The highlight of this transmission of knowledge was epitomized by the early narrative of the Islamic modernism in the Malay-Indonesian world, Indonesia in particular. The roots of Islamic modernism were deeply anchored in the distinctive context of Egypt of the turn of the twentieth century and its early decades, as a stimulating center of intellectual thought and production. For centuries, Egypt was also a destination for seekers of Islamic knowledge from the Malay-speaking lands. According to Peter Riddle, the absence in Southeast Asia of a long-established center of Islamic learning, not to mention the lack of a center to play the type of world-wide role enjoyed by al-Azhar University in Cairo, "has ensured that Malay-Indonesian students have continued to 'head westward' for advanced study in Islamic sciences down the centuries."[339] However, it was only since the second half of the nineteenth century that Egypt, Cairo in particular, started to play a much more significant role as center of transmitting ideas to the Malay-Indonesian world. Though this transmission should be seen in an Islamic context initially, it was not limited to it, and also addressed diverse fields, including politics. The opening of the Suez Canal in 1869, further facilitated the movement of Malay-Indonesian students to Cairo. Also important, was the position that Egypt, and Cairo in particular, had achieved since the second half of the nineteenth century, as a center for print and press of the Arabic-speaking lands. As a result, in this earlier period, Mecca-based Jawi scholars started to find Cairo as a proper place for printing their manuscripts, both in Arabic and Jawi, Malay written in Arabic script; whereas the printing technology arrived to Cairo during the early nineteenth century, its arrival to Mecca was at the later part of that century.³⁴⁰ Similarly, since the turn of the twentieth century, more students from the Malay-Indonesian world chose Cairo, primarily al-Azhar University, as their most favorite destination; Cairo offered students not just knowledge, in both basic Islamic studies and Arabic, but also a ground to freely express political ideas, including anti-colonial sentiments. In addition, during their sojourn in Egypt, they were exposed to the energetic, political atmosphere of the early decades of the twentieth century; it exposed them to diversified movements, and streams of thoughts, as well as acquainted them with the parliamentary mechanism, modern political institutions and parties. Some members of this community were even active in al-Hizb al-Watani (The National Party);³⁴¹ which was founded during the first decade of the twentieth century by Mustafa Kamil (1874-1908), whose name is strongly connected with the roots of the national resistance against the British occupation of Egypt. The opportunities that Cairo offered to Malay-Indonesian students during 1920s were summarized by a former student: "In Mecca one could study religion only; in Cairo, politics as well".³⁴² Thus, the community of the Malay-Indonesians students increased during 1920s to almost three hundred. This period of time, which stands as the focus of this book, constituted to some extent a Golden Age in the narrative of Malay speaking students and scholars in Cairo.³⁴³ It also seems that Cairo of the interwar period, more than Mecca and Medina, paved the way for young people from the Malay-Indonesian world to become involved in their homeland in emerging modern fields, such as academic life, politics and modern journalism.

Islamic modernism in the Malay-Indonesian world: Highlighting the process of the globalization of ideas, originated in Egypt

The most illustrative case of globalization in Islamic context at the turn of the twentieth century, in which Egypt played the prominent role in projecting ideas to the Malay-Indonesian world, was the significant, formative narrative in this region of Islamic modernism; the significant stream of thought, whose name is strongly connected with Jamal al-Din al-Afghani, and with the name of the Egyptian Muhammad 'Abduh, in particular. Referring to the first four decades of the twentieth century, Deliar Noer argued that ideas like those of Muhammad 'Abduh and his disciple, Rashid Rida, fired the imagination of Indonesian youth.[344] Fred R. Von der Mehden went even further, by saying that the modernist movement was an intellectual import from the Middle East, having its greatest impact on public Islam in Southeast Asia, during the century before World War II.[345]

It was early in the late nineteenth century that the primary ideas of al-Afghani and 'Abduh reached the Malay-Indonesian world, to a large extent, through the famous short-lived periodical, *al-'Urwa al-Wuthqa* ("The Firm Bond"), published by both of them in Paris in 1884.[346] Though it was more than a decade later that Islamic modernist ideas started to substantially flow into the Malay-Indonesia world, an evolution in which a prominent role was played by printed texts, journals in particular. The leading centers in this cross-cultural connection were Cairo and Singapore, then under British rule. Since the second half of the nineteenth century, Singapore began to appear as a regional center of advanced information technology, including through usage of the telegraph which had linked Singapore to Europe since 1870, and through advanced printing, publishing and journalism, in English and in diverse vernacular languages. Since the turn of the twentieth century, the cosmopolitan city of Singapore also started to function as a regional nerve center for Islamic intellectual life and flourishing Islamic activity, including by acting as a very significant staging post for pilgrims to Mecca from the Malay Indonesian world. Journals in Singapore of that time largely used Middle Eastern Press, Egyptian press, in particular, as a source of news and an inspiration for journalistic style. The influence of the Egyptian press was also evident in Arabic newspapers published in Singapore during the 1930s.[347]

Even Middle Eastern media of that time showed some degree of interest in Malay-Indonesian Muslims; newspapers in Egypt, Constantinople (Istanbul), and Beirut had correspondents in Indonesia and in Singapore, as early as the late nineteenth century, who also reported regularly on alleged mistreatment of their fellow Muslims by the Dutch.[348]

Main role in this historical chapter was played by the Cairo-based journal *al-Manar* (1898–1935), founded by the Syrian Rashid Rida (1865–1935), who made Egypt his home from 1897 and became 'Abduh's prominent disciple, biographer, and spokesman. Rida used his journal for promulgating 'Abduh's reformist ideas, while taking his heritage in the direction of a puritan approach, and calling for a return to the strict, purist values and ideals of the *salaf* (from *al-salaf al-salih*, the "righteous forefathers"). *Al-Manar's* influence reached across Arabic-speaking lands, and even far beyond, throughout the Islamic world; many of its articles were translated and published in diverse parts of *umma*. This journal was circulated in the Malay-Indonesian world through a number of avenues, including by smuggling, since the Dutch colonial rule in Indonesia suspected the Islamic modernist movement of maintaining an anti-colonialist stance. *Al-Manar*'s copies were also brought to the region by hajjis, upon their return from the pilgrimage in Mecca, and via students studying in Egypt and Arabia returning home. The wider circulation of *al-Manar* in the Malay-speaking world fostered a dialogue between supporters of the Islamic modernist movement and the journal. They considered *al-Manar* as a theological authority for 'Abduh's teachings, in particular, for his central reformist, theological tenet of *ijtihad;* the individual and independent rational legal interpretation of theological questions, based on the formative scriptures; the Qur'an and the Hadith. 'Abduh called to replace the blind and uncritical acceptance (*taqlid*) of the dogmas already formulated by the four schools of canon law, *al-madhahib*, by *ijtihad*. Hence, supporters of the Islamic modernism from the Malay-Indonesian world asked Rida for *fatwas* (legal opinion). They also wrote to the *al-Manar* journal to suggest articles for publications, request opinion on various theological matters and to address diverse issues, including current political concern. They expressed opposition to the Dutch colonial rule in Indonesian archipelago, as well. Interestingly, opponents of the Islamic modernist movement from the Malay-speaking lands were also involved in correspondence with *al-Manar*, which is what made its pages a platform for debate within educated circles from the region.[349]

In addition, a significant role was also played by the Singapore-based *al-Imam* (1906–1908), the first and primary Malay newspaper to carry the reformist goals of Islamic modernism to the Malay-Muslim world. It was founded in Singapore by Hadramis; many Hadramis played very important roles in the early formative stage of the Islamic modernist movement in the Malay-Indonesian world. *Al-Imam* was printed in Jawi and was closely modeled on *al-Manar*; many of its articles were Malay translations of articles from *al-Manar*. Its circulation reached 5,000 individuals; the majority of its copies were sent to subscribers from the Malay Peninsula, Sumatra, Java, and Borneo.[350] *Al-Imam* analyzed the ills of Malay society in a manner and language resembling al-Afghani and 'Abduh's diagnosis of the state of Muslim society, pointing to the "backwardness" of the Malays, their domination by aliens, their ignorance of modern fields of knowledge, and their laziness. *Al-Imam* did not limit its reformist message to religious-theological aspects and also addressed social and socio-political aspects, by fighting to modernize the educational system, for example. *Al-Manar* enjoyed a relative liberal climate in Singapore, then a British-governed enclave. This location also enabled the journal to be beyond the reach of the sultans, the *rajas*, the top of traditional ruling elite in the Malay Peninsular states. Thus *al-Imam*, which seems to deem the sultans as the source of most ills suffered by the local Muslim communities, did not hesitate to aim arrows of criticism at them. Being inspired by a basic premise in Islam, particularly prominent within Islamic modernist ideas — i.e. that all believers are equal in the eyes of God — *al-Imam* brought into question the whole royal ideology in the Malay peninsula, known as *kerajaan*, including the sultans' claims of divine power and authority and their basic position as the focus of loyalty and symbol of Muslim unity. Thus, the paper, for example, criticized the sultans for not enforcing the Islamic law, *shari'a*. They were also censured for failure to respond to the European challenge, neglecting the welfare of the Malay community, and turning a blind eye to injustice. The lifestyle of the court elites was also criticized. The titles and ceremony involved in the *kerajaan* were rejected as being frivolous and an emphasis on luxurious displays was condemned. The divine law of God, *shari'a*, not the royal court, was presented by *al-Manar* as the ideal legitimate basis of the Islamic community, the *umat* (Arabic: *umma*). The journal's arguments also implied that the *'ulama'*, not the sultans, should guide the Muslim community for the challenges posed by the new world. In other words, *al-Imam* implicitly gave priority to the unified Islamic identity, presented by the concept of *umma*, over a traditional, local collective identity of, *kerajaan*, that was based on the Malay race, *bangsa*.[351]

Al-Imam was a short-lived journal. After it ceased being published, a number of new Islamic modernist publications appeared; it was *al-Munir* (1911-6), founded in Padang (West Sumatra) that stood out among them as platform for the emerging Islamic modernist movement in the region. Like its predecessor, *al-Munir* also published translated articles from *al-Manar,* as well as from other Middle East journals.[352] However, although it had remained in print for barely two years, it seems it was *al-Imam* that significantly wrote its name in the formative narrative of Islamic modernism in the region, by propagating comprehensive Islamic reformist vision and program, strengthening bonds to the center of the Islamic world and advancing the pivotal concept of the *umma*. In this way it actually delivered a sort of pan-Islamic message that the blowing winds from the Middle East brought with them to the region. Notably, *al-Imam* translated the new ideas, transmitted mainly from Cairo, into the local context of Muslim communities in the Malay-Indonesia world.

Malay journals, founded in the Middle East, played a parallel role. *Al-Ittiihad* was the first Malay journal in the Middle East to serve as a platform for Islamic modernist ideas. It was founded in Cairo and its first issue appeared in late 1912. This journal was associated with Rashid Rida's worldview. The city of Cairo was highly praised by editors of *al-Ittihad*, as an intellectual metropolis and a center for learning of diverse studies. For that purpose, the journal's editors quoted an Egyptian saying in the first issue: "He who has not gone to Cairo has not yet seen the world!".[353] Also important were two Islamic modernist-oriented journals published by Indonesian and Malay students at the al-Azhar University: *Seruan Azhar* ("Call of al-Azhar"), published in the years 1925–8, and *Pilihan Timur* ("Choice of the East"), published in the years 1927–8. These two journals were also involved in transmitting overt political discussions that included expression of pan-Islamic ideas and expectations; these discussions were largely influenced by the contemporary political activity in Egypt, pertaining the 'Caliphate Question', following the abolition of the Caliphate in 1924. The two journals were also used as a stage for the expression of support for the idea of pan-Malayanism (union between Indonesia and Malaya), as well as for anti-colonial nationalism. It was hardly surprising that the Dutch colonial government in Indonesia banned both journals, and at the same time, they were also freely available in the Straits Settlements, the three British colonies, Singapore, Penang, and Malacca.[354]

This multi-faceted complex of conduits for transmitting the corpus of ideas of the Islamic modernism, while Cairo constituted the influential center, largely explains the success of this stream of thought to deeply set roots in the Malay-Indonesian world, and the Indonesian archipelago in particular, during the early decades of the twentieth century. Actually, the Islamic modernist movement in Indonesia, marked by orthodox purist doctrine, strongly challenged then the local traditional order, that was still largely regulated by the *adat*, local traditions and customary law. Being inspired by Muhammad 'Abduh's ideas on improving the level of religious education and modernizing the educational system, the modernists also strongly challenged the traditionalists in this field. Hence, a type of modern school, *madrasa*, was established by the Islamic modernist movement, both by organizations and individuals in the Indonesian archipelago and in the Malay Peninsula. This type of school was set up as a reaction to the old-fashioned Islamic school, *pondok* or *pesantren*. The traditional method of teaching, the *halaqa* ("study group"), where students, irrespective of age, sat in a circle around the teacher and learned the material by rote, was dropped; a new classroom method was introduced by the modernists. Now the students sat in rows, used graded texts, and were encouraged to participate actively in the class. In addition to the religious subjects, secular subjects were also included in the curriculum. In Indonesia, where the modernist Muslims recognized the advantages of adopting Western methods and techniques in the field of education, science was also incorporated into the curriculum, following its introduction into Dutch government schools.[355]

Of particular interest was the strong defiance by the Islamic modernists within the Hadrami community of the strict traditional stratification and the division of power; they even made efforts to delegitimize the source of authority of the traditional elite. This clash was clearly demonstrated in the heated conflict that erupted during the second decade of the twentieth century within this large and influential Hadrami community. Basically, members of this community in Indonesia were classified according to the immobile and dominant stratification employed in their homeland, Hadramaut; the *sada* (singular: *sayyid*) traditionally stood at the top of Hadrami society, due to their claim of being descent from the Prophet Muhammad, as well as their pietism; then there were the middle level of *mashayikh*, whose social status was largely based on their Islamic knowledge; and the lower stratum of *masakin*. Inspired by Islamic modernist perceptions and arguments related to equality, members of the Hadrami community started to oppose the religious and socially privileged position assigned to the *sada* in attempts to change their own social position in their new land, Indonesia. They argued, among other things, that all Muslim believers enjoy equality before God, that all should have equal rights, and that no man is superior to any other by virtue of his blood. Consequently, the Islamic modernists primarily argued that the *sada* should be deprived of any particular social privileges. A prominent role in this struggle was played by the Islamic modernist association Jam'iyyat al-Islah wa-al-Irshad al-'Arabiyya ("The Arab Association for Reform and Guidance"), established in Batavia (Jakarta) by the Hadramis. Knowing that the *sada* dominated society through the field of education, by shaping private and public opinion, the Hadrami modernists sharply criticized their opponents' monopoly on the education system as an inferior, stagnant platform for spreading superstitions, and as such, constituted an obstacle for development in Hadrami society. Under the guidance of Jam'iyyat al-Islah wa-al-l-Irshad al-'Arabiyya, an alternative educational system was established. In this way, they also sought to realize the reformist call for a more flexible and mobile society, by providing the population with proper education and training for modern life. This entire religious-socio-political development is regarded as one of the main manifestations of the "awakening" (*nahda*) of the Hadrami community in Indonesia during the early years of the twentieth century.[356]

The multi-faceted challenge posed by the rising Islamic modernist movement to the traditional order and status quo, along with the opposition with which that resistance was met in its formative period during the early decades of the twentieth century, has entered the pages of history as the conflict between the *Kaum Muda* ("young group"), namely Islamic modernists/reformists, and the *Kaum Tua* ("old group"), Islamic traditionalists. The strength of this conflict was clearly illustrated by William R. Roff in the following way:

> It needed only one haji to return from the Middle East fired with reformist ideas, one religious teacher to study at a *Kaum Muda* madrassah in Singapore, Perak or Penang, to divide a village temporarily into two embittered factions.[357]

The implications of this bitter conflict of the earlier decades of the twentieth century transcended the Islamic religious sphere, to include educational, social, and political aspects. Its acrimony gradually diminished during the 1930s, but its long-term implications were far-reaching across the diverse Islamic landscape of Indonesia.

From a broader historical perspective, the case of the Islamic modernist movement in the Indonesian archipelago demonstrates a successful narrative. Muhammadiyah, the massive Islamic modernist organization, established in 1912, now claims more than 30 million members and has marked a deep imprint on the entire "Islam space" in Indonesia and beyond, through which, the Islamic modernist movement has strengthened the orthodox Great Tradition of Islam in the region. Inspired by Muhammad 'Abduh's ideas, the movement in Indonesia has even functioned as an agent of social change and modernization, including reforming education and promoting women's opportunities in both education and employment. The *ijtihad*, the individual and independent rational-legal interpretation of theological questions, has served the movement for advancing modern ideas. Indeed, several decades after Islamic modernist movement started to establish the concept of *ijtihad* in the theological discourse in Indonesia, the neo-modernist stream of thought, considered to be the formative phase of liberal Islamic thought in this archipelago, would further advance the *ijtihad* as an effective tool for reforms and modernization, including to promote progressive, pluralistic concepts within the Muslim mainstream there.[358] However, the concept of *ijtihad*, in the Indonesian context, is primarily connected with the heritage of the Egyptian Muhammad 'Abduh, in general, and the success of the Islamic modernist stream of thought in Indonesia, in particular.

Moreover, the Islamic modernist organization, Muhammadiya, plays an important role, along with the Islamic traditionalist organization, Nahdlatul Ulama (NU), in the process of building democracy in Indonesia, since 1998. Both organizations shared efforts since 1980s for laying down the foundation for building an Islamic civil society, inspired by progressive values and ideals. This distinctive civil society, portrayed by Robert W. Hefner as "civil pluralist" Muslims, [359] was essential for enabling transition to democracy. It seems the during the years Muhammadiya has become more conservative; it is even argued that over the course of time Muhammadiya has lost some of its preliminary intellectual momentum and strong affinity to the original reformist ideas of 'Abduh.[360] However, it has been proved that the two of the largest and most significant Muslim organizations in Indonesia, the NU and Muhammadiya, the pillars of the huge moderate Muslim mainstream, provide a significant platform for the principles and goals of the Indonesian polity, including tolerance, development and modernity, and even safeguard the basic national tenet of separation between state and religion.

The distinct success of Islamic modernism in Indonesia sharply contrasts its destiny in Egypt. There in his own homeland, during his lifetime, 'Abduh faced fierce opposition to his reformist ideas and projects, that frustrated many of his efforts to put his reformist agenda into practice. After he died, his legacy was dissolved quite early on into various, contradicting conceptual trends, ideologies, and movements. Indeed, diverse traces of his ideas could be easily detected almost everywhere in the intellectual discourse in Egypt, as is shown in this book. Nevertheless, his heritage, as a solid corpus of ideas, failed to develop into an effective, influential, stream of thought and movement. Actually, in Egypt his heritage has been diluted and transmogrified into disparate sets of values and ideologies, as Malcolm H. Kerr relates:

> Such diverse individuals as the liberal constitutionalist Ahmad Lutfi as-Sayyid, the militant fundamentalist Hassan al-Bana of the Muslim Brethren, and Gamal 'Abd an-Nasir can all be identified, each in a different way, as heirs of 'Abduh. 'Abduh's historical role was simply to fling open the doors and expose a musty tradition to fresh currents. His intention may have been more specific, but the effect was not.[361]

No doubt, 'Abduh's ideas, formulated mainly in Egypt, during early decades of the twentieth century, have been transformed in the far-away Indonesian archipelago, into a very effective vehicle for a distinctive reformist agenda that covered diverse fields; religious theology and practice, education, society and even politics. Hence, this case does illustrate that through a process of globalization the destiny of "transmitted ideas" is largely decided by the distinctive contours of the new habitat in which they have been replanted. Perhaps this case also offers us, at least indirectly, an additional lens for thinking about the intellectual discourse in interbellum Egypt.

CHAPTER SIX
Epilogue:
A distinctive intellectual chapter in the modern history of Egypt

The rapid processes of both modernization and Westernization that ran in parallel, and not necessarily in the same pace, provided significant backdrop for the stormy stage of interbellum Egypt. The scale of the conceptual responses to the rapidly changing reality was extended between two opposite poles — on one extreme edge, were located ultra-conservatives and traditionalists, who sought to remain fortified deeply in their "trenches," and the zealous Islamists, including Salafists, who sought to struggle fiercely against the "Western attack". On the other opposite pole, were the radical advocates of comprehensive, rapid, unlimited Westernization. Obviously, the rhetoric of those who were placed in the two opposing poles of the public and intellectual discourse of that time could be easily identified, relatively speaking, mainly due to their use of clear uncompromising tones and expressing strong, bold and consistent arguments.

However, through a wider sample of Egyptian intellectuals, this book seeks to address a discourse located in a "grey area," in-between a strict denial of the winds of change on one hand, and devout advocates of Westernization, on the other hand. The voices of the participants of this discourse are prone to be less noticed. As such, the majority of the intellectuals focused upon in this book fall into the category of lesser-known intellectuals, set apart from the luminary thinkers and writers of their time. These intellectuals maintain differing positions, in-between the extreme edges of the ideological continuum; traditionalism/ conservatism, on one hand and modernism/progressivism/Westernization on the other hand. Their voices might sometimes be considered vague, inconsistent and apologetic. Pehaps it can also be explained by an assumption that they were more vulnerable to cultural confusion, uncertainty, and indecision, while wandering often between the "old" and "new," and seeking to bind together a belief in Islam as the ultimate truth and the basis also for modern life, with an understanding of the urgent need to enjoy the fruits of modernity; in particular the scientific, technological achievements of the West. There is no wonder that the apologetic approach was one of the main strategies employed to settle between the collective memory of the successful, winning Islamic civilization of the Golden Age, and the current reality; a reality in which Western civilization is victorious powerful and advanced, and in which European powers rule over Arab lands, which are even "conquered" allegedly by the Western culture.

The intellectual discourse examined here was produced by those who were born into a religious, traditional society, but were also exposed to new thoughts, such as nationalism, Darwinism, rationalism, liberalism, and even feminism, as is clearly demonstrated through their argumentation and reasoning. The dominant voice in this discourse gathers, implicitly, around an understanding about the need to create a middle ground by bridging between tradition and modernity. Thus, for example, in the question of cultural borrowing, a belief in the importance of setting limits for borrowing from Western civilization was evident. Perhaps, the desire to establish such restrictions reflects a somewhat naive notion that it is possible to hold sticks in both ends, namely, to enjoy the achievements of modernity, without shaking the foundations of the traditional society and its values. In the debate on the status of women and their rights, a common understanding of the significance of improving women education can be observed; less can be said about the openness to affording women true equal rights in employment. Moreover, women voices raised to claim their rights seem to be more determent, progressive, and courageous than male voices on the matter; traditional, patriarchal perceptions were still evident, albeit sometimes hidden in the backdrop.

Certainly linguistic questions largely concerned the intellectuals; their intellectual, literary thought and creations placed them on the front line of such questions in the wider context of Westernization and modernization. In other words, as men of letters; writers, belletrists, journalist, academic scholars and teachers, the process of Westernization and modernization strongly confronted them in their own "stronghold" of writing and literature. Hence, they were among those required to tackle questions regarding language, style, content, literary aesthetics, sources of inspiration etc. Intellectuals in Egypt during the interwar period did show strong, traditionalist belief in the Arabic language as a religious and cultural treasure. But this approach was blended into a rationalist, functionalist, communicative approach, side-by-side with rising nationalist aspirations and an emerging, distinctive Egyptian patriotism. This conceptual mixture seems to implicitly shape, a wider understanding about the need to promote balanced, moderate reforms of both the standard literary Arabic and the Egyptian colloquial language, in order to meet the challenges of the modern era and enable a real cultural, literary renaissance. This approach was strongly based on a belief that the Arabic language, through a process of reform, could overcome its temporary weakness, respond to the needs of the modern era, and serve as a rich, effective communicative tool. Thus, here again, the major voice within the discussed discourse indicates a sort of a middle of the road, by shying away from strict traditionalist-religious linguistic purism on one hand, and from radical linguistic reforms, such as sweeping lexical borrowing of words from foreign languages, free from the traditional linguistic molds, incorporating loan-words without modification to fit Arabic patterns, on the other hand.

Hence, there is no wonder that in the discussed discourse, that was largely marked by belief in the possibility of realizing reforms without shaking the foundations of the traditional Egyptian society, it was Japan that was deemed as a model for inspiration. For the same reason, as a counter-point, the modern Turkey of Ataturk was largely perceived as a wrong example, a blind imitation of the West that inevitably led to destruction of significant traditional values, loss of ancestral heritage, spiritual slavery and moral decline. Perhaps, due to its distinctive traits, this intellectual discourse significantly illustrates varied aspects of interwar Egypt, in general, and considerable outlooks within educated circles in particular, while being challenged, even tossed, by strong winds of change, modernity, and Westernization. The illustration already mentioned, i.e., of intellectuals moving between al-Azhar University and the Egyptian University, appears to tell the story of many educated Egyptians; feeling a sense of cultural confusion, of being puzzled, and even torn, between the "old" and the "new", wandering and fluctuating between contradictions in an epoch of transition, and seeking to bind together conflicting perceptions and values.

Perhaps this is precisely what did make Egypt, in general, and Cairo, in particular, a stimulating nerve-center, for educated Muslims — not just from Arab-speaking lands, but also from further territories, who experienced parallel challenges in an era of early globalization. It is really amazing to learn how rapidly and effectively ideas made their way across Muslim societies more than hundred years ago. Certainly it was not just *al-'Urwa al-Wuthqa* of al-Afghani and 'Abduh, published in Paris of 1884, that brought the formative, inspiring reformist message earlier to the Malay-Indonesian Muslims in Singapore, the "remote," cosmopolitan city, "corresponded" at that time with the dramatic developments in the Arab speaking lands. Torsten Tschacher interestingly showed how Muslims in Singapore even learned during late 1890s, mainly through newspapers published there, not only about Egypt, but even about the ongoing rebellion of the Mahdist movement (1881–1898) against the Ottoman-Egyptian rule of Sudan and British efforts to expand from Egypt into Sudan. [362] In the introduction to his article, Tschacher brought an insightful quotation of words written in May 1889, by an editor of Colombo-based Muslim newspaper, *Muslim Nesan*: "News of what is going on in one corner of the world is quickly known in another corner."[363] It is likely that a feeling of Islamic solidarity, and the fact that Singapore was then under British colonial rule, also sustained curiosity about events in Sudan — including the Egyptian and British connection. Hence, such kind of global transmission of news in those early years should be seen in the relevant context, as well. The same, and even more so, can also be said about the narrative of Islamic modernism in Indonesia, in particular. Much evidence indicates that both the transmission of 'Abduh's ideas to the Malay-Indonesian world and the transplantation of those understandings there, was initiated by more than merely an unavoidable traffic of ideas from the "center" of Islamic world to its "periphery" or a random imitation of fashionable concepts. It is likely that this process was the expression of a clever, intuitive historical choice. Due to the threatening clash between tradition and modernity, as well as, the collective mood among Muslims during the interwar period, together with an overall decline and weakness in a changing world, the Muslim communities in the Malay-Indonesian world were receptive to the conceptual heritage of Islamic modernism. It was slightly earlier, towards the end of the nineteenth century, that the collective experience of political and military weakness, decline, backwardness and cultural confusion among Muslim communities, pushed al-Afghani and 'Abduh to lay the foundation of Islamic modernism. They hoped, in this way, to respond constructively to Muslims' deep feeling of historical predicament.

Muhammad Basyuni 'Imran (1885–1953) from Sambas in West Borneo belonged to respected family of *'ulama'*. In 1906, after studying for several years in Mecca, he returned to Sambas. 'Imran subscribed there to Islamic reformist journal, *al-Manar*, and even began a correspondence with its editor, Rashid Rida, as other readers of *al-Manar* from the Malay-speaking world. Being attracted by the Islamic modernist thought, which originated primarily in Egypt, 'Imran travelled to that country in 1910 and enrolled at al-Azhar University, at Rashid Rida's newly established *madrasa*, Dar al-Da'wa wa-al-Irshad, founded in 1912. In 1913, after his father's death, 'Imran succeeded him as the Maharaja Imam, the highly religious, official position in his homeland, Sambas. In 1916, guided by Islamic reformist ideas, 'Imran established a modern *madrasa*. At the same time, he continued corresponding with Rashid Rida and also translated two of Rida's works into Malay. Based on his observation of the conditions of Muslims, in particular in Java, the central island of Indonesia, and in the Malay archipelago, 'Imran sent in 1930 a query to Rida asking what had caused the Muslims to become weak and declined in contrast to the great advance experienced by Europe, America and Japan. He asked Rida to refer his question to Shakib Arslan (1869-1946), Lebanese Druze politician, writer, poet and historian, who was influenced by al-Afghani and 'Abduh.[364] Arslan, who was deeply engaged in the Ottoman cause and Pan-Islamic ideas and later also in Arab nationalist politics, was exiled from the Middle East to Europe, with the defeat of the Ottoman Empire in 1918 to the Allied Powers. Arslan lived mainly in Western Europe, until his death in 1946.[365] The question posed by 'Imran prompted Arslan to answer through a series of articles published in *al-Manar* and later compiled in a well-known treatise entitled, "*Li-madha ta'akhkhara al-muslimun wa-li-madha taqaddama ghayruhun?*" ("Why are the Muslims in decline while others progress?"), published in Cairo in early 1930s.[366]

Indeed, this case remarkably illustrates the unique position of Egypt, and Cairo in particular, at the turn of the twentieth century and its early decades, as a creative, stimulating intellectual hub within two circles of globalization of ideas. Perhaps, we can illustrate this duel capacity of Egypt by envisaging two circles that intersect at two points; Egypt is positioned in an overlapping space — acting as both a significant "receiver" in the circle of the Western-oriented globalization, and as a "projective center" in another circle of globalization of ideas in Islamic context, which included a kind of processing and adaption of those Western-oriented ideas. This pattern is thoroughly demonstrated by the case of Muhammad 'Abduh; the great Egyptian thinker who formulated his reformist thought through his own intellectual journey also into European philosophy and literature. Shortly after his death, his legacy made significant inroads, mainly through Egypt, into the wider "Islamic space" of the Indonesian archipelago. Indeed, a journey back in time to Egypt of the early decades of the twentieth century, through its intellectual history, does expose a very distinctive chapter in the modern history of Egypt, whose ramifications reached far beyond its territorial boundaries.

Notes

1 Hisham Melhem, "The Barbarians Within Our Gates," *Politico Magazine*, 18 September 2014, http://www.politico.com/magazine/story/2014/09/the-barbarians-within-our-gates-111116 (last accessed, 9 March 2018).

2 On Muhammad 'Ali reign and his successors see, P. J. Vatikiotis, *The Modern History of Egypt*, Asia-Africa Series of Modern Histories (London: Weidenfeld and Nicholson, 1969), pp. 449-89; On exposure of educated Muslims to European knowledge and ideas through wider historical perspective, see Bernard Lewis, *Islam and the West* (New York and Oxford: Oxford University Press, 1993), pp. 29-42.

3 On al-Nahda, see Elizabeth Suzanne Kassab, *Contemporary Arab Thought: Cultural Critique in Comparative Perspective* (New York: Columbia University Press, 2010), pp. 17-47.

4 For the British colonial rule in Egypt see, Robert L. Tignor, *Modernization and British Colonial Rule in Egypt, 1882-1914* (Princeton, Princeton University Press, 1966).

5 For the *Shawam* see for example, Hussam Eldin Raafat Ahmed, *From Nahda to Exile: A History of the Shawam in Egypt in the Early Twentieth Century*. A thesis submitted to McGill University, Montreal: McGill University, Institute of Islamic Studies, June 2011.

6 See Marwa Elshakry, *Reading Darwin in* Arabic, 1860-1950 (Chicago: University of Chicago Press, 2014).

7 See Ibid., pp. 25-36.

8 Israel Gershoni and James P. Jankowski, *Egypt, Islam, and the Arabs: The Search for Egyptian Nationhood, 1900-1930* (Oxford: Oxford University Press, 1986), p. 83. See also p. 82.

9 See Richard P. Mitchell, *The Society of the Muslim Brethren* (New York and Oxford: Oxford University Press, 1993), pp. 224-31.

10 On the theory of Western "cultural attack" in Egypt of the turn of the twentieth century and its early decades see Uriya Shavit, *Islamism and the West: From "Cultural Attack" to "Missionary Migrant"* (London and New York: Routledge, 2014), pp. 29-34.

11 On the rise and decline of the constitutional parliamentary government in Egypt see Israel Gershoni and James P. Jankowski, *Confronting Fascism in Egypt: Dictatorship versus Democracy in the 1930s* (Stanford: Stanford University Press, 2009); Israel Gershoni and James P. Jankowski, *Redefining the Egyptian Nation, 1930-1945* (Cambridge: Cambridge University Press, Cambridge, 1995); Vatikiotis, *The Modern History of Egypt*, pp. 265-342.

12 See Gershoni and Jankowski, *Confronting Fascism in Egypt;* On the liberal experience in Egypt during 1920s and 1930s and its decline see also Nadav Safran, *Egypt in Search of Political Community* (Cambridge, MA: Harvard University Press, 1961), pp. 102-228; Charles D. Smith, "The Crisis of Orientation: The Shift of Egyptian Intellectuals to Islamic Subjects in the 1930s," *IJMES* 4(1973), pp. 382-410; Israel Gershoni, "Intellectual History in Twentieth-Century Middle Eastern Studies." In Israel Gershoni and Amy Singer (eds.), *Middle East Historiographies: Narrating the Twentieth Century* (Seattle: Washington University Press, 2006). pp. 131-182; Meir Hatina, *Identity Politics in the Middle East* (London and New York: I.B. Tauris. 2007), pp. 13-29; Meir Hatina, "On the Margins of Consensus: The Call to Separate Religion and State in Modern Egypt," *Middle Eastern Studies*, vol.36, no.1 (January 2000), pp.35-54.

13 S. N. Eisenstadt, "Intellectuals and Tradition," *Daedalus,* vol. 101, no.2 (Spring 1972), p. 18.

14 See Edward Shils, "Intellectuals, Tradition, and the Traditions of Intellectuals: Some Preliminary Considerations," *Daedalus*, vol. 101, no. 2 (Spring 1972), pp. 22-6.

15 Zachary Lockman, "Explorations in the Field: Lost Voices and Emerging Practices in Egypt, 1882-1914". In Israeli Gershoni, Hakan Erdem, and Ursula Wokoeck (eds.), *Histories of the Modern Middle East: New Directions*. Boulder: Lynn Rienner Publishers, 2002, pp. 137-153.

16 Gershoni, "Intellectual History in Twentieth-Century Middle Eastern Studies," p. 171.

17 See Israel Gershoni, "Secondary Intellectuals, Readers, and Readership as Agents of National-Cultural Reproduction in Modern Egypt". In Yaakov Elman and Israel Gershoni (eds.), *Transmitting Jewish Traditions: Orality, Textuality, and Cultural Diffusion* (New Haven: Yale University Press, 2000), pp. 324-48.

18 On the New *effendiyya* see Lucie Ryzova. *The Age of the Efendiyya: Passages to Modernity in National-Colonial Egypt,* Oxford Historical Monographs (New York: Oxford University Press, 2014); Lucie Ryzova, "Egyptianizing Modernity through the 'New *Effendiya*': Social and Cultural Constructions of the Middle Class in Egypt under the Monarchy." In Arthur Goldschmidt JR, Amy J. Johnson, and Barak A. Salmoni (eds.), *Re-envisioning Egypt 1919-1952* (Cairo; New York: American University in Cairo Press, 2005), pp. 124-63; Gershoni and Jankowski,

Redefining the Egyptian Nation, pp. 7-22; Gershoni and Jankowski, *Confronting Fascism in Egypt*, pp. 49-55; Yoav Di-Capua, *The Thought and Practice of Modern Egyptian Historiography, 1890-1970* (PhD dissertation, Princeton: Princeton University, November 2004), pp. 112-115; Yoav Di-Capua, "The Professional Worldview of the *Effendi* Historian, *History Compass*, vol. 7, issue 1 (Fall 2009), pp. 306-28.

19 James L. Gelvin and Nile Green, "Introduction." In James L. Gelvin and Nile Green (eds.), *Global Muslims in the Age of Steam and Print* (Berkeley Los Angeles London: University of California Press, 2014), p. 1.

20 Gustave E. von Grunebaum, *Modern Islam: The Search for Cultural Identity* (New York, 1964), p. 32.

21 See Bernard Lewis, *Islam in History: Ideas, Men and Events in the Middle East* (London: Alcove Press, 1973), pp. 290-1; Gustave E. von Grunebaum, *Medieval Islam: A Study in Cultural Orientation* (Chicago & London: University of Chicago Press, 1953), pp. 320-1; Nikki R. Keddie, "Symbol and Sincerity in Islam," *Studia Islamica*," vol. XIX (1963), pp. 30-1.

22 Jürgen Osterhammel, *The Transformation of the World: A Global History of the Nineteenth Century*. Translated by Patrick Camiller (Princeton: Princeton University Press, 2014), p. 915.

23 See Albert Hourani, *Arabic Thought in the Liberal Age: 1798–1939* (London: Oxford University Press, 1970), p. 101-29, 139-40, 150-1, 161; P.J. Vatikiotis, *Arab and Regional Politics in the Middle East* (London & Sydney: Croom Helm, 2001), pp. 1-18; Wilfred Cantwell Smith, *Islam in Modern History: The Tension between Faith and History in the Islamic World* (New York: Mentor Book/New American Library, 1957), pp. 54-8; Hisham Sharabi, *Arab Intellectuals and the West: the Formative Years*, 1875-1914 (Baltimore and London: Johns Hopkins Press, 1970), pp. 46-7.

24 The Egyptian University (*al-Jami'ah al-Misriyah*) was known in this name during the period 1908-1940. During 1940–1952 it was named King Fuad I University and since 1952 its name is Cairo University. On the Cairo University, see, Donald Malcolm Reid, Cairo University and the Making of Modern Egypt (Cambridge University Press, Cambridge, 1990).

25 Husni al-Shantawi, "Tawhid al-Thaqafa fi Misr," *Al-Balagh al-Usbu'i*, 10 August, 1928, p. 8. For other talks on cultural confusion and anxiety and a sense of chaos see Ahmad Hassan al-Zayyat, "Al-Thaqafa al-Mudhabdhaba," *Al-Risala*, vol. 3, 28 January 1935, p. 122; Amin al-Khuli, "Adabuna Alan Yumathiluna," *Al-Hilal*, vol. 45, February 1937, p. 379; Amin al-Khuli, "Al-Asalib," *Al-Risala*, vol. 1, issue 22, 4 December 1933, pp. 5-6, 42; Muhammad Abu Tai'la, "Misr bayna Hadaratayn,"*Al-Balagh Al-Usbu'i*, 12 June 1929, p. 4; Sayyid Qutb, book review

of Taha Husayn's Mustaqbal al-Thaqafa fi Misr, *Sahifat Dar al-'Ulum*, vol. 5, April 1939, p. 44; Ahmad Khaki, "Qadiyyat al-I.ugha al-'Arabiyya," part 1, *Al-Risala*, vol, 6, 4 April 1938, p. 574; Ahmad Abu al-Khidr Mansi, "A1-Mar'a al-Sharqiyya," a reply to a survey conducted by *al-Hilal*, vol. 33, May 1925, p. 851; Fikri Abaza, "Al-Mar'a Malak wa-Shaytan," *Al-Hilal*, vol. 43, November 1934, p. 67.

26 See Gustave E. von Grunebaum, *Islam: Essays in the Nature and Growth of a Cultural Tradition*. 2nd edition (London: Routledge & Kegan Paul LTD, 1961), p. 6; Lewis, *Islam in History*; Smith, *Islam in Modern History*, p. 43.

27 See Ibrahim A. Ibrahim, "Isma'il Mazhar and Husayn Fawzi: Two Muslim 'Radical' Westernizers,"*Middle Eastern Studies*, vol. 9 (1973), pp. 35-41.

28 Isma'il Mazhar, "Al-Nahda al-Sharqiyya al-Haditha," *Al-Muqtataf*, vol. 70, June 1927, p. 612.

29 On Mustafa Sadiq al-Rafi'i See Giora Eliraz, "The Social and Cultural Conception of Mustafa Sadiq al-Rafi'i,"*Asian and African Studies*, vol. 13 (1979), pp. 101-29.

30 Mustafa Sadiq al-Rafi'i, *Tathta Rayat al-Qur'an: Al-Ma'raka bayna al-Qadim wa-al-Jadid* (Cairo, 1926), pp. 384-6, 391.

31 Mustafa Sadiq al-Rafi'i, *Wahy al-Qalam*, 5th ed. (*Cairo*: Matba'at al-Istiqama, 1954), vol. 2, pp. 81-2: Mustafa Sadiq al-Rafi'I, *Kitab al-Masakin*, 9th ed. (Beirut: Dar al-Katib al-'Arabi, 1973), pp.15-9

32 Al-Rafi'i, *Rayat al-Qur'an*, pp. 385-6, 388, 390-1; Al-Rafi'i, *Wahy al-Qalam*, vol. 1, pp. 332-3.

33 Mustafa Sadiq al-Rafi'i, "Al-Faqr wa-al-Fuqara,"*Al-Muqtataf*, vol. 42 (May 1913), p. 469; Al-Rafi'i, *Wahy al-Qalam*, vol. 2, pp. 50-1, 72, 232; Mustafa Sadiq al-Rafi'i, "Difa' 'an al-Madhhab al-Qadim fi al-Adab,"*Al-Hilal*, vol. 32, February 1924, p. 473.

34 Mustafa Sadiq al-Rafi'i, "Amin 'Asr al-'Aql ila 'Asr al-Qalb," *Al-Muqtataf*, vol. 74, January 1929, pp. 15-8.

35 'Abd al-Wahhab 'Azzam," 'Ibrat al-Hadhithat,"*Al-Risala*, vol. 3, 30 September 1935, pp. 1561-2.

36 See Ahmad Hassan al-Zayyat, "Al-Hajj...,"*Al-Risala*, vol. 3, 21 January 1935, p. 82; Muhammad 'Abdallah 'Inan, "Misr bayna Thaqafatayn,"*Al-Risala*, vol. 3, 25 March, 1935, pp. 448-51; 'Abd al-'Aziz al-Bishri, *Qutuf*, (Cairo: Dar al-Katib al-Misri, 1947), vol. 2, pp. 82-3; Husayn al-Harawi, *Al-Mustashriqun wa-al-Islam* (Cairo: Matba'at al-Manar, 1936); Husayn al-Harawi, "Nahnu wa-al-Mustashriqun," Al-*Ma'rifa*, June 1932, pp. 177-80.

37 Mansur Fahmi, "Nahwa Thaqafa Sharqiyya Khalisa" (an interview), *Al-Rabita al-'Arabiyya*, 21 July 1937, p.16. See also Mansur Fahmi, "Al-Sharq wa al-Hadara al-Gharbiyya,"*Al-Muqtataf*, vol. 77, October 1930, pp. 257-63.

38 See Gershoni and Jankowski, *Egypt, Islam, and the Arabs,* pp. 255-74; Gershoni and Jankowski, *Redefining the Egyptian Nation*, pp. 35-53.

39 See Gershoni and Jankowski, *Redefining the Egyptian Nation,* pp. 47-8.

40 See Mansur Fahmi, "Masir al-Madaniyya wa-Mauqif al-Sharq minha fi al-Mal," *Al-Hilal*, vol. February 1932, pp. 513-4; Muhammad Lutfi Jum'a, "Nasib al-Sharq fi Hahadat al-Mustaqbal",*Al-Rabita al-'Arabiyya,* 18 August 1937, pp. 11-14; 'Abd al-Fatah Habisha," "Taqalus Zill al-Madaniyya al-Gharbiyya,"*Al-Muqtataf,* vol. 74, March 1929, pp. 320-2.

41 See Smith, *Islam in Modern History*, pp. 149-50.

42 Grunebaum, *Modern Islam*, p. 35. See also pp. 32-3.

43 Lewis, *Islam in History*, pp. 294-5.

44 See Ibrahim Hassan Hassan, "Al-Futuh al-Islamiyya wa-Atharuha fi Taqaddum al-Madaniyya," *Al-Risala*, vol. 4, 20 April 1936, pp. 641-3; Tantawi Jawhari, "Al-Mukashafat al-Haditha wa-Hiya 'Arabiyya Qadima," *Al-Muqtataf,* vol. 6, August 1922, pp. 242-7; Muhammad Dayf, *Balaghat al-'Arab fi al-Andalus* [Cairo] Matba'at Misr, 1924; Muhammad Lutfi Jum'a, *Tārikh Falasifat al-Islam fi al-Mashriq wa al-Maghrib* (Cairo: Matba'at al-Ma'arif, 1927), pp. zal, lam and mim (in the Introduction);" Muhammad 'Abdallah 'Inan, "Athar al-Hadara al-Islamiyya fi al-'Ihya al-Urubbi," *Al-Risala*, vol. 4, 24 February 1936, p. 286.

45 'Inan, "Athar al-Hadara al-Islamiyya," p. 286. See also Fakhri Abu al-Saud, "Al-Sharq fi Adab al-Gharb," *Al-Thaqafa*, vol. 1, copy 14, 4 April 1939, p. 22; Muhammad Ghallab, *Al-Akhlaq al-Nazariyya* (Cairo: Al-Matba'a al-Misriyya al-Ahliyya al-Haditha, 1933), p. 31; Ahmad Hassan al-Zayyat, *Fi Usul al-Adab* (Cairo: Matba'at Lajnat al-Ta'lif wa-al-Tarjamah wa-al-Nashr, 1935), vol 1, pp. 77-84.

46 M. Alper Yalcinkaya, *Learned Patriots: Debating Science, State, and Society in the Nineteenth-Century Ottoman Empire* (Chicago; London: The University of Chicago Press, 2015), p. 1. See also p. 2.

47 On *Sayyid Qutb* see John Calvert, *Sayyid Qutb and the Origins of Radical Islamism* (New York: Columbia University Press, 2010); Olivier Carré, *Mysticism and Politics: A Critical Reading of Fi Zilal Al-Qur'an by Sayyid Qutb (1906–1966).* Translated from French by Carol Artigues and revised by W. Shepard (Leiden: Brill, 2003), pp. 1-20.

48 Qutb, book review of Taha Husayn's Mustaqbal al-Thaqafa fi Misr, p. 44.

49 Zaki Mubarak, "Kayfa Nunshi' Thaqafa Sharqiyya Mustaqila," a reply to survey conducted by *al-Rabita al-'Arabiyya*, 11 August, 1937, pp. 15-7.

50 Al-Rafi'i, "Difa'," pp. 469-71; Mustafa Sadiq al-Rafi'i, "Al-Jumla al-Qur'ānīya,"*Al-Zuhara'*, vol. 1, Jumada al-Akhira 1343h, pp. 353-9. See also Mustafa Sadiq al-Rafi'i, "Madha 'Ara fi al-Tajdid wa-al-Mujaddidin?," *Al-Hilal*, vol. 37, March 1929, p. 545-7; Mustafa Sadiq al-Rafi'i, "Al-Imam," *Al-Zuhara'*, vol. 5, Rabi' al-Awwal 1347h, p. 7; Mustafa Sadiq al-Rafi'i, *Wahy al-Qalam*, p. 292, 455.

51 'Abd al-Wahhab 'Azzam, "Al-Tajdid fi al-Adab," part 2, *Al-Risala*, vol. 1, copy 10, 1 June 1, 1933, p. 12. See also p. 7.

52 Muhammad Ahmad al-Ghamrawi, "Al-Qadim wa-al-Jadid,"*Al-Risala*, vol. 7, 23 January 1939, pp. 166-9; Muhammad Ahmad al-Ghamrawi, "Al-Qadim wa-al-Jadid: Naqd wa-Tahlil," part 1, *Al-Risala*, vol. 6, 4 July 1938, p. 1103.

53 Mustafa Jad Abu al-Ala', "Al-Mathal al-A'la li-al-Zaujiya," *Al-Ma'arifa*, 2nd year, May 1932, p. 60.

54 Amin al-Khuli, "Al-Tajdid fi al-Din,"*Al-Risala*, vol. 1, issue 2, 1 February 1933, pp. 12-3.

55 Ahmad Dayf, *Muqaddima li- Dirasat Balaghat al-'Arab* (Cairo: Matba'at al-Sufūr, 1921), p. 4-5.

56 'Ali al-Najdi Nasef, "Al-Shi'r al-Hadith,"*Sahifat Dar al-'Ulum*, vol. 3, February 1937, p. 63.

57 See Ibid., pp. 64-5.

58 'Abd al-'Aziz al-Bishri, "Al-Tajdid wa-al-Mujadidun,"*Al-Hilal*, vol. 24, March 1936, p. 513.

59 See for example, Muhammad Lutfi Jum'a, *Al-Shihab al-Rasid* (Cairo: Matba'at al-Muqtataf wa-al-Muqattam), p. dal (in the introduction); Jum'a, *Tārikh Falasifat al-Islam*, p. ha (in the Introduction); Muhammad Rida, " Nahdat al-Umam wa-'Alaqatuha bi-al-Azya',"*Al-Muqattam*, 22 September 1925, p.1; 'Ali al-'Anani. *Al-Thaqafa al-'Ama* [Cairo] Matba'at Shubra, pp. 2, 9-11; Ahmad Hassan al-Zayyat, "Al-Risala fi 'Amiha al-Rabi',"*Al-Risala*, vol. 4, 6 January 1936, p. 2; 'Abd al-Wahab 'Azam, *Rihlat* (Cairo., Matba'at al-Risala, 1939), p. 187.

60 Mustafa Sadiq al-Rafi'i, "Al-Imam,"*Al-Zahra,'* vol. 1, Rabi' al-Awwal, 1343 AH, p. 5. See also Muhammad Lutfi Jum'a, "Kayfa Nunshi' Thaqafa Sharqiyya Mustaqila," a reply to survey conducted by *Al-Rabita al-'Arabiyya*, September 1, 1937, p. 8.

61 Mustafa Sadiq al- Rafi'i, "Ra'y fi al-Tajdid wa-Mudda'i al-Tajdid,"*Al-Manar*, vol. 27, June 1926, pp. 206-7. See also Jum'a, *Tārikh falasifat al-Islam*, pp. hawaw (in the Introduction).

62 Mansur Fahmi, "Shabab al-'Arab,"*Al-Zahra'*, vol. 1, Al-Muharram, 1343 AH, pp. 31-4; Fahmi, "Al-Sharq wa-al-Hadara al-Gharbiyya, p. 260.

63 'Ali Mustafa Musharrafa, "Al-Athar al-'Ilmi fi al-Thaqafa al-Misriyya al-Haditha. In *Ara' Hurra*. Cairo: Al-Matba'a al-'Asriya [1936], pp. 119, 122.

64 Zaki Mubarak, "Al-Mujadidun wa-al-Muhafizun,"*Al-Rabita al-'Arabiyya*, 21 October 1936, p. 20.

65 Ibid., p. 21.

66 Zaki Mubarak, *Al-Lugha wa-al-Din wa-al-Taqalid fi Hayat al-Istiqlal* (Cairo: Matba'at 'Issa al-Babi al- Halabi, 1936), p. 103. See also Jum'a, *Al-Shihab al-Rasid*, p. dal (in the Introduction).

67 Ibrahim Bayumi Madkur, "Falafat al-Islam," part 1, *Al-Risala*, vol. 4, 16 March 1936, p. 411.

68 Ahmad al-Iskandari, "Hamla 'ala al-Mujaddidin fi al-Adab,"*Al-Rabita al-'Arabiyya*, 25 May 1938, pp. 18-9.

69 'Abd al-Rahim Mahmud, "Nizamuna al-Ijtimaa'i," part 18, *Al-Muqtataf*, vol. 68, January 1926, p. 70.

70 Ibid.

71 Mazhar Sa'id, "Siyasat al-Tarbiya wa- al-Ta'alim fi al-Kharij,"*Al-Muqtataf*, vol. 80, March 1932, p. 312.

72 'Abd al-Rahman Shukri, "Al-Shabab wa-al-Mashib ka-al-Mitraqa wa-al-Sandan,"*Al-Hilal*, vol. 44, May 1936, pp. 769-71.

73 'Abd al-Rahman Shukri, "Ikhtilaf Hudud al-Haqq wa-al-Wajib," *Al-Risala*. Vol.6, 28 February 1938, p. 326.

74 Ibid.

75 Ibrahim 'Abd al-Qadir al-Mazini, *Hasad al-Hashim*, (Cairo: Al-Matba'a al-'Asriya, 1925), p. 65.

76 See Arthur Goldschmidt JR, "Book Review of Gershoni and Jankowski, Egypt, Islam, and the Arabs: The Search for Egyptian Nationhood, 1900-1930", *International Journal of African Historical Studies*, vol. 20, no. 4 (1987), p. 731.

77 Ibrahim al-Misri, "Al-Shabab wa-Ruh al-Quwa, *Al-Hilal*, vol.46, May 1936, pp. 463-4. See also Ibrahim al-Misri, *Al-Adab al-Hayy* (Cairo: Dar al-'Usur li-al-Tiba'a wa-al-Nashr, 1930), p. 112.

78 Isma'il Mazhar, "Huriyat al-Fikr," *Al-'Usur*, vol. 2, July 1928, p. 1180.

79 On the concept of cultural classicism including in Islamic context, see Grunebaum, *Modern Islam*, pp. 98-128.

80 On ways of facilitating acceptance of new ideas and doctrines, including of Western origin see Lewis, *Islam in History*, pp. 294, 302; Grunebaum, *Modern Islam*, p. 112.

81 See Israel Gershoni, "Reconstructing Tradition — Islam, Modernity, and National Identity in Egyptian Intellectual Discourse, 1930-1952." In Moshe Zuckermann (ed.), *Ethnizität, Moderne und Enttraditionalisierung.* Tel Aviver Jahrbuch für deutsche Geschichte, 2002), pp. 184-88.

82 Al-Zayyat, "Al-Thaqafa al-Mudhabdhaba, p. 122.

83 'Abd al-Wahhab 'Azzam, "Al-Nahda al-Turkiyya al-Akhira," part 2, *Al-Risala*, vol. 3, 24 June 24, 1935, p. 1009.

84 Fahmi, " Nahwa Thaqafa Sharqiyya Khalisa", p.17. See also Mansur Fahmi, "Hudud al-Taqlid wa-al-Iftida'," *Al-Ahram*, 24 June, 1939, p.1; Mansur Fahmi, "'Illat al-'Illal fi Mashakilina al-'Ijtimaiyya," *Al-Ahram*, 20 June, 1939, p. 1; 'Abd al-'Aziz al-Bishri, "Mas'ala,"*Al-Thaqafa*, vol. 1, 1 August 1939, p. 1518; Muhammad Lutfi Jum'a, *Hayat al-Sharq* (Cairo: Dar Ihya' al-Kutub al-'Arabiyya, 1932, pp. 120, 142; 'Azzam, "Al-Nahda al-Turkiyya al-Akhira,", p. 1009; Muhammad Rida, "Muharabat al-Khumur," part 1, *Al-Muqtataf*, vol. 59, July 1921, p. 26.

85 Nabawiyya Musa, "'Adatuna wa-'Adatuhum," *Al-Balagh al-Usbu'i*, 17 February 1928, p. 20.

86 'Abd al-Rahman Ibn Khaldun, *The Muqaddimah: An Introduction to History*, translated by Franz Rosenthal (Princeton: Princeton University Press, 1967) vol. 1, pp. 299-300.

87 For the debate in Egypt on the tarboosh, see: James Whidden, "The Generation of 1919." In Arthur Goldschmidt JR, Amy J. Johnson, and Barak A. Salmoni (eds.), *Re-envisioning Egypt 1919-1952* (Cairo; New York: American University in Cairo Press, 2005), pp. 37-8.

88 On Salama Musa see Vernon Egger, *A Fabian in Egypt: Salamah Musa and the Rise of the Professional Classes in Egypt, 1909-1939* (Lanham: University Press of America, 1986).

89 Salama Musa, "Al-Khat al-Latini li-al-Lugha al-'Arabiyya,"*Al-Majalla al-Jadida*, vol. 4 (November 1935), p. 70. See also Salama Musa, *Al-Yaum wa-al-Ghad* (Cairo: Al-Matba'a al-'Asriya, 1927), pp. 254-5; Salama Musa, "Fi Falsafat al-Libas,"*Al-Hilal*, vol. 33, February 1925, p. 465; "Salah al-Din Kamil, "'Aqaliyat al-Tarbush wa-'Aqaliyat al-Qubb'a,"*Al-Majalla al-Jadida*, vol. 6, July 1937, pp. 17-8.

90 Mahmud 'Azmi, "Al-Tarbush am al-Qubb'a: Limadha Labistu al-Qubb'a, *Al-Hilal*, vol. 36, November 1927, pp. 52-6.

91 Ahmad Hassan al-Zayyat, "Al-Tarbush wa- al-Qubb'a,"*Al-Risala*, vol. 5, June 7, 1937, p. 922.

92 Ahmad Wahbi al-Hariri, "Du'at al-Jadid,"*Al-Muqattam*, 11 July 1925, p. 1.

93 Muhammad Rida, " Al-Azya' al-Sharqiyya, *Al-Muqattam*, 18 September 1925, p.1.

94 Rida, "Nahdat al-Umam wa-'Alaqatuha bi-al-Azya', p.1.

95 Mustafa Sadiq al- Rafi'i, "Al-Tarbush am al-Qubb'a: Limadha Astamsik bi-al-Tarbush,"*Al-Hilal*, vol. 36, November 1927, p. 51. See also pp. 49-50, 52.

96 Fahmi, "Al-Sharq wa al-Hadara al-Gharbiyya, p. 257.

97 Ibid., pp. 258-9; Mansur Fahmi, "Mauqif al-Sharq min Hadarat al-Gharb, *Al-Hilal*, vol. 40, November 1931, pp. 55-7; Mansur Fahmi, "Fi Usul al-Tarbiyya wa-al-Ta'lim," part 3, *Al-Ahram*, 20 February 1926, p. 1.

98 Ahmad Hassan al-Zayyat, "Al-Thaqafa al-Mudhabdhaba,"*Al-Risala*, vol. 3, January 28, 1935, p. 122.

99 Ibid., p. 122.

100 'Azzam, "Al-Nahda al-Turkiyya al-Akhira," part 2, p. 1009.

101 Muhammad Ahmad al-Ghamrawi, *Al- Naqd al-Tahlili li-Kitab fi al-Adab al-Jahili"* (Cairo, Al-Matba'ah al-Salafiyah 1929), pp. 44-55. See also al-Bishri, "Al-Tajdid wa-al-Mujadidun, pp. 513-4.

102 Al-Zayyat, "Tat'im al-Adab al-'Arabi," p. 1861. See al-Zayyat, *Fi Usul al-Adab*, vol. 1, p. 28.

103 See al-Rafi'i, *Tata Rayat al-Qur'an*, p. 374; Al-Rafi'i, "Madha Ara fi al-Tajdid wa-al-Mujaddidin?, p. 547; Al-Rafi'i, *Wahy al-Qalam*, vol. 3, pp. 203, 457; vol. 2, p. 84; Mustafa Sadiq al-Rafi'I, "Al-Kutub allati Afadatni,"*Al-Hilal*, vol. 35, January 1927, p. 275.

104 See al-Rafi'i, *Wahy al-Qalam*, vol. 2, pp. 83-4.

105 Ibid., vol. 3, p. 204.

106 Ibid., vol. 2, p. 84.

107 See Carl Brockelmann, *Geschichte der Arabischen Literatur*. Supplementband III (Leiden: E.J. Brill 1943), p. 73; Mustafa Nu'man Husayn al-Badri, *Al-Imam Mustafa Sadiq al-Rafi'i* (Baghdad, 1968), pp. 53, 58.

108 See Al-Rafi'i, *Wahy al-Qalam*, vol. 3, pp. 204-5.

109 See Eliraz, "The Social and Cultural Conception of Mustafa Sadiq al-Rafi'i," pp. 101-6.

110 See Al-Rafi'i, *Wahy al-Qalam*, vol. 3, p. 204.

111 Rida, "Muharabat al-Khumur, p. 25. See also Sa'id, "Siyasat al-Tarbiya wa-al-Ta'alim fi al-Harij," p. 312.

112 Mohammad Tawfik Diab, "Ghayat al-Nahda al-Nisa'iyya fi Misr,"*Al- Siyasa al-Usbu'iyya*, 10 December 1927, p. 9.

113 'Abd al-Khalik Islam'il, "Tahawwul al-Sharq," *Al-Muqattam*, 9 July 1925, p. 1. See also Muhammad 'Abd al-Qadir Hamza, A'da' al-Adab al-'Arabi,"*Al-Balagh*, 4 June 1934, p. 3; 'Inan, "Misr bayna Thaqafatayn," p. 450; Nazla al-Hakim Sa'id, "Ikhtilat al-Jinsayn, *al-Ma'rifa*, 1st year, February 1932, p. 1262; Amin Wasif, "Nahdat al-Sharq al-'Arabi,"*Al-Hilal*, vol. 31, March 1923, p. 611; 'Abd al-Majid Nafi', "Tabi' al-Haya al-Misriyya al-Yawm," a reply to survey conducted by *Al-Rabita al-'Arabiyya*, 26 May 1937, p.13.

114 'Abd al-'Aziz al-Bishri, "Kaifa Yanba'ith al-Adab wa-Kayfa Natarawwahu?," part 2, *Al-Risala*, vol. 3, April 1, 1935, pp. 491; 'Abd al-'Aziz al-Bishri, "Hairat al-Adab al-Misri,"*Al-Ma'rifa*, 1st year, February 1932, pp. 1187, 1192.

115 Al-Bishri, "Kaifa Yanba'ith al-Adab wa-Kayfa Natarawwahu?," part. 2, pp. 491.

116 Ibid., p. 493.

117 Al-Bishri, "Al-Tajdid wa-al-Mujadidun," pp. 513-4. See also 'Abd al-'Aziz al-Bishri, "Kayfa Yanba'ith al-Adab wa-Kayfa Natarawwahu?," *Al-Risala*, part 1, vol. 3, 25 March 1935, p. 453; Al-Bishri, *Qutuf*, vol. 2, pp. 81-6; 'Abd al-'Aziz al-Bishri, "Shawqi...!,"*Al-Risala*, vol. 2, 15 October 1934, p. 1684. On the connection between national literature and local customs, morals and characteristics, see also Ahmad Dayf, "Al-Adab al-Misri fi al-Qarn al-Tasi' 'Ashar," *Al-Muqttaf*, part 1, vol. 68, April 1926, p. 401; Al-Khuli, "Adabuna Alan Yumathiluna," p. 377.

118 Ahmad Hassan al-Zayyat, "Al-Imtiyazat wa -al-Adab !,"*Al-Risala*, vol. 2, 28 May 1934, pp. 881-2.

119 About the discourse on collective identities in Egypt see, Gershoni and Jankowski, *Egypt, Islam, and the Arabs*; Gershoni and Jankowski, *Redefining the Egyptian Nation* ; Gershoni, "Reconstructing Tradition," pp. 155-211; Gabriel Piterberg, "The Tropes of Stagnation and Awakening in Nationalist Historical Consciousness: The Egyptian Case." In James P. Jankowski and Israel Gershoni (eds.), *Rethinking Nationalism in the Arab Middle East* (Columbia University Press, New York, 1997), pp. 42-61; Whidden, "The Generation of 1919." pp. 19-46.

120 See Gershoni and Jankowski, *Egypt, Islam, and the Arabs;* pp. 35-6, 39, 101, 116, 131-2, 134, 193. See also Whidden, "The Generation of 1919," p. 28. Even Sayyid Qutb, who years later has become well known as the influential zealous ideologue of radical Islam, shared in his earlier period a perception of Egypt as a living organic entity. See Calvert, *Sayyid Qutb and the Origins of Radical Islamism*, pp. 88.

121 See Hourani, *Arabic Thought in the Liberal Age*, pp. 20, 144, 171, 344.

122 Mubarak, *Al-Lugha wa-al-Din wa- al-Taqalid fi Hayat al-Istiqlal*, p. 94.

123 Al-Bishri, *Al-Mukhtar*, vol. 1, p.58.

124 Abu Tai'la, "Misr bayna Hadaratayn," p. 5. See also 'Abd al-Latif Hamza, "Tabi' al-Haya al-Misriyya al-Yawm,"a reply to survey conducted by *Al-Rabita al-'Arabiyya*, 26 May 1937, p.12.

125 See Ahmad Amin, "Halqa Mafquda," *Al-Risala*, vol. 1, issue no. 1, 15 January 1933, pp. 6-7.

126 Muhammad Mahdi 'Alam, "Al-Halqa al-Mafquda," *Sahifat Dar al-'Ulum*, 1st year, June 1934, pp. 19-26.

127 Fahmi, "Al-Sharq wa al-Hadara al-Gharbiyya,"*al-Muqtataf*, pp. 262-3.

128 Salama Musa, *Al- Youm aw- al-Ghad* (Cairo: Al-Matba'a al-'Asriya, 1927), pp. 229-57. See also Salama Musa, "Al-Sharq Sharq wa-al-Ghab Ghab,"*Al-Majalla al-Jadida*, vol. 1, May 1930, pp. 882-8; Gershoni and Jankowski, *Redefining the Egyptian Nation*, pp. 51, 129.

129 On Isma'il Ahmad Adham, see Juynboll, G.H.A, "Ismail Ahmad Adham (1911-1940), the Atheist," *Journal of Arabic Literature*, vol. 3 (1972), pp. 54-71.

130 Isma'il Ahmad Adham, "Al-Tatawwur al-Hadith fi Misr wa-Turkiya," *Al-Majalla al-Jadida*, vol. 6, April 1937, p. 28.

131 Isma'il Ahmad Adham, "Misr wa-al-Thaqafa al-Urubbiyya," *Al-Majalla al-Jadida*, vol. 6, May 1937, pp. 28-31. See also Isma'il Ahmad Adham, "Bayna al-Ghab wa-al-Sharq," part 2, *Al-Risala*, vol. 6, 27 June 1938, p.1055.

132 Ibrahim al-Misri, "Al-Mathal al-A'la li-al-Fard wa-al-Mujtama' 'Indana,"*Al-Majalla al-Jadida*, vol. 2, December 1930, pp. 164-71, 177. See also Ibrahim al-Misri, "Shakhsiyat al-Fanan,"*Al-Balagh al-Usbu'i,* 11 February 1927, pp. 35-6. Ibrahim al-Misri sometimes implicitly supported a moderate Westernization. See for example Ibrahim al-Misri, *Saut al-Jil* (Cairo: Maktabat Saba wa-Matba'atuha, 1934), p.89; Ibrahim al-Misiri, *Why al-'Asr* (Cairo: Maktabat al-Hilal) [1935], p. 85; Ibrahim al-Misri, "Al-Musiqa al-Sharqiya,"*Al-Hilal*, vol.46, July 1938, pp. 501-6. It is argued that though al-Misri shared Salama Musa's belief in radical Westernization he was afraid to fully express it. See Habib al-Zahlawi, "Udaba' Mua'sirun, *Al-Muqttaf*, 2 August 1935, pp. 11-2.

133 Ibrahim al-Misri, "Khalq Amthila 'Ulya li-al-Shabab al-Misriyin,"*Al-Hilal*, vol. 46, July 1938, p. 617.

134 See for example, Jum'a, *Hayat al-Sharq*, pp. 14-6 (in the introduction); Muhammad Lutfi Jum'a, "Al-Nahda al-Sharqiyya al-Haditha," *Al-Muqttaf*, vol. 71, August 1927, pp. 141-3; Qutb, book review of Taha Husayn's Mustaqbal al-Thaqafa fi Misr, p. 46; Nafi', "Tabi' al-Haya al-Misriyya al-Yawm," p.13.

135 Ibrahim al-Misiri, *Saut al-Jil*, pp. 45-55.

136 Grunebaum, *Islam: Essays in the Nature and Growth of a Cultural Tradition*, pp. 237-46.

137 Adham, "Bayna al-Ghab wa-al-Sharq," part 1, p.1014.

138 Ibid.

139 Adham, "Al-Tatawwur al-Hadith fi Misr wa-al-Turkiya," p. 18.

140 Ibrahim 'Abd al-Qadir al-Mazini, "Al-Hayat al-Misriyya wa-Hajatuha ila 'Anasir al-Quwa wa-al-Khayal," *Al-Hilal*, vol. 38, March 1930, p. 552.

141 Al-Mazini, Ibid.

142 Hamilton A.R, Gibb, *Studies on the Civilization of Islam*. Edited by Stanford J. Shaw and William R. Polk (Boston: Beacon Press, 1962), p. 322.

143 See Fahmi, " 'Illat al-'Illal fi Mashakilina al-'Ijtimaiyya".

144 Fahmi, "Mauqif al-Sharq min Hadarat al-Gharb", p. 58.

145 Qasim Amin, *Tahrir al-Mar'a* (Cairo 1928), pp. 128-59.

146 See Hourani, *Arabic Thought in the Liberal Age*, pp. 166-70; Charles C. Adams, *Islam and Modernism in Egypt* (New York: Russell & Russell, 1968), pp. 231-7.

147 On earlier feminist *consciousness* of late nineteenth century see Margot Badran, *Feminists, Islam, and Nation: Gender and the Making of Modern Egypt* (Princeton University Press, 1995), pp. 3-19. On Egyptian women in nineteenth-century Egypt, see Judith Tucker, *Women in Nineteenth-Century Egypt* (Cambridge: Cambridge University Press, 1985); Liat Kozma, *Policing Egyptian Women: Law, Sex and Medicine in Khedival Egypt* (Syracuse, Syracuse University Press, 2011).

148 See Malak Hifni Nasif ("Bahithat al-Badiyya"), *Al-Nisa'iyyat*. Cairo n.d. 2 vols; Hoda Yousef, "Malak Hifni Nasif: Negotiations of a feminist agenda between the European and the Colonial," *Journal of Middle East Women's Studies*, vol 7, no.1 (Winter 2011), p. 74.

149 See Malak Hifni Nasif ("Bahithat Al-Badiyya"), *Al-Nisa'iyyat*, 2 vols. (Cairo n.d.): Hoda Yousef, "Malak Hifni Nasif: Negotiations of a Feminist Agenda between the European and the Colonial, " *Journal of Middle East Women's Studies*, vol 7, no.1 (Winter 2011), pp. 70–89; Omnia Shakry, "Schooled Mothers and Structured Play: Child-Rearing in Turn-of-the-Century Egypt. In Lila Abu-Lughod (ed.), *Remaking Women: Feminism and Modernity in the Middle East* by (Princeton: Princeton University Press and Cairo: American University in Cairo Press, 1998), pp. 143-8.

150 On Mayy Ziyadaj see Boutheina Khaldi, *Egypt Awakening in the Early Twentieth Century : Mayy Ziyadah's Intellectual Circles* (New York: Palgrave Macmillan, 2012).

151 For in-depth discussion about the connections between Egyptian nationalism, feminism and gender see Beth Baron, *Egypt as a Woman; Nationalism, Gender, and Politics* (Cairo: The American University in Cairo Press, 2005). See also Nabila Ramdani, "Women in the 1919 Egyptian Revolution: From Feminist Awakening to Nationalist Political Activism," *Journal of International Women's Studies*, vol. 14, issue 2 (March 2013), pp. 39-52; Thomas Philipp, "Feminism and Nationalist Politics in Egypt." In Lois Beck and Nikki Keddie (eds.), *Women in the Muslim World* (Cambridge: Harvard University Press, 1978), pp. 277-95.

152 Badran, *Feminists, Islam, and Nation,* pp. 19-21. See also Pernille Arenfeldt and Nawar al-Hassan Golley, "Arab Women's Movements: Developments, Priorities, and Challenges." In Pernille Arenfeldt and Nawar al-Hassan Golley (eds.), *Mapping Arab Women's Movements; A Century of Transformations from Within* (Cairo: American University in Cairo Press, 2012), pp. 7-13.

153 On Huda Sha'rawi see Rula B. Quawas, "A Sea Captain in Her Own Right": "Navigating the Feminist Thought of Huda Shaarawi," *Journal of International Women's Studies*, vol. 8, issue 1, pp. 219-35; Badran, *Feminists, Islam, and Nation,* pp. 32-8.

154 On reforming women's education in Egypt see Badran, *Feminists, Islam, and Nation,* pp. 8-10, 95, 142-64; Margot Badran, *Feminism in Islam: Secular and Religious Convergences* (London: Oneworld Publications, 2009), pp. 78-82.

155 See Kozma, *Policing Egyptian Women,* p. xxii (in the Introduction); Morroe Berger, *The Arab World Today* (New York: Doubleday & Company, Inc., 1961), pp. 100-102.

156 See Beth Baron, *Egypt as a Woman; Nationalism, Gender, and Politics* (Cairo: The American University in Cairo Press, 2005), pp. 151-88; Badran, *Feminists, Islam, and Nation,* p. 208-12.

157 Badran, *Feminists, Islam, and Nation,* p. 124.

158 See Ibid., pp. 124-41.

159 See Ira M. Lapdus, A History of Islamic Societies, 3rd ed. (Cambridge: Cambridge University Press, 2015), p. 659; Badran, *Feminists, Islam, and Nation,* pp 126, 209; Vatikiotis, *The Modern History of Egypt,* 302.

160 On Nabawiyya Musa see Christina Civantos, "Reading and Writing the Turn-of-the-Century Egyptian Woman Intellectual: Nabawiyya Musa's Ta'rikhi bi-Qalami, *Journal of Middle East Women's Studies,* vol. 9, no. 2 (Spring 2013), pp. 4-31; Badran, *Feminists, Islam, and Nation,* pp. 38-46. On the feminist discourse see, Cathlyn Mariscotti, *Gender and Class in the Egyptian Women's Movement, 1925-1939: Changing Perspectives* (New York: Syracuse University Press, 2008), pp. 1-33 ; Badran, *Feminism in Islam,* pp. 55-65.

161 On patriarchy and women's situation through a wider historical perspective see Gerda Lerner, *The Creation of Patriarchy* (New York, NY: Oxford University Press, 1986).

162 Amin, *Tahrir al-Mar'a.* pp. 9-10; see also Qasim Amin, *Al-Mar'a al-Jadida* (Cairo: Matba'at al-Ma'arif 1900), p. viii.

163 On the thought and ideas of Gamal al-Din al-Afghani, Muhammad 'Abduh and Rashid Rida see: Adams, *Islam and Modernism in Egypt*; Hamilton A. R. Gibb, *Modern Trends in Islam* (Chicago: The University of Chicago Press, 1947); Malcolm H. Kerr, *Islamic Reform: The Political and Legal Theories of Muhammad 'Abduh and Rashid Rida* (Berkeley and Los Angeles: University of California Press, 1966); Hourani, *Arabic Thought in the Liberal Age,* pp. 103-60, 222-244; Safran, *Egypt in Search of Political Community,* pp. 43-50, 62-84.

164 Husayn Al-Harawi, *Al-Mustashriqun wa- al-Islam* (Cairo: Matba'at al-Manar, 1936), pp. 98-9, 103. cf. Muhammad Rashid Rida, *Al-Wahy al-Muhammadi,* 2nd ed. (Cairo: Matba'at al-Manar, 1352 H), pp. 267-9. See also Nabawiyya

Musa, "Al-Nahda al-Nisawiyya fi Misr wa-Ahamm Asbabuha," *Al-Balagh al-Usbu'i*, 24 June 1927, p. 32; Nabawiyya Musa, "Al-'Ilm wa-al-Din," *Al-Balagh al-Usbu'i*, 3 June, 1927, p.33; Nabawiyya Musa, "Qanun al-Zawaj al-Jadid," *Al-Balagh al-Usbu'i*, 25 March 1927, p.30.

165 See for example 'Abd al-Fatah 'Ibada, "Nahdat al-Mar'a al-Misriyya,", part 1, *Al-Hilal*, April 1927, p. 708; Fakhri Abu Al-Su'ud, "Al-Mar'a fi al-Adabayn al-'Arabi wa-al-Inglizi," *Al-Risala*, 7 September 1936, p. 1447.

166 See Nabawiyya Musa, "Al-Mutazawwij wa-al-A'mal al-'Amma," *Al-Balagh Al-Usbu'i*, 16 September 1927, p. 31; Nabawiyya Musa, "Al-Qarn al-'Ishrun wa-lima Summiya bi-'Asr al-Mar'a," *Al-Balagh al-Usbu'i*, 11 May 1928, p. 28; Nabawiyya Musa, "Shay' 'an al-Mar'a," *Al-Balagh al-Usbu'i*, 30 December 1927, p. 20; Sherifa Zuhur, *Revealing Revealing: Islamist Gender Ideology in Contemporary Egypt* (Albany, State University of New York Press, 1992), p.15.

167 Quawas, "A Sea Captain in Her Own Right," pp. 218-35. See also Interview with Huda Sha'rawi, *Al-Hilal*, vol. 35, April 1927, p. 653; Huda Sha'rawi, "Hadaratina al-Qadima," a reply to survey conducted by *al-Hilal*, vol, 39, April 1930, p. 825.

168 Al- Rafi'i, *Wahy al-Qalam*, vol.2, p. 299, vol. 3, p. 163.

169 Sayyid Qutb, 'Ayy Rajul Turiduhu al-mar'a?,' *Al-Balagh Al-Usbu'i*, 27 March 1929, p. 28.

170 Ibid.

171 'Ali, Shukri Khamis, "Al-Mar'a al-Misriyya wa-al-Mar'a al-Gharbiyya," *Al-Muqattam*, 3 March 1927, p. 10.

172 Abaza, "Al-Mar'a Malak wa-Shaytan,", pp. 65-8.

173 Salim Salih, "Al-Mar'a wa-Atharuha fi al-Hayah," *Al-Muqattam*, 14 December 1924, p.1.

174 Al-Mazini, *Hasad Al-Hashim*, pp. 111-4.

175 Mustafa Lutfi al-Manfaluti, "Ihtiram al-Mar'a," *Al-Hilal*, vol. 30, July 1922, p. 914.

176 Ibid., p. 915.

177 Ahmad Shukri, "Hal fi Istita'at al-Rajul an Yafahama al-Mar'a,," *Al-Balagh al-Usbu'i*, 16 April 1930, p. 27.

178 Mansur Fahmi, "'Aqliyat al-Mar'a wa-'Aqliyat al-Rajul," *Al-Hilal*, vol. 38, February 1930, pp. 404-6.

179 Amin, *Tahrir al-Mar'a*, pp. 54-96.

180 On the custom of veiling see *Gabriel Baer, Population and Society in the Arab East*. Translated by *Hanna Szoke* (London: Routledge & Kegan Paul, 1964), pp. 41-2.

181 See Badran, *Feminism in Islam*, pp. 75, 83; Badran, *Feminists, Islam, and Nation*, pp. 23, 67; Werner Ende and Udo Steinback (eds.), *Islam in the World Today: A Handbook of Politics, Religion, Culture, and Society* (Ithaca, N.Y. : Cornell University Press, 2010), p. 646.

182 See Yousef, "Malak Hifni Nasif," pp. 70–89; Nasif, *Al-Nisa'iyyat*, vol. 1, pp. 24-9; Arina Angerman, Geerte Binnema, Annemieke Keunen, Vefie Poels, and Jacqueline Zirkzee (eds.), *Current Issues in Women's History*. By International Conference on Women's History (London/New York: Routledge, 1989), pp. 161-2.

183 Ahmad Hassan al-Zayyat, "Shuruh wa-Hawash, *Al-Risala*, vol., 15 May 1933, pp. 3-4.

184 Al-Harawi, *Al-Mustashriqun wa- al-Islam*, p. 105.

185 Muhammad Zaki 'Abd Al-Qadir, "Al-Ihjam 'an al-Zawaj," Al-Siyasa al-Usbu'iyya, part 1, 10 September 1927, p. 6; part 3, 24 September 1927, p.8.

186 See Muhammad Ahmad al-Ghamrawi, "Al-Bi'a al-Islamiyya," *Al-Risalas*, vol.6, 21 March 1938, p. 491; Muhammad Lutfi Jum'a, *Hayat Al-Sharq*, Cairo 1932, p. 117.

187 Al- Rafi'i, *Wahy al-Qalam*, vol. I, pp. 207-26.

188 *Gabriel Baer, Population and Society in the Arab East*. Translated by *Hanna Szoke* (London: Routledge & Kegan Paul, 1964), p. 42.

189 See Mariscotti, *Gender and Class in the Egyptian Women's Movement*, pp. 4, 25, 47-61.

190 Ahmad Hassan al-Zayyat, "Al-'Id...," *Al-Risala*, vol. 1, 15 April 1933, p. 4.

191 Salih, p. 2. See also 'Ibada, "Nahdat al-Mar'a al-Misriyya,", part 2, pp. 841-2, 849. cf. Amin, *Tahrir*, pp. 14, 79.

192 Hafiz Mahmud, "Al-Adab al-Makshuf wa-al-Adab al-Mastur," *Al-Siyasa al-Usbui'yya*, vol. 3, December 1927, p. 9.

193 Ibrahim Naji, "Al-Shabab al-Misri wa-al-Mushkila al-Jinsiyya," *Al-Hilal*, vol. 47. November 1938: 57-60.

194 Amin, *Tahrir al-Mar'a*, pp. 122-128; Amin, Al-*Mar'a al-Jadida*, pp. 33-4.

195 Nasif, *Al-Nisa'iyyat*, vol. 1, pp. 20, 26, 36-41, 62, 113, 116-17, 136-37. For earlier discourse on women's veiling see also Leila Ahmed, *Women and Gender in Islam: Historical Roots of a Modern Debate* (New Haven and London: Yale University Press, 1992), pp. 144-68.

196 Saʻid, "Ikhtilat al-Jinsayn," pp. 1255-61.

197 Rashid Mustafa al-Barradi, "Fi ʻAlam al-Tarbiya: Al-Taʻlim al-Mushtarik," *Al-Balagh Al-Usbuʻi*, vol. 7, September 1928, p. 29.

198 Hafiz Mahmud, "Muqaddimat al-Zawaj kama Yaraha Shabb," *Al-Majalla al-Jadida*, vol. 2, March 1931, pp. 583-5.

199 Muhammad ʻAbdallah Muhibb, "Tafashshi al-Talaq wa-Turuq 'Ilajuhu," *al-Siyasa al-Usbuiʻyya*, 15 October 1927, p. 27. See also Lutfi al-Mandarawi, "Bahth fi Mushkilat al-ʻUzuba wa-Azmat al-Zawaj," *a/-Muqattam*, 9 November 1934, pp. 1, 10.

200 ʻAbd al-Qadir, "Al-Ihjam," part 3, p. 8.

201 Abu Taʼila, "Misr bayna Hadaratayn," p.5.

202 ʻAbd al-Hamid Ahmad Thabit, "Tarbiyat al-Marʼa al-Misriyya," *Al-Siyasa al-Usbuʻiyya*, 20 August 1927, p. 8.

203 On the difficulties to promote the idea of social intercourse between the sexes in Arab traditional society see Baer, *Population and Society in the Arab East*, pp. 67-8.

204 Al-Rafiʻi, *Wahy al-Qalam*, vol. 1, p. 300.

205 Muhammad Muhammad al-Sayhi, "Al-Ikhtilat," *Al-Balagh*, 27 June 1934, p. 10.

206 Sayyid Qutb, "Al-Azma al-Zawjiyya," *Al-Balagh al-Usbuʻi*, 10 April 1929, pp. 28-9.

207 Sayyid Qutb, "Al-Ikhtilat fi al-Aryaf,' *Al-Balagh al-Usbuʻi*, 8 May 1929, p. 29.

208 Abd al-Munʻim Mursi ʻAlam, "Wazifat al-Marʼa al-Haqiqiyya, *Al-Muqattam*, 23 July 1933, p. 1.

209 Amina Ahmad Taha, "Al-Sufur," *Al-Balagh al-UsbuʻI*, 9 December 1927, p. 22.

210 Amin, *Tahrir al-Marʼa,* pp. 16-22, 31, 41-54. See also Amin, *Al-Marʼa al-Jadida*, pp. 110-122, 160-3.

211 Nasif, *Al-Nisa'iyyat*, vol. 1, pp. 72-3, 110-11, 123. See also Mayy Ziyada, *Bahithat al-Badiyya* (Cairo: Matbaʻat al-Muqtataf, 1920), pp. 93-5.

212 Nabawiyya Musa, "Al-Thaqafa al-'Amma," *Al-Balagh al-Usbu'i*, 31 December 1926, p. 27; Nabawiyya Musa, "Al-Zawaj bi-al-Ajnabiyyat," *Al-Balagh al-Usbu'i*,18 November 1927, p. 20; Nabawiyya Musa, "Ta'lim al-Banat wa-'Alaqatuhu bi-Ta'lim al-Banin," *Sahafat al-Mu'alliminn*, 3rd year, July-October 1925, pp. 445-50 ; Nabawiyya Musa, "Hajat Misr ila al-Nisa' al-'Amilat," *Al-Balagh al-Usbu'i*, 17 June 1927, pp. 32-3; Nabawiyya Musa, "Madaris al-Ummahat wa-al-Tadbir al-Manzili," *Al-Balagh al-Usbu'i*, 7 January 1927, p. 24; Musa, "Shay," p. 20.

213 Asma Fahmi, "Al-Ta'lim al-'Ali li-al-Nisa'," *Al-Risala*, vol. 2, 22 January 1934, pp. 141-2; Asma Fahmi, "Thaqafat al-Mar'a," *Al-Risala*, vol. 1, 15 June 1933, pp. 17-8. See also 'Abd al-Hamid Ahmad Thabit, "Taqaddum al-Mar'a al-Misriyya," *Al-Siyasa al-Usbu'iiyya*, 18 June 1927, p. 6.

214 Muhammad Shafiq Ghurbal, "Hal Yakun Nizam Ta'lim al-Banat Huwa Nafs Nizam Ta'lim al-Banin," *Sahifat al-Mualimin*, 3rd year, July-October 1925, pp. 438-44.

215 Sulaiman Darwish Sayyid, "Wazifat al-Mar'a," *Al-Muqattam*, 30 July 1933, p. 7.

216 Muhammad 'Ali Majdhub, "Al-Tarbiya al-Mushtaraka," *Sahifat al-Mu'allimin*, 3rd year, July-October 1925, p. 467.

217 Sayyid Qutb, "Tawhid Baramij al-Ta'lim li-al-Jinsayn," *Al-Balagh al-Usbu'i*, 20 March 1929, p. 28.

218 Ihsan Ahmad al-Qusi, "Istithmar Nahdat al-Mar'a li-Khayr al-Bilad," *Al-Risala*, vol. 4, 18 May 1936, pp. 824-6.

219 Muhammad 'Abdallah 'Inan, "Malikat wa-Wazirat," *al-Risala*, vol. 3, 20 July 1936, pp. 1165-7.

220 Musa, "Hajat Misr ila al-Nisa' al-'Amilat," p. 32; Nabawiyya Musa, "Al-Mar'a al-Jadida," *Al-Balagh al-Usbu'i*, 23 December 1927, p. 21. See also Fahmi (Asma), "Ta'lim," p. 142.

221 Musa, "Mutazawwijat," p. 31.

222 Sa'id, "Ikhtilat," p. 1255.

223 Nazla al-Hakim Sa'id, "Al-Fata al-Misriyya fi al-Madrasa wa-al-Ba'tha wa-al-Manzil," *Al-Ma'rifa*, October 1932, 2nd year, p. 659.

224 Suheir al-Qalamawi, "Makanat al-Mar'a fi al-Nahda al-Misriyya," *Al-Rabita al-'Arabiyya*, 16 December 1936, pp.172-4.

225 Sayyid Qutb, "Tawhid Baramij al-Ta'lim li-al-Jinsayn," p. 28.

226 Sayyid Qutb, "Al-Mar'a fi Maydan al-'Amal," *Al-Balagh al-Usbu'i*, 20 March 1929, p. 28.

227 Al- Rafi'i, *Wahy al-Qalam*, vol. 1, p. 222. See also Al- Mansi, "Al-Mar'a al-Sharqiyya,", p. 852.

228 Al-Harawi, *Al-Mustashriqun wa- al-Islam*, p. 96.

229 Sulayman Darwish Sayyid, "Wazifat al-Mar'a," *Al-Muqattam*, 10 August 1933, p. 8.

230 Al-Zayyat, "Shuruh wa-Hawash," p. 4.

231 Muhammad Lutfi Jum'a, "Nahdat al-Sharq al-'Arabi,'" in reply to survey conducted by *al-Hilal*, 31 December 1922, p. 241.

232 *Population and Society in the Arab East*, pp. 50-2.

233 Ayman A. El-Desouky, *The Intellectual and the People in Egyptian Literature and Culture : Amāra and the 2011 Revolution (*Hampshire ; New York : Palgrave Macmillan, 2014), p. 49.

234 On the role of Arabic in forming and articulating national identity in the Middle East since nineteenth century see Yasir Suleiman, *The Arabic Language and National Identity: A Study in Ideology* (Washington, D.C.: Georgetown University Press, 2003).

235 See Helge Daniëls, "Linguistic Conservatism as the Basis for Political Revolution? The fusha-'ammiya Debate in Nineteenth-century Ottoman-Arab Middle Eastern Society", *Antwerp Papers in Linguistics,* vol. 106 (2004), pp. 79-92.

236 On the Egyptian territorial nationalism, including Egyptian national literature see Gershoni and Jankowski, *Egypt, Islam, and the Arabs*, pp. 77-227. See also Charles Wendell, *The Evolution of the Egyptian National Image: From its Origins to Ahmad Lutfi al-Sayyid* (Berkeley and Los Angeles: University of California Press, 1972); Donald M. Reid, "Nationalizing the Pharaonic Past: Egypt 1922—1952." In James Jankowski and Israel Gershoni (eds.), *Rethinking Nationalism in the Arab Middle East* (New York: Columbia University Press, 1997), pp. 127-67. For the debate in Egypt of the late nineteenth century and the early decades of the twentieth century on the literary and colloquial language see also Yasir Sulaiman, *The Arabic Language and National Identity: A Study in Ideology* (Washington, D.C.: Georgetown University Press, 2003), 169-97; John Cornelius Baskerville, *From Tahdhiib al-Amma to Tahmiish al-Ammiyya: In Search of Social and Literary Roles for Standard and Colloquial Arabic in late 19th Century Egypt*. PhD dissertation (The University of Texas, 2009); David Semah, *Four Egyptian Literary Critics* (Leiden: E. J. Brill, 1974), pp. 13, 32, 75-95, 118-20.

237 See Kees Versteegh, *The Arabic Language* (Edinburgh: Edinburgh University Press, 2014), pp. 74-7, 108; Anwar Chejne, *The Arabic Language: Its Role in History* (Minneapolis, Minn: University of Minnesota Press, 1969), pp. 8-13, 146.

238 On idea of linguistic evolution see Mario Alinei, "Darwinism, Traditional Linguistics and the New Palaeolithic Continuity Theory of Language Evolution." In Jean Paul Van Bendegem and Diederik Aerts, (eds.), *Evolutionary Epistemology, Language and Culture. A Non-Adaptationist, Systems Theoretical Approach* (Berlin-Heidelberg-New York: Springer, 2006), pp.121-47; Pierre-Yves Oudeyer and Frédéric Kaplan, "Language Evolution as a Darwinian Process: Computational Studies," *Cognitive Processing*, vol. 8, no. 1 (2007), pp. 21–35 2007. On the purist-modernist controversy on language see also: Jaroslav Stetkevych, The Modern Arabic Literary Language: Lexical and Stylistic Developments (Chicago: University of Chicago Press, 1970), pp. xvii-xviii (in the introduction by W.R. Polk) and p. 6.

239 Hassan al-Sharif, "Al-Lugha al-'Arabiyya Aghna min al-Faransiyya", *Al-Hilal*, vol. 47, January 1939, p. 303. See also p. 302.

240 Ibid., 303. See also Hassan Al-Sharif, "Tabsit Qawa'id al-Lugha al-'Arabiyya", *Al-Hilal*, vol. 46, August 1938, p. 1110.

241 Mansur Fahmi, "Hawla Majma' al-Lugha al-'Arabiyya al-Malaki", part 2, *Al-Siyasa Al-Usbu'iyya*, 19 June 1937, p. 5.

242 Muhammad 'Abd al-Qadir Hamza, "Al-Lugha al-'Arabiyya wa-al-Huruf al-Latiniyya", *Al-Balagh al-Usbu'i*, 1 June 1928, p.4. See also al-Bishri, "Mas'ala", p. 1519: Mustafu Lutfi al-Manfaluti, " "Al-Bayan," *Al-Hilal*, vol. 27, October 1918, p. 63.

243 'Ali Mustafa Musharrafa, "Al-Lugha al-'Arabiyya ka-Adah 'Ilmiyya", *Al-Risala*, vol. 1, 15 January 1933, p. 10.

244 'Abd al-'Aziz al-Bishri, "Kifah al-Lugha al-'Arabiyya fi Sabil al-Hayah wa-al-Nuhud", *Al-Hilal*, vol.45, April 1937, p. 645. See also al-Bishri, *Al-Mukhtir*, vol. 1, pp. 57-60; Al-Bishri, "Kayfa Yanba'ith al-Adab wa-Kayfa Natarawwahu?," part 2, p. 494.

245 Khaki, "Qadiyyat al-I.ugha al-'Arabiyya", part I, p. 574.

246 Ahmad 'Isa, "Kayfa Takhdum al-Lugha al-'Arabiyya", *Al-Hilal*, vol. 42, August 1934, p. 1209.

247 Muhammad Sharaf, "Hadaratuna al-Qadima," in reply to survey conducted by *al-Hilal*, vol. 39, April 1930, p. 827.

248 Mubammad Muhammad Baraniq, "Qissat al-Lugha al-'Arabiyya", *Al-Ahram*, 28 March 1938, p. 7. See also Hamza, "Al-Lugha al-'Arabiyya wa-al-Huruf al-Latiniyya", p. 3; Mansur Fahmi, "Al-Lugha al-'Arabiyya", in reply to survey conducted by *al-Hilal*, vol. 47, August 1939, pp. 989-90; Ahmad Abu al-Khidr al-Mansi, "Ma'ani al-Hubb fi al-Lugha al-'Arabiyya wa-al-Lughatt al-Ukhra", *Al-Ahram*, vol. 3 July 1937, p. 3: Al-Zayyat, "Tat'im al-Adab al-'Arabi," p.1861; Fakhri Abu al-Su'ud, "Al-Taswir fi al-Shi'r al-'Arabt," *Al-Risala*, vol. 2, 7 May 1934, p. 780.

249 Amin Wasif, "Al-Shi'r wa-al-Musiqa", *Al-Hilal*, vol. 28 (May 1919), p. 686; cf. Semah, *Four Egyptian Literary Critics*, p. 91.

250 Musharrafa, "Al-Lugha al-'Arabiyya ka-Adah 'Ilmiyya", p.10.

251 Muhammad Sharaf, "Al-Lugha al-'Arabiyya wa-al-Mustalahat al-'Ilmiyya", part 2, *Al-Muqtataf,* vol. 74, March 1929, p. 279. See also Ahmad al-Iskandari, "Ta'rib", *Al-Zahara'*, vol. 1, Rabi' al-Awwal 1343 AH, p. 171.

252 Sharaf, "Al-Lugha al-'Arabiyya wa-al-Mustalahat al-'Ilmiyya", part 2, p. 280.

253 Hafiz Mahmud, "Fi-al-Tataawwar al-Lugha", *Al-Majalla al-Jadida*, vol. 1, July 1930, p. 1095.

254 Ibrahim 'Abd al-Qadir al-Mazini, "Al-Lugha al-'Ammiyya wa-al-Lugha al-Fusha", *Al-Majalla al-Jadida*, vol. 7, October 1938, p. 86.

255 Ibrahim 'Abd Al-Qadir al-Mazini, "Al-Lugha wa-al-Qawalib al-Mawrutha", *Al-Risala*, vol. 7, August 1939, p. 1528.

256 Khaki, "Qadiyyat al-I.ugha al-'Arabiyya", part 1, p. 574.

257 Hamza, "Al-Lugha al-'Arabiyya wa-al-Huruf al-Latiniyya", p. 4.

258 Sharif, "Tabsit Qawa'id al-Lugha al-'Arabiyya," p. 1110. See also Ahmad Zaki Abu Shadi, "Fi Sabil al-'Arabiyya", *Al-Muqtataf,* vol. 75, July 1929, p. 168.

259 See Salama Musa, "Al-Lugha al-Fusha wa-al-Lugha al-'Ammiyya," *Al-Hilal*, vol. 34, July 1926, pp. 1073-77; Salama Musa, *Al-Yawm wa-al-Ghad* (Cairo: Al-Matba'a al-'Asriya, l927), pp. 237-8; Salama Musa, *Al-Dunya ba'd Thalathin Sana* (Cairo: Salama Musa li-al-Nashar wa-al-Tawzi', n.d.), pp. 67-8 For Musa's ideas on language in the context of the debate on national identity see Sulaiman, *The Arabic Language and National Identity,* pp. 180-90.

260 Adham, "Misr wa-al-Thaqafa al-Urubiyya", p. 30.

261 See G.E. von Grunebaum, "I'jaz", *Encyclopedia of Islam* (Leiden: E. J. Brill, 1969), vol. 3, pp. 1018-20; Chejne, *The Arabic Language: Its Role in History*, p. 8.

262 Al- Rafi'i, *Tahta Rayat Al-Qur'an*, pp. 53-63. For al- Rafi'i's notion of relation between Arabic and the Qur'an see also Mustafa Sadiq al- Rafi'i, "Falsafat al-Adab," *Al-Muqtataf*, vol. 81, July 1932, p. 155; Mustafa Sadiq al-Rafi'i, "Mustaqbal al-Lugha al-'Arabiyya", *Al-Hilal*, vol. 28, February 1920, p. 399-400.

263 Al- Rafi'i, *Wahy al-Qalam*, vol. 3, p. 435.

264 Muhammad 'Abd al-Qadir Hamza, "Hadith al-Ithnayn: Al-Qissa fi al-Adab al-Misri al-Hadith", *Al-Balagh*, 10 December 1934, p. 3. See also Muhammad 'Abd al-Qadir Hamza, "Hadith al-Ithnayn: Bayna al-Shuyukh wa-al-Shabab", *Al-Balagh*, 29 October 1934, p. 3.

265 Muhammad Lutfi Jum'a, "Al-Hadara al-'Arabiyya wa-Ahamm Muqawwamatuha", *Al-Rabita*, al-'Arabiyya, 10 November 1937, p. 12. See also p. 11. For the relation between the Arabic language and Islam see also Muhammad Ahmad al-Ghamrawi, *Al-Naqd al-Tahlili li-al-Kitab Fi al-Adab al-Jahili* (Cairo 1929), pp. 49-53.

266 Ahmad Ahmad Badawi, "Al-Wahda al-'Arabiyya wa-al-Adab al-Qaumi", *Al-Ma'rifa*, vol. 1, February 1932, pp. 1215-6.

267 Ahmad Ahmad Badawi, "Al-Lugha al-'Arabiyya fi Madarisina", *Al-Siyasa al-Usbu'iyya*, vol. 20, March 1937, p. 29.

268 On the use of colloquial language in Mahmud Taymur's literary writing see Nafusa Zakariyya Sa'id, *Ta'rikh al-Da'wa ila al-'Ammiyya wa-Atharuha fi Misr* (Alexandria: Dar Nashr al-Thaqafa, 1964), pp. 401-17. See also Mahmud Taymur, *Al-Shaykh Jum'a wa-Aqasis Ukhra*, 2nd ed. (Cairo Al-Matba'a al-Salafiyah, 1927), pp. 14-5.

269 Mahmud Taymur, "Al-Niza' bayna al-Fusha wa-al-'Ammiyya fi al-Adab al-Misri al-Hadith", *Al-Hilal*, vol. 4l, July 1933, pp. 1186-8.

270 See Gershoni and Jankowski, *Egypt, Islam, and the Arabs*, p. 192.

271 Dayf, *Muqaddima li-Dirasat Balaghat al-'Arab*, p. 6.

272 Ibid.

273 On the use of colloquial language in Ibrahim 'Abd Al-Qadir Al-Mazini's literary writing, see Sa'id, *Ta'rikh al-Da'wa ila al-'Ammiyya wa-Atharuha fi Misr*, pp. 417-36.

274 'Abd al-Qadir al-Mazini, "Al-'Aanmiyya wa-al-Fusha", *Al-Risala*, vol. 6, 24 October 1938, pp. 1721-4; Al-Mazini,"'Ammiyya", pp. 83-8; See also Ibrahim 'Abd al-Qadir al-Mazini, "Al-'Ammiyya wa-al- 'Arabiyya", *Al-Risala*, vol. 3, 7 October 1935, pp. 1616-7; Ibrahim 'Abd al-Qadir al-Mazini, "Al-'Ammiyya

wa-al-'Arabiyya Aydan," *Al-Risala*, vol. 3, 21 October 1935, pp. 1692-3. Ibrahim 'Abd al-Qadir al-Mazini, *Ibrahim al-Katib* (Cairo: Matba'at Dar al-Turki, 1931), pp. 12-3; Ibrahim 'Abd al-Qadir al-Mazini, "Al-Masrah al-Misri," *Al-Risala*, 16 September 1935, p. 1482. According to Dr. Ahmad 'Isa, many colloquial words which are regarded today as distasteful, actually originated in literary Arabic: Ahmad 'Isa, *Al-Muhkam fi Uszul al-Kalimat al-'Ammiyya* (Cairo: Matba'at 'Isa al-Babi al-Halabi, 1939), pp. 1209-11.

275 Ahmad Zaki Abu Shadi, *Al-Shu'la* (Cairo 1933), p. 10 of the introduction (the citation is based on Sa'id, *Ta'rikh al-Da'wa ila al-'Ammiyya wa-Atharuha fi Misr*, p. 375).

276 Ahmad Zaki Abu Shadi, "Al-Shi'r wa-al-Sha'ir," an essay published in the introduction to his *diwan*, *Al-Shafaq al-Baki* (Cairo: Al-Matba'ah al-Salafiyah, 1926), pp. 44-8. For Ahmad Zaki Abu Shadi's view about the colloquial language see Abu Shadi, "Fi Sabil al-'Arabiyya," p. 173; Sa'id, *Ta'rikh al-Da'wa ila al-'Ammiyya wa-Atharuha fi Misr*, pp. 374-9.

277 See Chejne, *The Arabic Language*, pp. 157-61. In 1943 'Abd al-'Aziz Fahmi submitted to the Royal Academy of Arabic Language a proposal for the adoption of the Latin script - the proposal was rejected (see Sa'id, *Ta'rikh al-Da'wa ila al-'Ammiyya wa-Atharuha fi Misr*, pp. 208-20).

278 See Uriel Heyd, *Language Reform in Modern Turkey* (Jerusalem: Israel Oriental Society, 1954), pp. 22-5; Bernard Lewis, *History: Remembered, Recovered, Invented* (Princeton: Princeton University Press, 1975), pp. 432-3.

279 See Musa, "Al-Khat al-Latini li-al-Lugha al-'Arabiyya," pp. 79-80; Musa, *Al-Dunya ba'd Thalathin Sana*, pp. 68-9.

280 See Muhammad 'Abdallah 'Inan, "Harb Munazzama Yashaharaha al-Kamaliyun 'ala al-Islam", *Al-Risala*, vol 3, 14 January 1935, pp. 45-6; Muhammad Amin Hassuna, *Wara'a al-Bihar* (Cairo: Matba'at al-Shams,1936), pp. 59-60; Abu Ta'ila, "Misr bayna Hadaratayn," p. 5; Hamza, "Al-Lugha al-'Arabiyya wa-al-Huruf al-Latiniyya", p. 3.

281 Hamza, "Al-Lugha al-'Arabiyya wa-al-Huruf al-Latiniyya", pp. 3-5.

282 Abu Shadi, "Fi Sabil al-'Arabiyya," pp. 165-6.

283 Tahir Ahmad al-Tanahi, "Hal Yumkinu Islah al-Huruf al-'Arabiyya," *Al-Hilal*, vol. 42, May 1934, p. 833.

284 Zaki Mubarak, *Al-Lugha al-Din wa-al-Taqalid fi Hayat al-Istiqlal* (Cairo: Matba'at 'Isa al-Babi al-Halabi, 1936), pp. 30-3. The Royal Academy of Arabic Language also examined methods to simplify Arabic writing. In 1944

it announced an award for the best proposal on the subject (see Sa'id, *Ta'rikh al-Da'wa ila al-'Ammiyya wa-Atharuha fi Misr*, pp. 207, 221-3). See also Ahmad al-Iskandari, "Taysir al-Hija' al-'Arabi," *Majallat Majma' al-Lugha al-'Arabiyya al-Malaki*, vol. 1, October 1934, pp. 369-80; interview with the Minister of Education, Bahey al-Din Barakat, "Qadiyat al-Lugha al-'Arabiyya" , *Al-Ahram*, 28 February 1938, p. 1; Stetkevych, *The Modern Arabic Literary Language*, pp. 88-90.

285 See: Stetkevych, *The Modern Arabic Literary Language*, pp. 1-78: Chejne, *The Arabic Language*, pp. 151-7.

286 See Stetkevych, *The Modern Arabic Literary Language*, pp. 1-7, 57-61. On the development of Arabic political vocabulary during the nineteenth century see Ami Ayalon, *Language and Change in the Arab Middle East* (New York: Oxford University Press, 1987).

287 For the use of foreign languages in the Egyptian University see Grunebaum, *Modern Islam*, pp. 267-8. See also Ahmad Hassan al-Zayyat, "Istiqlal al-Lugha", *Al-Risala*, vol. 4, 7 December 1936, p. 1982; Muhammad Qabil, "Al-Qari' al-'Arabi wa-Fikruhu fi al-Thaqafa al-Hadirtha," *Al-Ahram*, 22 October 1937, p. 3; 'Inan, "Misr bayna thaqafatayn", pp. 448-51.

288 Mubarak, *Al-Lugha wa-al-Din wa- al-Taqalid fi Hayat al-Istiqlal*, p. 15.

289 For the principle of *naht* see Stetkevych, *The Modern Arabic Literary Language*, pp. 48-55.

290 Sharif, "Al-Lugha al-'Arabiyya Aghna min al-Faransiyya," p. 303.

291 'Isa, "Kayfa Takhdum al-Lugha al-'Arabiyya," p. 1209. See also, Stetkevych, *The Modern Arabic Literary Language*, pp. 6-7, 57; Wendell, *The Evolution of the Egyptian National Image*, p. 277.

292 Musharrafa, "Al-Lugha al-'Arabiyya ka-Adah 'Ilmiyya", p. 11.

293 For the *majaz,* see Chejne, *The Arabic Language*, p. 151.

294 Fahmi, "Al-Lugha al-'Arabiyya"pp. 989-90.

295 The decision of the Royal Academy of Arabic Language of 1934 regarding the question of *ta'rib* stated: "The Academy allows the use of a number of non-Arabic words (*alfaz 'ajamiyya*) — when necessary — in accordance with the Arabs' methods in their Arabization.": "Qararat al-Majma," *Majallat Majma' al-Lugha al-'Arabiyya al-Malaki*, vol. 1, October 1934, p. 33. See also, p. 37; Stetkevych, *The Modern Arabic Literary Language*, p. 63.

296 Sharaf, "Al-Lugha al-'Arabiyya wa-al-Mustalahat al-'Ilmiyya," part 2, pp. 278-82. For the Arabization of foreign words see also Muhammad Sharaf, "Al-Lugha al-'Arabiyya wa-al-Mustalahat al-'Ilmiyya," part 1, *al-Muqtaaf*, vol, 74, February 1929, p. 127; Abu Shadi, "Fi Sabil al-'Arabiyya," pp. 172-74;Al-Bishri, "Mas'ala," pp. 1518-9.

297 See for example al-Bishri, "Mas'ala," p. 1519; Stetkevych, p. 62.

298 Iskandart, "Al-Ta'rib," pp. 168-77.

299 Salama Musa, "Islah al-Lugha", *Al-Balagh*, vol. 23, February 1935, p. 1.

300 Ibid.

301 Musa, "Al-Khat al-Latini li-al-Lugha al-'Arabiyya," pp. 69-70. See also Salama Musa, *Al-Dunya ba'd Thalathin Sana*, p. 69. In the second decade of the twentieth century, Muhammad Husayn Haykal suggested permanent adoption of foreign technical and scientific terms, which had already found their way into everyday language, instead of trying to coin new terms based on Arabic roots (see Semah, *Four Egyptian Literary Critics*. p. 92).

302 See J. Heyworth-Dunne, *An Introduction to the History of Education in Modern Egypt* (London: Taylor & Francis Group, 1968), pp. 2-7; Abu al-Futouh Ahmad Radwan, *Old and New Forces in Egyptian Education* (New York: Teachers College Columbia University, 1951), pp. 59-68; H.A.R. Gibb, "The Heritage of Islam in the Modern World," part 3, *IJMES*, vol. 2 (1971): 141-4; Vatikiotis, *The Modern History of Egypt*, pp. 91-2. For the education in Islam see Ignaz Goldziher, "Education (Muslim)", *Encyclopaedia of Religion and Ethics*, vol. 5 (1912), pp. 198-201; A.L. Tibawi, *Islamic Education* (London: London: Luzac & Co., 1972), pp. 23-46.

303 See Heyworth-Dunne, *An Introduction to the History of Education in Modern Egypt*; Vatikiotis, *The Modern History of Egypt*, pp. 90-125.

304 Gibb, "The Heritage of Islam in the Modern World," p. 146.

305 Radwan, pp. 59, 101.

306 Amir Boktor, "Thaqafatuna al-Qawmiyya wa-ma Yanqusuha min 'Awamil al-Quwa," *Al-Hilal*, vol. 45, April 1937, pp. 658-60; Amir Boktor, "Al-Jil al-Misri al-Muqbil," *Al-Hilal*, vol. 46, February 1938, pp. 366-73. See also Mahmud 'Azmi, "Ittijah al-Ta'lim fi al-Jami'at," *Al-Hilal*, vol. 37, April 1929, p. 676; Ibrahim al-Misri , "Li-man Yaktubu al-Katib al-Misri," *Al-Hilal*, vol. 46, July 1938, pp. 988-9.

307 Al-Mazini, "Al-Hayah al-Misriyya wa-Hajatuha ila 'Anasir al-Quwa wa-al-Khayal," p. 552. See also 'Abd al-Hamid Hassan, "Bayna al-Qadim wa-al-Hadith fi Tarbiya wa-al-Ta'lim," *Sahifat Dar al-'Ulum*, vol. 1, June 1934, pp. 64-72.

308 Barakat, interview, p. 1.

309 See *al-Risala*, vol. 6, 14 March 1938, pp. 435-6 and 18 July 1938, p. 1197; "Silat al-Tullab bi-Harakat al-Tajdid wa-al-Thaqafa al-'Arabiyya," *Al-Ahram*, 2 August 1938, pp. 3, 15; "Taysir Qawa'id al-Nahw wa-al-Sarf wa-al-Balagha," *Al-Muqtalaf*, vol. 93, November 1938, pp. 401-3. On the simplification of the rules of Arabic grammar see also Stetkevych, *The Modern Arabic Literary Language*, pp. 79-94; Sa'id, *Ta'rikh al-Da'wa ila al-'Ammiyya wa-Atharuha fi Misr*, pp. 95-206.

310 Muhammad 'Abd al-Qadir Hamza, "Hadith al-Ithnayn: Khata' Tariqat Ta'lim al-Lugha al 'Arabiyya", *Al-Balagh al-Usbu'i*, 23 March 1936, p. 10.

311 Hamza, "Al-Lugha al-'Arabiyya wa-al-Huruf al-Latiniyya", p. 4.

312 Mustafa Muhammad Salam, "Islah al-Lugha al-'Arabiyya", *Al-Ahram*, 27 August 1937, p. 13.

313 Ahmad Hassan al-Zayyat, "'Afat al-Lugha Hadha al-Nahw...", *Al-Risala*, vol. 1, issue 13, 15 July 1933, pp. 7-8; Ahmad Hassan al-Zayyat, "Tadris al-Lugha al-'Arabiyya", *Al-Risala*, vol. 7, 8 May 1939, pp. 895-6.

314 'Afifi, *'Ala Hamish al-Siyasa*, p. 75.

315 Ibid., pp. 72-3, 75.

316 In a reply to this study by Ibrahim Mustafa, Muhammad 'Arafah, a lecturer in the department of Arabic Language at al-Azhar University, published a book entitled *Al-Nahw wa-al-Nuhah* (Cairo: Matba'at al-Sa'ada 1937).

317 See Ibrahim Mustafa, *Ihya' al-Nahw* (Cairo: Matba'at Lajnat al-Ta'lif wa-al-Tarjamah wa-al-Nashr, 1937), pp. v-viii.

318 Sharif, "Tabsit Qawa'id al-Lugha al-'Arabiyya," pp. 1109-15. Hafiz Mahmud also supported reforming the rules of Arabic grammar. Notable his proposal for changing the principles of construction of the inflection of verbs in the future tense (see Mahmud, "Fi-al-Tataawwur al-Lugha", pp. 1095-98).

319 Sharif, "Tabsit Qawa'id al-Lugha al-'Arabiyya", pp. 1115-9.

320 Ibid, p. 1110.

321 Badawi, "Al-Lugha al-'Arabiyya fi Madarisina," p. 29.

322 Muhammad Taha al-Hajiri, "Athar al-Nahw fi Taqwim al-Lisan," *Al-Risala*, vol. 4, 3 August, 1936, p. 1250.

323 Ibrahim 'Abd al-Qadir al-Mazini, "Al-Nahw", *Al-Risala*, 1 March 1937, p. 325. For the reform in Arabic language teaching in general and of Arabic grammar in particular see Khaki, "Qadiyyat al-Lugha al-'Arabiyya", part 2, pp. 643-6; 'Abd al Mun'im al-Khalaf, " 'Afat al-Lugha al-'Arabiyya", *Al-Ahram*, 26 August 1937, p. 15.

324 Ibrahtm 'Abd al-Qadir al-Mazini, "Al-Adab al-"Arabi wa-Tariqat Tadrisihi fi al-Madaris,' *al Balagh*, 20 November 1934, p. 1. See also Ibrahim 'Abd al-Qadir al-Mazini, "Al-Adab al-'Arabi wa-Tariqat Tadrisihi fi al-Madaris: Al-Adab wa-Ta'rikh al-Adab", *Al-Balagh*, 21 November 1934, pp. 1,9. Dr. Zaki Mubarak shared the view that modern Arabic literature should serve as a starting point for the teaching of Arabic literature (see Zaki Mubarak, "Al-Hadith Dhu Shujun: Ila Ma'ali Wazir al-Ma'arif," *Al-Balagh*, 12 June 1936, p. 11). This idea was rejected by 'Abd al-Qadir Hamza. In his opinion, every field of knowledge should be taught from its natural starting point, be it easy to understand or not (see 'Abd al-Qadir Hamza, "Hadith al Ithnayn: Tadris al-Adab al-'Arabi fi al-Madaris al-Misriyya", *Al-Balagh*, 26 November 1934, pp. 3, 11).

325 See Vatikiotis, *The Modern History of Egypt*, pp. 292-312.

326 William Scheuerman, "Globalization". In Edward N. Zalta (ed.), *The Stanford Encyclopedia of Philosophy* (Summer 2014 Edition), http://plato.stanford.edu/archives/sum2014/entries/globalization/ (last accessed, 20 March 2018).

327 See C.A. Bayly, *The Birth of the Modern World, 1780-1914: Global Connections and Comparisons*. (Maiden, MA and Oxford: Blackwell, 2004), pp. 1-21.

328 Gelvin and Green, "Introduction." p. 1.

329 Azyumardi Azra. "Globalization of Indonesian Muslim Discourse: Contemporary Religio-Intellectual Connections between Indonesia and the Middle East." In Johan Meuleman (ed.), *Islam in the Era of Globalization: Muslim Attitude Towards Modernity and Identity* (London: RoutledgeCurzon, 2002), p. 31.

330 M. F. Laffan, *Islamic Nationhood and Colonial Indonesia: The Umma Below the Winds* (London and New York: Routledge Curzon, 2003) , p. 13.

331 Christine Dobbin, *Islamic Revivalism in a Changing Peasant Economy: Central Sumatra, 1784–1847*, Scandinavian Institute of Asian Studies, Monograph Series no. 47 (London and Malmo: Curzon Press, 1983), pp. 117–224; Christine Dobbin, "Islamic Revivalism in Minangkabau at the Turn of the Nineteenth Century," *Modern Asian Studies*, vol. 8, no. 3 (1974), pp. 319–56; Taufik Abdullah, "Adat and Islam: An Examination of Conflict in Minangkabau," *Indonesia*, II (October 1966), pp. 1–24; Taufik Abdullah, "Modernization in the Minangkabau World: West Sumatra in the Early Decades of the Twentieth Century,". In Claire Holt (ed.), *Culture and Politics in Indonesia* (Ithaca: Cornell University Press, 1972),

pp. 198–205; William R. Roff, "South-East Asian Islam in the Nineteenth Century". In P. M. Holt, Ann K. S. Lambton and Bernard Lewis (eds.), *The Cambridge History of Islam*, vol. 2: *The Further Islamic Lands, Islamic Society and Civilization*, (London: Cambridge University Press, 1970), pp. 155-70; Anthony Crothers Milner, "Islam and the Muslim State". In M.B. Hooker (ed.), *Islam in Southeast Asia* (Leiden: E.J. Brill, 1993), pp. 45-49.

332 For a discussion on the Arab Peninsula role in the narrative of Islam in the Malay-Indonesia World see Azyumardi Azra, *The Transmission of Islamic Reformism to Indonesia: Networks of Middle Eastern and Malay-Indonesian 'Ulama' in the Seventeenth and Eighteenth Centuries* (Honolulu: ALLEN & UNWIN and University of Hawaii Press, 2004); Giora Eliraz, *Islam in Indonesia: Modernism, Radicalism and the Middle East Dimension* (Brighton: Sussex Academic Press, 2004), pp. 42-56; Laffan, *Islamic Nationhood and Colonial Indonesia,* pp. 3-76.

333 Clifford Geertz, *Islam Observed: Religious Development in Morocco and Indonesia* (New Haven and London: Yale University Press, 1968), p. 67.

334 Ibid.

335 On the Dutch suspicion of the Pilgrimage and its implications see Syed M.K. Aljunied, Western Images of Meccan Pilgrims in the Dutch East Indies, 1800-1900", *SARI* (2005), pp. 105-22; C. van Dijk, "Colonial Fears, 1890–1918: Pan-Islamism and the Germano-Indian Plot.". In Huub de Jonge and Nico Kaptein (eds.), *Transcending Borders: Arabs, Politics, Trade and Islam in Southeast Asia* (Leiden: KITLV Press: 2002), pp. 53–89; Huub de Jonge, "Dutch Colonial Policy pertaining to Hadhrami Immigrants". In Ulrike Freitag and William G. Clarence-Smith, *Hadhrami Traders, Scholars and Statesmen in the Indian Ocean,1750s–1960s* (Leiden: Brill, 1997), pp. 106–11; Roff, "South-East Asian Islam in the Nineteenth Century", pp. 180-1; Laffan, *Islamic Nationhood and Colonial Indonesia*, pp. 37-9.

336 William G. Clarence-Smith, "Hadramaut and the Hadrami Diaspora in the Modern Colonial Era: An Introductory Survey". In Ulrike Freitag and William G. Clarence-Smith (eds.), *Hadhrami Traders, Scholars and Statesmen in the Indian Ocean, 1750s–1960s* (Leiden: Brill, 1997), p. 5; Natalie Mobini-Kesheh, *The Hadrami Awakening: Community and Identity in the NetherlandsEast Indies, 1900–1942* (Ithaca: Cornell University Press, 1999), p. 21; William R. Roff, *The Origins of Malay Nationalism* (New Haven and London: Yale University Press, 1967), p. 40; Delphine Alles, *Transnational Islamic Actors and Indonesia's Foreign Policy* (London: Routledge, 2015), p. 25.

337 See Leif Manger, *The Hadrami Diaspora: Community-Building on the Indian Ocean Rim* (New York: Berghahn Books, 2010), p. 1.

338 See Alles, *Transnational Islamic Actors and Indonesia's Foreign Policy*, pp. 24-5, 27.

339 Peter G. Riddell, *Islam and the Malay-Indonesian World: Transmission and Responses* (Honolulu: University of Hawai'i Press, 2001), p. 9.

340 Michael Laffan, "An Indonesian Community in Cairo: Continuity and Change in a Cosmopolitan Islamic Milieu", *Indonesia*, vol. 77, (April 2004), pp. 4-5. See also Laffan, *Islamic Nationhood and Colonial Indonesia*, pp. 127-33; Numan Hayimasae, "The Intellectual Network of Patani and the Haramayn". In P. Jory (ed.), *The Ghosts of the Past in Southern Thailand; Essays on the History and Historiography of Patani* (Singapore: NUS press, 2013), p. 117.

341 Laffan, *Islamic Nationhood and Colonial Indonesia*, p.219; Deliar Noer, *The Modernist Muslim Movement in Indonesia: 1900–1942* (Oxford: Oxford University Press, 1978), p. 153.

342 William R. Roff, "Indonesian and Malay Students in Cairo in the 1920's". *Indonesia*, vol. 9 (April 1970), p. 74.

343 On the community of the Malay-Indonesian students and scholars in Cairo see Mona Abaza, *Changing Images of Three Generations of Azharites in Indonesia* (Singapore: Institute of Southeast Asian Studies, 1993); Mona Abaza, "Some Research Notes on Living Conditions and Perceptions Among Indonesian Students in Cairo". *Journal of Southeast Asia Studies*, vol. 22, no. 2 (1991), pp. 347-60; Mona Abaza, "Indonesian Azharites, Fifteen Years Later", *Sojourn*, vol. 18, no. 1 (2003), pp. 139-53; Roff, "Indonesian and Malay Students in Cairo in the 1920s". pp. 73-87; Roff, *The Origins of Malay Nationalism*, pp. 87-8; Laffan, *Islamic Nationhood and Colonial Indonesia*, pp. 215-22; Laffan, "An Indonesian Community in Cairo, pp. 1-26; Alles, Transnational Islamic Actors and Indonesia's Foreign Policy, pp. 24-5; Mohammad Redzuan Othman, "The Origins and Contribution of the Early Arabs in Malaya". In Eric Tagliacozzo (ed.), *Southeast Asia and the Middle East: Islam, Movement, and the Longue Duree* (Stanford: Stanford University Press, 2009), p. 92.

344 Noer, *The Modernist Muslim Movement in Indonesia*, p. 296.

345 Fred R. von der Mehden, *Two Worlds of Islam: Interaction between Southeast Asia and the Middle East* (Gainesville: University Press of Florida, 1993), p. 13.

346 See Hafiz Zakariya, "Cairo and the Printing Press as the Modes in the Dissemination of Muhammad 'Abduh's Reformism to Colonial Malaya", *International Proceedings of Economics Development & Research* (IPEDR), vol. 17 (2011), p.125; Jan Stark, *Malaysia and the Developing World: The Asian Tiger on the Cinnamon Road* (London and New York: Routledge, 2013), p. 67.

347 See Roff, *The Origins of Malay Nationalism*, pp. 32-55; Michael Laffan, *The Makings of Indonesian Islam: Orientalism and the Narration of a Sufi Past* (Princeton, NJ: Princeton University Press, 2011), pp. 183-196; C. M. Turnbull,

A History of Modern Singapore 1819 - 2005 (published posthumously). Singapore: NUS Press, 2009), pp. 125-32; Carl A. Trocki, *Singapore: Wealth, Power and the Culture of Control* (New York, NY: Routledge, 2006), pp. 59-61; Torsten Tschacher, " 'Walls of Illusion': Information Generation in Colonial Singapore and the Reporting of the Mahdi-Rebellion in Sudan, 1887-1890". In Derek Heng and Syed Muhd Khairudin Aljuneid (eds.), *Singapore in Global History* (Amsterdam: Amsterdam University Press, 2011), pp. 67-88.

348 von der Mehden, *Two Worlds of Islam*, p. 6.

349 On *al-Manar* and its dialogue with its readers in the Malay-Indonesian World see Bluhm-Warn, J., "Al-Manar and Ahmad Soorkattie". In P. G. Riddell and T. Street (eds.), *Islam: Essays on Scripture, Thought and Society* (Leiden: E.J. Brill, 1997), pp. 295-308; Jutta E. Bluhm, "A Preliminary Statement on the Dialogue Established between the Reform Magazine *al-Manar* and the Malayo-Indonesian World", *Indonesia Circle*, no. 32 (November 1983), pp. 35-42; Azyumardi Azra, "The Transmission of al-*Manar*'s Reformism to the Malay-Indonesian World: The Cases of *al-Imam* and *al-Munir*", *Studia Islamika*, vol. 6, no. 3 (1999), pp. 79–97; William R. Roff, *The Origins of Malay Nationalism*, pp. 87–90; Abaza, *Changing Images of Three Generations of Azharites in Indonesia*, pp. 56-67: Zvi Ben-Dor Benite, "Taking 'Abduh to China: Chinese-Egyptian Intellectual Contact in the Early Twentieth Century". In Gelvin and Green (eds.), *Global Muslims in the Age of Steam and Print* (Berkeley Los Angeles London: University of California Press, 2014), pp. 253, 258; Ilham Khuri-Makdisi, " Fin-de-Siècle Egypt: A Nexus for Mediterranean and Global Radical Networks". In James L. Gelvin and Nile Green (eds.), *Global Muslims in the Age of Steam and Print* (Berkeley Los Angeles London: University of California Press, 2014), pp. 88-9 ; Peter G. Riddell, "Religious Links between Hadhramaut and the Malay-Indonesian World c.1850 to c.1950." In Ulrike Freitag and William G. Clarence-Smith (eds.), *Hadhrami Traders, Scholars and Statesmen in the Indian Ocean, 1750s-1960s* (Leiden: Brill, 1997), p. 225; William L. Cleveland, *Islam Against the West: Shakib Arslan and the. Campaign for Islamic Nationalism* (Austin: University of Texas Press, 1985), pp. 94, 97, 99; Zakariya, "Cairo and the Printing Press as the Modes in the Dissemination of Muhammad 'Abduh's Reformism to Colonial Malaya," pp. 121-6.

350 Roff, *The Origins of Malay Nationalism*, p. 59; Azra, "The Transmission of *al-Manar*'s Reformism to the Malay-Indonesian World, p. 82; Laffan, *The Making of Indonesian Islam*, p. 183; Christopher M. Joll, "Islam's Creole Ambassadors." In P. Jory (ed.), The Ghosts of the Past in Southern Thailand; Essays on the History and Historiography of Patani (Singapore: NUS press, 2013), p. 143.

351 See Anthony Milner, *The Invention of Politics in Colonial Malaya: Contesting Nationalism and the Expansion of the Public Sphere* (Cambridge: Cambridge University Press, 1994), pp. 137-79; William R. Roff, "Kaum Muda – Kaum Tua:

Innovation and Reaction Amongst the Malays, 1900–1941". In K. G. Tregonning (ed.), *Papers on Malayan History*. Singapore: Journal South-East Asian History, 1962, pp. 165-71.

352 On *al-Munir*, see: Laffan, *Islamic Nationhood and Colonial Indonesia*, pp. 172-8; Azra, "The Transmission of *al-Manar*'s Reformism to the Malay-Indonesian World," pp. 75-100; Noer, *The Modernist Muslim Movement in Indonesia*, pp. 39-40.

353 Laffan, *Islamic Nationhood and Colonial Indonesia*, p. 140. See also Laffan, *The Makings of Indonesian Islam*, p. 188; Laffan, "An Indonesian Community in Cairo", pp. 5-6.

354 On the modernist-oriented journals, *Seruan Azhar* and *Pilihan Timur* and on the Indonesian and Malay students in Cairo during 1920s see Roff, "Indonesian and Malay Students in Cairo in the 1920s", pp. 73–87; Roff, "Kaum Muda – Kaum Tua", pp. 183–5; Roff, *The Origins of Malay Nationalism*, pp. 87–90; Abaza, *Changing Images of Three Generations of Azharites in Indonesia*,, p. 3; Laffan, *Islamic Nationhood and Colonial Indonesia*, pp. 215-22; Hussin Mutalib, *Islam in Malaysia: From Revivalism to Islamic State* (Singapore: Singapore University Press, 1993), p. 22; Noer, *The Modernist Muslim Movement in Indonesia*, pp. 153–7.

355 See A. H. Johns "Islam in Southeast Asia." In Mircea Eliade (ed.), *The Encyclopedia of Religion* (New York: Macmillan Publishing Company, 1987), vol. 7, pp. 411–2; Roff, *The Origins of Malay Nationalism*, 58, 75–7; Roff, "Kaum Muda – Kaum Tua", pp. 167, 171, note 29; Howard M. Federspiel, "The Muhammadijah: A Study of an Orthodox Islamic Movement in Indonesia". *Indonesia*, 10 (1970), pp. 61–4; Noer, *The Modernist Muslim Movement in Indonesia*, pp. 306–7.

356 On the Arabs, the Hadrami Arabs in particular, in the Malay-Indonesian World and the significant role played by them in the formative narrative of the Islamic modernism in this region see Mobini-Kesheh, *The Hadrami Awakening*; Riddell, "Religious Links between Hadhramaut and the Malay-Indonesian World, *c.* 1850 to *c.* 1950," pp. 217–30; Peter G. Riddell, "Arab Migrants and Islamization in the Malay World during the Colonial Period," *Indonesia and the Malay World*, vol. 29, no. 84 (2001), pp. 113–28; Manger, *The Hadrami Diaspora*, pp. 128-49; Roff, *The Origins of Malay Nationalism*, pp. 39–43; Joseph Kostiner, "Impact of the Hadrami Emigrants in the East Indies on Islamic Modernism and Social Change in the Hadramawi during the 20th Century." In Raphael Israeli and Anthony H. Johns (eds.), *Islam in Asia*, vol. II: *Southeast and East Asia* (Jerusalem: The Magnes Press, 1984), pp. 206–37; de Gonge," Dutch Colonial Policy pertaining to Hadhrami Immigrants," pp. 94–111; Sumit K. Mandal, "Natural Leaders of Native Muslims: Arab Ethnicity and Politics in Java under Dutch Rule." In Ulrike Freitag and William G. Clarence-Smith (eds.), *Hadhrami*

Traders, Scholars and Statesmen in the Indian Ocean, 1750s–1960s (Leiden: Brill, 1997), pp. 185-98; Sumit K. Mandal, "Forging a Modern Arab Identity in Java in the Early Twentieth Century." In Huub De Jonge and Nico Kaptein (eds.), *Transcending Borders: Arabs, Politics, Trade and Islam in Southeast Asia* (Leiden: KITLV Press, 2002), pp. 163–84; Sumit K. Mandal, "Challenging Inequality in a Modern Islamic idiom: Social Ferment amongst Arabs in Early 20th-century Java. In Eric Tagliacozzo (ed.), *Southeast Asia and the Middle East: Islam, Movement, and the Longue Durée* (Stanford, CA: Stanford University Press, working with NUS Press in Singapore, 2009), pp. 156-175; Eliraz, *Islam in Indonesia: Modernism, Radicalism and the Middle East Dimension*, pp. 10-1, 48-52; Othman, "The Origins and Contribution of the Early Arabs in Malaya," pp. 83-107; Dijk, "'Colonial fears, 1890-1918," pp. 53-89 ; William R. Roof, *The Origins of Malay Nationalism*, pp. 87–90; Abaza, *Changing Images of Three Generations of Azharites in Indonesia*, pp. 39-43.

357 Roff, "Kaum Muda – Kaum Tua, p. 182. On the controversial issues between the modernists and the traditionalists see John R. Bowen, "Modern Intentions: Reshaping Subjectivities in an Indonesian Muslim Society. " In Robert W. Hefner and Patricia Horvatich (eds.), *Islam in an Era of Nation-States: Politics and Religious Renewal in Muslim Southeast Asia* (Honolulu: University of Hawai'i Press, 1997), pp. 157–81; G. W. J. Drewes, "Indonesia Mysticism and Activism."In Gustav E. von Grunebaum (ed.), *Unity and Variety in Muslim Civilization* (Chicago & London: The University of Chicago Press, 1963), p. 294; Noer, *The Modernist Muslim Movement in Indonesia*, pp. 86–7, 95, 220–1, 226; Roff, "Kaum Muda – Kaum Tua,", p. 176; Roff, *The Origins of Malay Nationalism*, p. 78, note 73; Federspiel, "The Muhammadijah", p. 66; Howard M Federspiel, *Islam and Ideology in the Emerging Indonesian State: The Persatuan Islam (PERSIS), 1923 to 1957* (Leiden: Brill, 2001), pp. 58–9.

358 On the neo-modernism, see: Bahtiar Effendy, *Islam and the State in Indonesia* (Singapore: Institute of Southeast Asian Studies, 2003), pp. 65–123; Bahtiar Effendy, "Islam and the State in Indonesia: Munawir Sjadzali and the Development of a New Theological Underpinning of Political Islam," *Studia Islamika*, vol. 2, no. 2 (1995), pp. 97–121; M. Din Syamsuddin, "Islamic Political Thought and Cultural Revival in Modern Indonesia," *Studia Islamika*, vol. 2, no. 4 (1995), pp. 47–68; Greg Barton, "Islamic Liberalism and the Prospects for Democracy in Indonesia." In Michèle Schmiegelow (ed.), *Democracy in Asia* (New York: St. Martin's Press, 1997), pp. 427–51; Greg Barton, "Neo-Modernism: A Vital Synthesis of Traditionalist and Modernist Islamic Thought in Indonesia," *Studia Islamika*, vol. 2, no. 3 (1995), pp. 1-75; Greg Barton, "Indonesia's Nurcholish Madjid and Abdurrahman Wahid as Intellectual 'Ulama': The Meeting of Islamic Traditionalism and Modernism in neo-Modernist Thought," *Studia Islamika*, vol. 4, no. 1 (1997), pp. 29–81; Luthfi Assyaukanie, *Islam and the Secular State in Indonesia* (Singapore : Institute of Southeast Asian Studies, 2009), pp. 97-139,

205; Robert W. Hefner, "Secularization and Citizenship in Muslim Indonesia". In David Martin, Paul Heelas and Paul Morris (eds.), *Religion, Modernity, and Postmodernity* (Oxford: Blackwell Publishers, 1998), pp. 147-68; Giora Eliraz, "Distinctive Contemporary Voice: Liberal Islam Thought in Indonesia," *Studia Islamika*, vol. 15, no. 3 (2008), pp. 1-38; Ali Munhanif, "Islam and the Struggle for Religious Pluralism in Indonesia: A Political Reading of the Religious Thought of Mukti Ali," *Studia Islamika*, pp. 79-126; Bakti Andi Faisal, "Islam and Modernity; Nurcholish Madjid's Interpretation of Civil Society, Pluralism, Secularization, and Democracy", *Asian Journal of Social Science*, vol. 33, no. 3 (2005), pp. 486-505.

359 See Robert W. Hefner, *Civil Islam: Muslims and Democratization in Indonesia* (Princeton and Oxford: Princeton University Press, 2000); Hefner, "Secularization and Citizenship in Muslim Indonesia," p. 148.

360 See M. Din Syamsuddin, *Religion and Politics in Islam: The Case of Muhammadiyah in Indonesia's New Order* (PhD. dissertation, Los Angeles: University of California, 1991), pp. 268-70, 287-8; M. Din Syamsuddin, "The Muhammadiyah Da'wah and Allocative Politics in the New Order Indonesia," *Studia Islamika*, vol. 2, no. 2 (1995): 63-4. See also Azra, "The Transmission of *al-Manar's* Reformism to the Malay-Indonesian World," p. 97.

361 Kerr, *Islamic Reform*, p. 15

362 Tschacher, "'Walls of Illusion'," pp. 67-88.

363 Ibid, p. 67.

364 On Muhammad Basyuni 'Imran see: Jutta Bluhm-Warn, "Al-Manar and Ahmad Soorkattie". In P. G. Riddell and T.Street (eds.), *Islam: Essays on Scripture, Thought and Society* (Leiden: E.J. Brill, 1997), pp. 295-6; Martin van Bruinessen, "Basyuni Imran." In *Dictionnaire biographique des savants et grandes figures du monde musulman périphérique, in du XIXe siècle à nos jours*, Fasc. no 1. Paris: CNRS-EHESS, 1992, p.26; Umar Ryad, *Islamic Reformism and Christianity: A Critical Reading of the Works of Muhammad Rashid Rida and his Associates (1898-1935)* (Leiden: Brill, 2009), pp. 47-8; Ahmad N. Amir, Abdi O. Shuriye and Jamal I. Daoud, "Muhammad Abduh's Influence in Southeast Asia," *Middle-East Journal of Scientific Research* (MEJSR), vol.13 (2013). p. 125.

365 On Shakib Arslan see William L. Cleveland. *Islam Against the West: Shakib Arslan and the. Campaign for Islamic Nationalism* (Austin: University of Texas Press, 1985). On his contribution to *al-Manar* see Ryad, *Islamic Reformism and Christianity*, pp. 43-50.

366 Shakib Arslan, *Li-madha ta'akhkhara al-muslimun wa li-madha taqaddama ghayruhum*, 2nd ed. (Cairo: Matba'at 'Isa al-Babi al-Halabi, 1358 AH 1939 AD).

Bibliography

Egyptian Newspapers and Periodicals
Al-Ahram

Al-'Alam

Al-Balagh

Al-Balagh al-Usbu'i

Al-Hilal

Al-Majalla al-Jadida

Majallat Majma' al-Lugha al-'Arabiyya al-Malaki

Al-Ma'rifa

Al-Muayyad

Al-Muqattam

Al-Muqtataf

Al-Rabita al-'Arabiyya

Al-Risala

Sahifat al-Mu'alimin

Sahifat Dar al-'Ulum

Al-Siyyasa

Al-Siyyasa al-Usbu'iyya

Al-Zuhara'

Books and Articles in Arabic
Abaza, Fikri, "Al-Mar'a Malak wa-Shaytan," *Al-Hilal*, vol. 43, November 1934, pp. 65-8.

'Abd al-Qadir, Muhammad Zaki, "Al-Ihjam 'an al-Zawaj," Al-Siyasa al-Usbu'iyya, part 1, 10 September 1927, p. 6; part 3, 24 September 1927, p.8.

Abu al-'Ala' Mustafa Jad, "Al-Mathal al-A'la li-al-Zaujiya," *Al-Ma'arifa*, 2nd year, May 1932, pp. 60-4.

Abu Shadi, Ahmad Zaki, "Fi Sabil al-'Arabiyya", *Al-Muqtataf*, vol. 75, July 1929, pp. 165-74.

_____, "Al-Shi'r wa-al-Sha'ir". In the introduction to his *diwan, Al-Shafaq al-Baki,* Cairo: Al-Matba'ah al-Salafiyah, 1926, pp. 44-8.

Abu al-Su'ud, Fakhri, "Al-Mar'a fi al-Adabayn al-'Arabi wa-al-Inglizi," *Al-Risala*, 7 September 1936, pp. 1447-9.

_____, "Al-Sharq fi Adab al-Gharb," *Al-Thaqafa*, vol. 1, copy 14, 4 April 1939, pp. 22-5.

_____, "Al-Taswir fi al-Shi'r al-'Arabi," *Al-Risala*, vol. 2, 7 May 1934, pp. 779-80.

Abu Tai'la, Muhammad, "Misr bayna Hadaratayn," *Al-Balagh al-Usbu'i*, 12 June 1929, pp. 4-5.

Adham, Isma'il Ahmad, "Bayna al-Ghab wa al-Sharq," *Al-Risala*, part 1. vol. 6, 20 June 1938, p.1012-4; part 2, vol. 6, 27 June 1938, pp. 1054-5.

_____, "Misr wa-al-Thaqafa al-Urubbiyya," *Al-Majalla al-Jadida*, vol. 6, May 1937, pp. 28-31.

_____, "Al- Tatawwur al-Hadith fi Misr wa-al-Turkiya," *Al-Majalla al-Jadida*, vol. 6, April 1937, pp. 17-28.

'Aftfi, Hafiz, *'Ala Hamish al-Siyasa*. Cairo: Matba'at Dar al-Kutub al-Misriyah, 1938.

'Alam, Muhammad Mahdi, "Al-Halqa al-Mafquda, " *Sahifat Dar al- 'Ulum*, 1st year, June 1934, pp. 19-26.

'Alam, Abd al-Mun'im Mursi, "Wazifat al- al-Mar'a al-Haqiqiyya, *Al-Muqattam*, 23 July 1933, p. 1.

Amin, Ahmad, "Halqa Mafquda", *Al-Risala*, vol. 1, issue no. 1, 15 January 1933, pp. 6-7.

Amin, Qasim, *Al-Mar'a al-Jadida*. Cairo: Matba'at al-Ma'arif, 1900.

_____, *Tahrir al-Mar'a*. Cairo 1928.

Al-'Anani, 'Ali. *Al-Thaqafa al-'Amma*. [Cairo] Matba'at Shubra.

'Arafah, Muhammad, *Al-Nahw wa-al-Nuhah*. Cairo: Matba'at al-Sa'ada 1937.

Arslan, Shakib, *Li-madha ta'akhkhara al-muslimun wa li-madha taqaddama ghayruhum*, 2nd ed. Cairo: Matba'at 'Isa al-Babi al-Halabi, 1358 AH 1939 AD.

'Azzam, 'Abd al-Wahhab, "'Ibrat al-Hadhithat", *Al-Risala*, vol. 3, 30 September 1935, pp. 1561-2.

_____, "Al-Nahda al-Turkiyya al-Akhira," *Al-Risala*, part 2, vol. 3, 24 June 1935, pp. 1009-11.

_____, *Rihlat*. Cairo, Matba`at al-Risala., 1939.

_____, "Al-Tajdid fi al-Adab," part 2, *Al-Risala*, vol. 1, copy 10, 1 June, 1933, pp. 11-4.

'Azmi, Mahmud, "Ittijah al-Ta'lim fi al-Jami'at", *Al-Hilal*, vol. 37, April 1929, pp. 673-6.

_____, "Al-Tarbush am al-Qubb'a: Limadha Labistu al- Qubb'a," *Al-Hilal*, vol. 36, November 1927, pp. 52-6.

Badawi, Ahmad Ahmad, "Al-Lugha al-'Arabiyya fi Madarisina," *Al-Siyasa al-Usbu'iyya*, vol. 20,

March 1937, p. 29.

_____, "Al-Wahda al-'Arabiyya wa-al-Adab al-Qaumi," *Al-Ma'rifa*, vol. 1, February 1932, pp. 1213-6.

Al-Badri, Mustafa Nu'man Husayn, *Al-lmam Mustafa Sadiq al-Rafi'i*. Baghdad, 1968.

Baraniq, Mubammad Muhammad, "Qissat al-Lugha al-'Arabiyya," *Al-Ahram*, 28 March 1938, pp. 7, 14.

Barakat, Bahey al-Din, "Qadiyat al-Lugha al-'Arabiyya" (interview), *Al-Ahram*, 28 February 1938, pp, 1, 3.

Al-Barradi, Rashid Mustafa, "Fi 'Alam al-Tarbiya: Al-Ta'lim al-Mushtarik," *Al-Balagh Al-Usbu'i*, vol. 7, September 1928, p. 29.

Al-Bishri, 'Abd al-'Aziz, "Hairat al-Adab al-Misri,"*Al-Ma'rifa*, 1st year, February 1932, pp. 1185-87, 1192.

_____, Kayfa Yanba'ith al-Adab wa-Kayfa Natarawwahu?," *Al-Risala*, part 1, vol. 3 25 March 1935, pp. 451-3; part. 2, vol. 3, 1 April 1935, pp. 491-4.

_____, "Kifah al-Lugha al-'Arabiyya fi Sabil al-Hayah wa-al-Nuhud," *Al-Hilal*, vol.45, April 1937, pp. 641-5.

_____, "Mas'ala," *Al-Thaqafa*, vol. 1, 1 August, 1939, pp. 1518-9.

_____, *Al-Mukhtar*. 2 vols: vol.1, 2nd ed., 1938 ; vol. 2, 1937. Cairo: Matba'at al-Ma'arif.

_____, *Qutuf*. Cairo: Dar al-Katib al-Misri, 1947, vol. 2.

_____, "Shawqi…!,"*Al-Risala*, vol. 2, 15 October 1934, pp. 1681-4.

_____, "Al-Tajdid wa-al-Mujadidun," *Al-Hilal*, vol. 24, March 1936, pp. 512-6.

Boktor, Amir, "Al-Jil al-Misri al-Muqbil," *Al-Hilal*, vol. 46, February 1938, pp. 366-73.

_____, "Thaqafatuna al-Qawmiyya wa-ma Yanqusuha min 'Awamil al-Quwa," *Al-Hilal*, vol. 45, April 1937, pp. 657-63.

Dayf, Ahmad, "Al-Adab al-Misri fi al-Qarn al-Tasi' 'Ashar," *Al-Muqttaf*, part 1, vol. 68, April 1926, pp. 401-5.

_____, *Balaghat al-'Arab fi al-Andalus* [Cairo] Matba'at Misr, 1924

_____, *Muqaddima li-Dirasat Balaghat al-'Arab*. Cairo: Matba'at al-Sufur, 1921.

Dayf, Muhammad, *Balaghat al-'Arab fi al-Andalus*. [Cairo] Matba'at Misr, 1924

Diab, Mohammad Tawfik, "Ghayat al-Nahda al-Nisa'iyya fi Misr," *Al- Siyasa Al-Usbu'iyya*, 10 December, 1927, pp. 9-10.

Fahmi, Asma, "Al-Ta'lim al-'Ali li-al-Nisa'," *Al-Risala*, vol. 2, 22 January 1934, pp. 141-3.

_____, "Thaqafat al-Mar'a," *Al-Risala*, vol. 1, 15 June 1933, pp. 17-8.

Fahmi, Mansur, "'Aqliyat al-Mar'a wa-'Aqliyat al-Rajul," *Al-Hilal*, vol. 38, February 1930, pp. 404-6.

_____, "Fi Usul al-Tarbiyya wa-al-Ta'lim," part 3, *Al-Ahram*, 20 February 1926, p. 1

_____, "Hawla Majma' al-Lugha al-'Arabiyya al-Malaki", part 2, *Al-Siyasa al-Usbu'iyya*, 19 June 1937, p. 5.

_____, "Hudud al-Taqlid wa-al-Iftida'," *Al-Ahram*, 24 June, 1939, p.1.

_____, " 'Illat al-'Illal fi Mashakilina al-'Ijtimaiyya," *Al-Ahram*, 20 June 1939, p. 1.

_____, "Al-Lugha al-'Arabiyya," a reply to survey conducted by *Al-Hilal*, vol. 47, August 1939, pp. 989-90.

_____, "Masir al-Madaniyya wa-Mauqif al-Sharq minha fi al-Mal," *Al-Hilal*, vol. February 1932, pp. 513-20.

_____, "Mauqif al-Sharq min Hadarat al-Gharb, *Al-Hilal*, vol. 40, November 1931, pp. 49-59.

_____, " Nahwa Thaqafa Sharqiyya Khalisa" (interview), *Al-Rabita Al-'Arabiyya*, 21 July, 1937, pp. 16-7.

_____, "Shabab al-'Arab,"*Al-Zahra'*, vol. 1, Al-Muharram, 1343 AH, pp. 31-4.

_____, "Al-Sharq wa-al-Hadara al-Gharbiyya," *Al-Muqtataf*, vol. 77, October 1930, pp. 257-63.

Ghallab, Muhammad, *Al-Akhlaq al-Nazariyya*. Cairo: Al-Matba'a al-Misriyya al-Ahliyya al-Haditha, 1933.

Al-Ghamrawi, Muhammad Ahmad, "Al-Bi'a al-Islamiyya," *Al-Risalas*, vol.6, 21 March 1938, pp.490-92.

_____, "Al-Naqd al-Tahlili li-Kitab fi al-Aadab al-Jahili. Cairo: Al-Matba'ah al-Salafiyah, 1929.

_____, "Al-Qadim wa-al-Jadid,"*Al-Risala*, vol. 7, 23 January 1939, pp. 166-9.

_____, "Al-Qadim wa-al-Jadid: Naqd wa-Tahlil," *Al-Risala*, Part 1, vol. 6, 4 July 1938, pp. 1103-5.

_____, "Hal Yakun Nizam Ta'lim al-Banat Huwa Nafs Nizam Ta'lim al-Banin," *Sahifat al-Mualimin*, 3rd year, July-October 1925, pp. 438-44.

Habisha, 'Abd al-Fatah, "Taqalus Zill al-Madaniyya al-Gharbiyya", *Al-Muqtataf*, vol. 74, March 1929, pp. 320-2.

Al-Hajiri, Muhammad Taha, "Athar al-Nahw fi Taqwim al-Lisan," *Al-Risala*, vol. 4, 3 August, 1936, pp. 1249-51.

Hamza, Muhammad 'Abd al-Qadir, "A'da' al-Adab al-'Arabi," *Al-Balagh*, 4 June 1934, p. 3.

_____, "Hadith Al-Ithnayn: Bayna al-Shuyukh wa-al-Shabab," *Al-Balagh*, 29 October 1934, p. 3.

_____, "Hadith al-Ithnayn: Khata' Tariqat Ta'lim al-Lugha al 'Arabiyya", *Al-Balagh al-Usbu'i*, 23 March 1936, p. 10.

_____, "Hadith al-Ithnayn: Al-Qissa fi al-Adab al-Misri al-Hadith," *Al-Balagh*, 10 December 1934, p. 3.

_____, "Hadith al Ithnayn: Tadris al-Adab al-'Arabi fi al-Madaris al-Misriyya," *Al-Balagh*, 26 November 1934, pp. 3, 11.

_____, "Al-Lugha al-'Arabiyya wa-al-Huruf al-Latiniyya", *Al-Balagh al-Usbu'i*, 1 June 1928, pp. 3-5.

Hamza, 'Abd al-Latif, "Tabi' al-Haya al-Misriyya al-Yawm," a reply to survey conducted by *Al-Rabita al-'Arabiyya*, 26 May, 1937, pp. 10-12.

Al-Hariri, Ahmad Wahbi, "Du'at Al-Jadid," *Al-Muqattam*, 11 July, 1925, p. 1.

Al-Harawi, Husayn, *Al-Mustashriqun wa- al-Islam*. Cairo: Matba'at al-Manar, 1936.

_____, "Nahnu wa-al-Mustashriqun", Al-*Ma'rifa*, June 1932, pp. 177-80.

Hassan, 'Abd al-Hamid, "Bayna al-Qadim wa-al-Hadith fi Tarbiya wa-al-Ta'lim", *Sahifat Dar al-'Ulum*, vol. 1, June 1934, pp. 64-72.

Hassan, Ibrahim Hassan, "Al-Futuh al-Islamiyya wa-Atharuha fi Taqaddum al-Madaniyya," *Al-Risala*, vol. 4, 20 April 1936, pp. 641-3.

Hassuna, Muhammad Amin, *Wara'a al-Bihar*. Cairo: Matba'at al-Shams,1936.

'Ibada, 'Abd al-Fatah, "Nahdat al-Mar'a al-Misriyya, *Al-Hilal*, part 1, vol. 27, April 1919, pp. 705-12; part 2, vol. 27, May 1919, pp. 841-9.

'Inan, Muhammad 'Abdallah, "Athar al-Hadara al-Islamiyya fi al-'Ihya al-Urubbi," *Al-Risala*, vol. 4, 24 February 1936, pp. 286-8.

_____, "Harb Munazzama Yashaharaha al-Kamaliyun 'ala al-Islam", *Al-Risala,* vol 3, 14 January 1935, pp. 45-7.

_____, "Malikat wa-Wazirat," *Al-Risala*, vol. 3, 20 July 1936, pp. 1165-7.

_____, "Misr bayna Thaqafatayn," *Al-Risala*, vol. 3, 25 March 1935, pp. 448-51.

'Isa, Ahmad, "Kayfa Takhdum al-Lugha al-'Arabiyya," *Al-Hilal*, vol. 42, August 1934, pp. 1209-11.

_____, *Al-Muhkam fi Usul al-Kalimat al-'Ammiyya*. Cairo: Matba'at 'Isa al-Babi al-Halabi, 1939.

Al-Iskandari, Ahmad, "Hamla 'ala al-Mujaddidin fi al-Adab,"*Al-Rabita al-'Arabiyya*, 25 May 1938, pp. 18-9.

_____, "Al-Ta'rib", *Al-Zahara'*, vol. 1, Rabi' al-Awwal, 1343 AH, pp. 168-77..

_____, "Taysir al-Hija' al-'Arabi," *Majallat Majma' al-Lugha al-'Arabiyya al-Malaki*, vol. 1, October 1934, pp. 369-80.

Islam'il, 'Abd al-Khalik, "Tahawwul al-Sharq," *Al-Muqattam*, 9 July 1925, p. 1.

Jawhari, Tantawi, "Al-Mukashafat al-Haditha wa-Hiya 'Arabiyya Qadima," *Al-Muqtataf*, vol. 6, August 1922, pp. 242-7.

Jum'a, Muhammad Lutfi, "Al-Hadara al-'Arabiyya wa-Ahamm Muqawwamatuha," Al-*Rabita* al-'Arabiyya, 10 November 1937, pp. 11-5.

_____, *Hayat al-Sharq*. Cairo: Dar Ihya' al-Kutub al-'Arabiyya, 1932.

_____, "Kayfa Nunshi' Thaqafa Sharqiyya Mustaqila," a reply to survey conducted by *Al-Rabita al-'Arabiyya*, 1 September 1937, p. 8.

_____, "Al-Nahda al-Sharqiyya al-Haditha," *Al-Muqttaf*, vol. 71, August 1927, pp. 141-3.

_____, "Al-Nahda al-Sharqiyya al-Haditha," *Al-Muqttaf*, vol. 71, August 1927, pp. 141-3.

_____, "Nahdat al-Sharq al-'Arabi', " a reply to survey conducted by *Al-Hilal*, 31 December 1922, p. 241.

_____, "Nasib al-Sharq fi Hahadat al-Mustaqbal,"*Al-Rabita Al-'Arabiyya,* 18 August, 1937, pp. 11-4.

_____, *Al-Shihab al-Rasid.* Cairo: Matba'at al-Muqtataf wa-al-Muqattam, 1926.

_____, *Tārikh Falasifat al-Islam fi al-Mashriq wa al-Maghrib.* Cairo: Matba'at Al-Ma'arif, 1927.

Kamil, Salah al-Din, "'Aqaliyat al-Tarbush wa-'Aqaliyat al-Qubb'a," *Al-Majalla al-Jadida*, vol. 6, July 1937, pp. 17-8.

Khaki, Ahmad, "Qadiyyat al-Lugha al-'Arabiyya," *Al-Risala*, part 1, vol. 6, 4 April 1938, pp. 574-77 and part 2, vol. 6, 18 April 1938, pp. 643-6.

Al-Khalaf, Mun'im, " 'Afat al-Lugha al-'Arabiyya," *Al-Ahram*, 26 August 1937, pp. 11, 15.

Khamis, 'Ali Shukri, "AI-Mar'a al-Misriyya wa-al-Mar'a al-Gharbiyya," *Al-Muqattam*, 3 March 1927, p. 10.

Al-Khuli, Amin, "Adabuna Alan Yumathiluna," *Al-Hilal*, vol. 45, February 1937, pp. 377-9.

_____, "Al-Asalib," *Al-Risala*, vol. 1, issue 22, 4 December 1933, pp, 5-6, 42.

_____, " Al-Tajdid fi al-Din," *Al-Risala*, vol. 1, issue 2, 1 February, 1933, pp. 12-3, 18.

Madkur, Ibrahim Bayumi, "Falasafat al-Islam," *Al-Risala*, part 1, vol. 4, 16 March 1936, p. 411-4.

Mahmud, 'Abd al-Rahim,, "Nizamuna al-Ijtimaa'i," part 18, *Al-Muqtataf*, vol. 68, January 1926, pp. 68-70.

Mahmud, Hafiz, "Al-Adab al-Makshuf wa-al-Adab al-Mastur," *Al-Siyasa al-Usbui'yya*, vol. 3, December 1927, p. 9.

_____, "Fi al-Tataawwar al-Lugha", *Al-Majalla al-Jadida*, vol. 1, July 1930, pp. 1095-8.

_____, "Muqaddimat al-Zawaj kama Yaraha Shabb," *Al-Majalla Al-Jadida*, vol. 2, March 1931, pp. 583-6.

Majala, "Qararat al-Majma'", *Majallat Majma' al-Lugha al-'Arabiyya al-Malaki*, vol. 1, October 1934.

Majdhub, Muhammad 'Ali, "Al-Tarbiya al-Mushtaraka," *Sahifat al-Mu'allimin*, 3rd year, July-October 1925, pp. 461-71.

Al-Mandarawi, Lutfi, "Bahth fi Mushkilat al-'Uzuba wa-Azmat al-Zawaj," *a/-Muqattam*, 9 November 1934, pp. 1, 10.

_____, "Al-Bayan", *Al-Hilal*, vol. 27, October 1918, pp. 61-6.

_____, "Ihtiram al-Mar'a," *Al-Hilal*, vol. 30, July 1922, pp. 913-5.

Mansi, Ahmad Abu al-Khidr, "Ma'ani al-Hubb fi al-Lugha al-'Arabiyya wa-al-Lughatt al-Ukhra," *Al-Ahram*, vol. 3, July 1937, p. 3.

_____, "Al-Mar'a al-Sharqiyya," a reply to survey conducted by *Al-Hilal*, vol. 33, May 1925, pp. 851-2.

Al-Misri, Ibrahim, *Al-Adab al-Hayy*. Cairo: Dar al-'Usur li-al-Tiba'a wa-al-Nashr, 1930.

_____, "Khalq Amthila 'Ulya li-al-Shabab al-Misriyin," *Al-Hilal*, vol. 46, July 1938, pp. 617-21.

_____, "Li-man Yaktubu al-Katib al-Misri", *Al-Hilal*, vol. 46, July 1938, pp. 987-91.

_____, "Al-Mathal al-A'la li-al-Fard wa-al-Mujtama' 'Indana," *Al-Majalla al-Jadida*, vol. 2, December 1930, pp. 164-71.

_____, "Al-Musiqa al-Sharqiya,"*Al-Hilal*, vol.46, July 1938, pp. 501-6.

_____, *Saut al-Jil*. Cairo: Maktabat Saba wa- Matba'atuha, 1934.

_____, "Al-Shabab wa-Ruh al-Quwa, *Al-Hilal*, vol.46, May 1936, pp. 463-68.

_____, "Shakhsiyat al-Fanan," *Al-Balagh al-Usbu'i,* 11 February 1927, pp. 35-6.

_____, *Why al-'Asr*. Cairo: Maktabat al-Hilal [1935].

Mazhar, Isma'il, Huriyat al-Fikr," *Al-'Usur*, vol. 2, July 1928, pp. 1169-80.

_____, "Al-Nahda al-Sharqiyya al-Haditha," *Al-Muqtataf*, vol. 70, June 1927, pp. 611-18.

Al-Mazini, Ibrahim 'Abd al-Qadir, "Al-Adab al-'Arabi wa-Tariqat Tadrisihi fi al-Madaris," *Al Balagh*, 20 November 1934, p. 1.

_____, "Al-Adab al-'Arabi wa-Tariqat Tadrisihi fi al-Madaris: Al-Adab wa-Ta'rikh al-Adab", *Al-Balagh*, 21 November 1934, pp. 1,9.

_____, "Al-'Ammiyya wa-al-'Arabiyya," *Al-Risala*, vol. 3, 7 October 1935, pp. 1616-7.

_____, "Al-'Ammiyya wa-al-'Arabiyya aydan," *Al-Risala*, vol. 3, 21 October 1935, pp. 1692-3.

_____, "Al-'Ammiyya wa-al-Fusha", *Al-Risala*, vol. 6, 24 October 1938, pp. 1721-4.

_____, "Al-Hayat al-Misriyya wa-Hajatuha ila 'Anasir al-Quwa wa-al-Hayal," *Al-Hilal*, vol. 38, March 1930, pp. 549- 52.

_____, *Hasad al-Hashim*. Cairo: Al-Matba'a al-'Asriya, 1925.

_____, *Ibrahim al-Katib*. Cairo: Matba'at Dar al-Turki, 1931.

_____, "Al-Lugha al-'Ammiyya wa-al-Lugha al-Fusha", *Al-Majalla Al-Jadida*, vol. 7, October 1938, pp. 83-6.

_____, "Al-Lugha wa-al-Qawalib al-Mawrutha", *Al-Risala*, vol. 7 August 1939, pp. 1527-9.

_____, "Al-Masrah al-Misri", *Al-Risala*, 16 September 1935, pp. 1481-3.

_____, "Al-Nahw," *Al-Risala*, 1 March 1937, pp. 323-5.

Mubarak, Zaki, "Al-Hadith Dhu Shujun: Ila Ma'ali Wazir al-Ma'arif," *Al-Balagh*, 12 June 1936, pp. 10-1.

_____, "Kayfa Nunshi' Thaqafa Sharqiyya Mustaqila," a reply to survey conducted by *Al-Rabita al-'Arabiyya*, 11 August, 1937, pp. 15-7.

_____, *Al-Lugha wa-al-Din wa- al-Taqalid fi Hayat al-Istiqlal*. Cairo: Matba'at 'Isa al-Babi al-Halabi, 1936.

_____, "Al-Mujadidun wa-al-Muhafizun," *Al-Rabita al-'Arabiyya*, 21 October 1936, p. 20-1.

Muhibb, Muhammad 'Abdallah, "Tafashi al-Talaq wa-Turuq 'Ilajuhu," *al-Siyasa Al-Usbui'yya*, 15 October 1927, pp. 7-8.

Musa, Nabawiyya, "'Adatuna wa-'Adatuhum," *Al-Balagh al-Usbu'i*, 17 February 1928, pp. 20-1.

_____, "Hajat Misr ila al-Nisa' al-'Amilat," *Al-Balagh al-Usbu'i*, 17 June 1927, pp. 32-3.

_____, "Al-'Ilm wa-al-Din," *Al-Balagh al-Usbu'i*, 3 June, 1927, pp. 32-3.

_____, "Madaris al-Ummahat wa-al-Tadbir al-Manzili," *Al-Balagh al-Usbu'i*, 7 January 1927, pp. 24, 26.

_____, "Al-Mar'a al-Jadida," *Al-Balagh al-Usbu'i*, 23 December 1927, p. 21.

_____, "Al-Mutazawwij wa-al-A'mal al-'Amma," *Al-Balagh al-Usbu'i*, 16 September 1927, p. 31.

_____, "Al-Nahda al-Nisawiyya fi Misr wa-Ahamm Asbabuha," *Al-Balagh al-Usbu'i*, 24 June 1927, pp. 32-3.

_____, "Qanun al-Zawaj al-Jadid," *Al-Balagh al-Usbu'i*, 25 March 1927, pp. 30-2.

_____, "Al-Qarn al-'Ishrun wa-lima Summiya bi-'Asr al-Mar'a," *Al-Balagh al-Usbu'i*, 11 May 1928, pp. 28-9.

_____, "Shay' 'an al-Mar'a," *Al-Balagh al-Usbu'i*, 30 December 1927, p. 20.

_____, "Ta'lim al-Banat wa-'Alaqatuhu bi-Ta'lim al-Banin," *Sahafat al-Mu'alliminn*, 3rd year, July-October 1925, pp. 445-50.

_____, "Al-Thaqafa al-'Amma," *Al-Balagh al-Usbu'i*, 31 December 1926, pp. 27-8.

_____, "Al-Zawaj bi-al-Ajnabiyyat," *Al-Balagh al-Usbu'i*, 18 November 1927, p. 20-1.

Musa, Salama, *Al-Dunya ba'd Thalathin Sana*. Cairo: Salama Musa li-al-Nashar wa-al-Tawzi', n.d.

_____, "Fi Falsafat al-Libas," *Al-Hilal*, vol. 33, February 1925, pp. 463-5.

_____, "Islah al-Lugha", *Al-Balagh*, vol. 23, February 1935, p. 1.

_____, "Al-Khat al-Latini li-al-Lugha al-'Arabiyya," *Al-Majala al-Jadida*, vol. 4, November 1935, pp. 69-70.

_____, Al-Lugha al-Fusha wa-al-Lugha al-'Ammiyya," *Al-Hilal*, vol. 34, July 1926, pp. 1073-77.

_____, *Al-Yaum wa*-al-*Ghad*. Cairo: Al-Matba'a al-'Asriya, 1927.

Musharrafa, 'Ali Mustafa, "Al-Athar al-'Ilmi fi al-Thaqafa al-Misriyya al-Haditha. In *Ara' Hurra*, a collection of articles, issued by the American University in Cairo. Cairo: Al-Matba'a al-'Asriya [1936], pp. 117-24.

_____,"Al-Lugha al-'Arabiyya ka-Adah 'Ilmiyya", *Al-Risala*, vol. 1, 15 January 1933, pp. 10-1.

Mustafa, Ibrahim, *Ihya' Al-Nahw*, Cairo: Matba'at Lajnat al-Ta'lif wa-al-Tarjamah wa-al-Nashr, 1937, pp. v-viii.

Nafi', 'Abd Al-Majid, "Tabi' al-Haya al-Misriyya al-Yawm," a reply to survey conducted by *Al-Rabita al-'Arabiyya*, 26 May 1937, pp. 12-3.

Naji, lbrahim, "Al-Shabab al-Misri wa-al-Mushkila al-Jinsiyya," *Al-Hilal*, vol. 47. November 1938, pp. 57-60.

Nasef, 'Ali al-Najdi, "Al-Shi'r al-Hadith," *Sahifat Dar al-'Ulum*, vol. 3, February 1937, pp. 63-9.

Nasif, Malak Hifni ("Bahithat al-Badiyya"), *Al-Nisa'iyyat*, 2 vols. Cairo n.d.

Qabil, Muhammad, "Al-Qari' al-'Arabi wa- Fikruhu fi al-Thaqafa al-Haditha", *Al-Ahram*, 22 October 1937, p. 3.

Al-Qalamawi, Suheir, "Makanat al-Mar'a fi al-Nahda al-Misriyya," *Al-Rabita al-'Arabiyya*, 16 December 1936, pp. 172-4.

Al-Qusi, lhsan Ahmad, "Istithmar Nahdat al-Mar'a li-Khayr al-Bilad," *Al-Risala*, vol. 4, 18 May 1936, pp. 824-6.

Qutb, Sayyid, book review of Taha Husayn's Mustaqbal al-Thaqafa fi Misr, *Sahifat Dar al-'Ulum*, vol. 5, April 1939, pp. 28-79.

_____, " 'Ayy Rajul Turiduhu al-Mar'a?," *Al-Balagh al-Usbu'i*, 27 March 1929, pp. 28-9.

_____, "Al-Azma al-Zawjiyya," *Al-Balagh al-Usbu'i*, 10 April l929, pp. 28-9.

_____, "Al-Ikhtilat fi al-Aryaf," *Al-Balagh al-Usbu'i*, 8 May 1929, p. 29.

_____, "Al-Mar'a fi Maydan al-'Amal," *Al-Balagh al-Usbu'i*, 20 March 1929, pp. 28-9.

_____, "Tawhid Baramij al-Ta'lim li-al-Jinsayn," *Al-Balagh al-Usbu'i*, 20 March 1929, p. 28.

Al-Rafi'i, Mustafa Sadiq, "Amin 'Asr al-'Aql ila 'Asr al-Qalb," *Al-Muqtataf*, vol. 74, January 1929, pp. 15-8.

_____, "Difa' 'an al-Madhhab al-Qadim fi al-Adab," *Al-Hilal*, vol. 32, February 1924, pp. 469-75..

_____, "Al-Faqr wa-al-Fuqara", *Al-Muqtataf*, vol. 42, May 1913, pp. 462-70.

_____, "Falsafat al-Adab," *Al-Muqtataf*, vol. 81, July 1932, pp. 149-55.

_____, "Al-Imam," *Al-Zuhara'*, vol. 5, Rabi' al-Awwal 1347 AH, pp. 2-7.

_____, "Al-Jumla al-Qur'ānīya," *Al-Zuhara'*, vol. 1, Jumada al-Akhira 1343 AH, pp. 353-9.

_____, *Kitab al-Masakin*, 9th ed., Beirut: Dar al-Katib al-'Arabi, 1973.

_____, "Al-Kutub allati Afadatni,"*Al-Hilal*, vol. 35, January 1927, p. 275.

_____, "Madha'Ara fi al-Tajdid wa-al-Mujaddidin?," *Al-Hilal*, vol. 37, March 1929, pp. 545-7.

_____, "Mustaqbal al-Lugha al-'Arabiyya," *Al-Hilal*, vol. 28, February 1920, pp. 399-402.

_____, "Ra'y fi al-Tajdid wa-Mudda'i al-Tajdid,"*Al-Manar*, vol. 27, June 1926, pp. 205-7.

_____, *Tahta Rayat al-Qur'an: Al-Ma'raka bayna al-Qadifm wa-al-Jadid*. Cairo: Al-Maktaba al-Ahliyya, 1926.

_____, "Al-Tarbush am al-Qubb'a: Limadha Astamsik bi-al-Tarbush,"*Al-Hilal*, vol. 36, November 1927, pp. 49-52.

_____, *Wahy al-Qalam*. 5th ed., 3 vols. Cairo: Matba'at Al-Istiqama, 1954.

Rida, Muhammad, "Al-Azya' al-Sharqiyya, *Al-Muqattam*, 18 September, 1925, p.1.

_____, "Muharabat al-Khumur," part 1, *Al-Muqtataf*, vol. 59, July 1921, pp. 24-32.

_____, " Nahdat al-Umam wa-'Alaqatuha bi-al-Azya',"*Al-Muqattam*, 22 September 1925, p.1.

Rida, Muhammad Rashid, *Al-Wahy al-Muhammadi*, 2nd ed. Cairo: Matba'at al-Manar, 1352 H.

Sa'id, Mazhar, "Siyasat al-Tarbiya wa- al-Ta'alim fi al-Kharij,"*Al-Muqtataf*, vol. 80, March 1932, pp. 312-7, 369.

Sa'id, Nafusa Zakariyya, *Ta'rikh al-Da'wa ila al-'Ammiyya wa-Atharuha fi Misr*. Alexandria: Dar Nashr al-Thaqafa, 1964.

Sa'id, Nazla al-Hakim, "Al-Fata al-Misriyya fi al-Madrasa wa-al-Ba'tha wa-al-Manzil," *Al-Ma'rifa*, October 1932, 2nd year, pp. 656-60.

_____, "Ikhtilat al-Jinsayn, *Al-Ma'rifa*, 1st year, February 1932, pp. 1255-62.

Salam, Mustafa Muhammad, "Islah al-Lugha al-'Arabiyya," *Al-Ahram*, 27 August 1937, p. 13.

Salih, Salim, "Al-Mar'a wa-Atharuha fi al-Hayah," *Al-Muqattam*, 14 December 1924, pp.1-2.

Al-Sayhi, Muhammad Muhammad, "Al-Ikhtilat," *Al-Balagh*, 27 June 1934, p. 10.

Sayyid, Sulayman Darwish, "Wazifat al-Mar'a," *Al-Muqattam*, 10 August 1933, pp. 1, 8.

Al-Shantawi, Husni, "Tawhid al-Thaqafa fi Misr," *Al-Balagh al-Usbu'i*, 10 August, 1928, p. 8

Sharaf, Muhammad, Hadaratuna al-Qadima," in reply to survey conducted by *Al-Hilal*, vol. 39, April 1930, pp. 826-7.

_____, "Al-Lugha al-'Arabiyya wa-al-Mustalahat al-'Ilmiyya", *Al-Muqtataf*, part 1, vol, 74, February 1929, pp. 123-7 and part 2, vol. 74, March 1929, pp. 278-82.

Sha'rawi, Huda, Interview, *Al-Hilal*, vol. 35, April 1927, pp. 650-4.

_____, "Hadaratina al-Qadima," in reply to survey conducted by *Al-Hilal*, vol, 39, April 1930, pp. 824-5.

Al-Sharif, Hassan, "Al-Lugha al-'Arabiyya Aghna min al-Faransiyya," *Al-Hilal*, vol. 47, January 1939, pp. 302-5.

_____, "Tabsit Qawa'id al-Lugha al-'Arabiyya," *Al-Hilal*, vol. 46, August 1938, pp. 1108-19.

Shukri, 'Abd al-Rahman, "Ikhtilaf Hudud al-Haqq wa-al-Wajib, *Al-Risala*. vol. 6, 28 February, 1938, pp. 325-6.

_____, "Al-Shabab wa-al-Mashib ka-al-Mitraqa wa-al-Sandan," *Al-Hilal*, vol.44, May 1936, pp. 769-71.

Shukri, Ahmad, "Hal fi Istita'at al-Rajul an Yafahama al-Mar'a,," *Al-Balagh al-Usbu'i*, 16 April 1930, p. 27.

Taha, Amina Ahmad, "Al-Sufur," *Al-Balagh al-Usbu'I*, 9 December 1927, pp. 22-3.

Al-Tanahi, Tahir Ahmad, "Hal Yumkinu Islah al-Huruf al-'Arabiyya," *Al-Hilal*, vol. 42, May 1934, pp. 829-33.

Taymur, Mahmud, "Al-Niza' bayna al-Fusha wa-al-'Ammiyya fi al-Adab al-Misri al-Hadith", *Al-Hilal*, vol. 4l, July 1933, pp. 1185-8.

_____, *Al-Shaykh Jum'a wa-Aqasis Ukhra*. 2nd ed. Cairo: Al-Matba'a al-Salafiyah, 1927.

Thabit, 'Abd al-Hamid Ahmad, "Taqaddum al-Mar'a al-Misriyya," *Al-Siyasa al-Usbu'iiyya*, 18 June 1927, p. 6.

_____, "Tarbiyat al-Mar'a al-Misriyya," *Al-Siyasa al-Usbu'iyya*, 20 August 1927, p. 8.

Wasif, Amin, "Nahdat al-Sharq al-'Arabi," a reply to survey conducted by *Al-Hilal*, vol. 31, March 1923, pp. 609-12.

_____, "Al-Shi'r wa'l-Musiqa", *Al-Hilal*, vol. 28, May 1919, p. 686-8.

Al-Zahlawi, Habib, "Udaba' Mua'sirun, *Al-Muqttaf*, 2 August 1935, pp. 11-2.

Al-Zayyat, Ahmad Hassan, "'Afat al-Lugha Hadha al-Nahw...," *Al-Risala*, vol. 1, issue 13, 15 July, 1933, pp. 7-8.

_____, *Fi Usul al-Adab*. Vol. 1. Cairo: Matba'at Lajnat al-Ta'lif wa-al-Tarjamah wa-al-Nashr, 1935.

_____, "Al-Hajj…", *Al-Risala*, vol. 3, 21 January 1935, pp. 81-2.

_____, "Al-'Id...," *Al-Risala*, vol. 1, 15 April 1933, pp. 3-4.

_____, "Al-Imtiyazat wa -al-Adab!,"*Al-Risala*, vol. 2, 28 May 1934, pp. 881-2.

_____, "Istiqlal al-Lugha", *Al-Risala*, vol. 4, 7 December 1936, p. 1982.

_____, "Al-Risala fi 'Amiha al-Rabi`,"*Al-Risala*, vol. 4, 6 January 1936, pp.1-2.

_____, "Shuruh wa-Hawash, *Al-Risala*, vol. 1f, 15 May 1933, pp. 3-4.

_____, "Tadris al-Lugha al-'Arabiyya," *Al-Risala*, vol. 7, 8 May 1939, pp. 895-6.

_____, "Al-Tarbush wa-al-Qubb'a," *Al-Risala*, vol. 5, 7 June, 1937, pp. 921-2.

_____, "Tat'im al-Adab al-'Arabi," *Al-Risala*, vol. 4, 16 November 1936, pp.1861-2.

_____, "Al-Thaqafa al-Mudhabdhaba," *Al-Risala*, vol. 3, 28 January, 1935, pp.121-2.

Ziyada, Mayy, *Bahithat al-Badiyya*, Cairo: Matba'at al-Muqtataf, 1920.

Books and Articles in English

Abaza, Mona, *Changing Images of Three Generations of Azharites in Indonesia*. Singapore: Institute of Southeast Asian Studies, 1993.

_____, "Indonesian Azharites, Fifteen Years Later", *Sojourn*, vol. 18, no. 1 (2003), pp. 139–53.

_____, "Some Research Notes on Living Conditions and Perceptions Among Indonesian Students in Cairo". *Journal of Southeast Asia Studies*, vol. 22, no. 2 (1991), pp. 347–60.

Abdullah, Taufik, "Adat and Islam: An Examination of Conflict in Minangkabau," *Indonesia*, II (October 1966), pp. 1–24.

_____, "Modernization in the Minangkabau World: West Sumatra in the Early Decades of the Twentieth Century." In Claire Holt (ed.), *Culture and Politics in Indonesia*. Ithaca: Cornell University Press, 1972, pp. 178-245.

Adams, Charles C., *Islam and Modernism in Egypt*. New York: Russell & Russell, 1968.

Ahmed, Hussam Eldin Raafat, *From Nahda to Exile: A History of the Shawam in Egypt in the Early Twentieth Century*. A thesis submitted to McGill University. Montreal: McGill University, Institute of Islamic Studies, June 2011.

Ahmed, Leila. *Women and Gender in Islam: Historical Roots of a Modern Debate*. New Haven and London: Yale University Press, 1992.

Alinei, Mario, "Darwinism, Traditional Linguistics and the New Palaeolithic Continuity Theory of Language Evolution." In Jean Paul Van Bendegem and Diederik Aerts (eds.), *Evolutionary Epistemology, Language and Culture. A Non-Adaptationist, Systems Theoretical Approach*. Berlin-Heidelberg-New York: Springer, 2006, pp.121-47.

Alles, Delphine, *Transnational Islamic Actors and Indonesia's Foreign Policy*. London: Routledge, 2015.

Aljunied, Syed M.K., "Western Images of Meccan Pilgrims in the Dutch East Indies, 1800-1900", *SARI* (2005), pp. 105-22.

Amir, Ahmad N., Abdi O. Shuriye and Jamal I. Daoud, "Muhammad Abduh's Influence in Southeast Asia." *Middle-East Journal of Scientific Research* (MEJSR), vol.13 (2013). pp. 124-38.

Angerman, Arina, Geerte Binnema, Annemieke Keunen, Vefie Poels, and Jacqueline Zirkzee (eds), *Current Issues in Women's History.* By International Conference on Women's History. London/New York: Routledge, 1989.

Arenfeldt, Pernille and Nawar al-Hassan Golley, in Pernille Arenfeldt and Nawar al-Hassan Golley (eds.), *Mapping Arab Women's Movements; A Century of Transformations from Within.* Cairo: American University in Cairo Press, 2012), pp. 7-42.

Assyaukanie, Luthfi, *Islam and the Secular State in Indonesia.* Singapore: Institute of Southeast Asian Studies, 2009.

Ayalon, Ami, *Language and Change in the Arab Middle East.* New York: Oxford University Press, 1987.

Azra Azyumardi, "Globalization of Indonesian Muslim Discourse: Contemporary Religio-Intellectual Connections between Indonesia and the Middle East." In Johan Meuleman (ed.), *Islam in the Era of Globalization: Muslim Attitude Towards Modernity and Identity.* London: RoutledgeCurzon, 2002, pp. 31-50.

_____, "The Transmission of al-Manar's Reformism to the Malay-Indonesian World: The Cases of al-Imam and al-Munir." *Studia Islamika,* vol. 6, no. 3 (1999), pp. 77–100.

_____, *The Transmission of Islamic Reformism to Indonesia: Networks of Middle Eastern and Malay-Indonesian 'Ulama' in the Seventeenth and Eighteenth Centuries.* Honolulu: ALLEN & UNWIN and University of Hawaii Press, 2004.

Bayly, C.A. *The Birth of the Modern World, 1780-1914: Global Connections and Comparisons*. Maiden, MA and Oxford: Blackwell, 2004.

Badran, Margot, *Feminism in Islam: Secular and Religious Convergences.* London: Oneworld Publications, 2009.

_____, *Feminists, Islam, and Nation: Gender and the Making of Modern Egypt.* Princeton University Press, 1995.

Baer, Gabriel, *Population and Society in the Arab East.* Translated by Hanna Szoke. London: Routledge & Kegan Paul, 1964.

Baron, Beth, *Egypt as a Woman; Nationalism, Gender, and Politics.* Cairo: The American University in Cairo Press, 2005.

Barton, Greg, "Indonesia's Nurcholish Madjid and Abdurrahman Wahid as Intellectual 'Ulama': The Meeting of Islamic Traditionalism and Modernism in neo-Modernist Thought." *Studia Islamika*, vol. 4, no. 1 (1997), pp. 29–81.

_____, "Islamic Liberalism and the Prospects for Democracy in Indonesia." In Michèle Schmiegelow (ed.), *Democracy in Asia.* New York: St. Martin's Press, 1997, pp. 427–51.

_____, "Neo-Modernism: A Vital Synthesis of Traditionalist and Modernist Islamic Thought in Indonesia," *Studia Islamika,* vol. 2, no. 3 (1995), pp. 1-75.

Baskerville, John Cornelius, *From Tahdhiib al-Amma to Tahmiish al-Ammiyya: In Search of Social and Literary Roles for Standard and Colloquial Arabic in late 19th Century Egypt.* PhD dissertation. The University of Texas, 2009.

Bayly, C.A., *The Birth of the Modern World, 1780-1914: Global Connections and Comparisons.* Maiden, MA and Oxford: Blackwell, 2004.

Benite, Zvi Ben-Dor, "Taking ʿAbduh to China: Chinese-Egyptian Intellectual Contact in the Early Twentieth Century". In James L. Gelvin and Nile Green (eds.), *Global Muslims in the Age of Steam and Print* (Berkeley Los Angeles London: University of California Press, 2014), pp. 249-68.

Berger, Morroe, *The Arab World Today.* New York: Doubleday & Company, Inc., 1961.

Bluhm, Jutta E., "A Preliminary Statement on the Dialogue Established between the Reform Magazine al-Manar and the Malayo-Indonesian World." *Indonesia Circle,* no. 32 (November 1983), pp. 35-42.

Bluhm-Warn, Jutta., "Al-Manar and Ahmad Soorkattie". In P. G. Riddell and T. Street (eds.), *Islam: Essays on Scripture, Thought and Society.* Leiden: E.J. Brill, 1997, pp. 295-308.

Browen, John R., "Modern Intentions: Reshaping Subjectivities in an Indonesian Muslim Society. In Robert W. Hefner and Patricia Horvatich (eds.), *Islam in an Era of Nation-States: Politics and Religious Renewal in Muslim Southeast Asia.* Honolulu: University of Hawai'i Press, 1997, pp. 157–81.

Brockelmann, Carl, *Geschichte der Arabischen Literatur.* Supplementband III. Leiden: E.J. Brill 1943.

Bruinessen, Martin van, "Basyuni Imran." In *Dictionnaire biographique des savants et grandes figures du monde musulman périphérique, in du XIXe siècle à nos jours,* Fasc. no 1. Paris: CNRS-EHESS, 1992, p.26.

Calvert, John, *Sayyid Qutb and the Origins of Radical Islamism.* New York: Columbia University Press, 2010.

Clarence-Smith, William G., "Hadramaut and the Hadrami Diaspora in the Modern Colonial Era: An Introductory Survey". In Ulrike Freitag and William G. Clarence-Smith (eds.), *Hadhrami Traders, Scholars and Statesmen in the Indian Ocean, 1750s–1960s.* Leiden: Brill, 1997.

Carré, Olivier, *Mysticism and Politics: A Critical Reading of Fi Zilal Al-Qur'an by Sayyid Qutb (1906–1966)*. Translated from French by Carol Artigues and revised by W. Shepard. Leiden: Brill, 2003.

Chejne, Anwar, *The Arabic Language: Its Role in History.* Minneapolis, Minn: University of Minnesota Press, 1969.

Civantos, Christina, "Reading and Writing the Turn-of-the-Century Egyptian Woman Intellectual: Nabawiyya Musa's Ta'rikhi bi-Qalami." *Journal of Middle East Women's Studies*, vol. 9, no. 2 (Spring 2013), pp. 4-31.

Cleveland, William L., *Islam Against the West: Shakib Arslan and the. Campaign for Islamic Nationalism.* Austin: University of Texas Press, 1985.

Daniëls, Helge, "Linguistic conservatism as the basis for political revolution? The fusha-'ammiya debate in nineteenth-century Ottoman-Aran Middle Eastern society." *Antwerp Papers in Linguistics,* vol. 106 (2004), pp. 79-92.

de Jonge, Huub, "Dutch Colonial Policy pertaining to Hadhrami Immigrants". In Ulrike Freitag and William G. Clarence-Smith, *Hadhrami Traders, Scholars and Statesmen in the Indian Ocean,1750s –1960s*. Leiden: Brill, 1997, pp. 94-111.

El-Desouky, Ayman A. *The Intellectual and the People in Egyptian Literature and Culture: Amāra and the 2011 Revolution.* Hampshire; New York : Palgrave Macmillan, 2014.

Di-Capua, Yoav, "The Professional Worldview of the Effendi Historian", *History Compass,* vol. 7, issue 1 (Fall 2009), pp. 306-28.

_____, *The Thought and Practice of Modern Egyptian Historiography, 1890–1970.* PhD dissertation. Princeton: Princeton University, November 2004.

Dijk, C. van. "Colonial Fears, 1890–1918: Pan-Islamism and the Germano-Indian Plot". In Huub De Jonge and Nico Kaptein (eds.), *Transcending Borders: Arabs, Politics, Trade and Islam in Southeast Asia.* Leiden: KITLV Press: 2002.

Dobbin, Christine, *Islamic Revivalism in a Changing Peasant Economy: Central Sumatra, 1784–1847.* Scandinavian Institute of Asian Studies, Monograph Series no. 47. London and Malmo: Curzon Press, 1983.

_____, "Islamic Revivalism in Minangkabau at the Turn of the Nineteenth Century." *Modern Asian Studies,* vol. 8, no. 3 (1974), pp. 319–56.

Drewes, G. W. J., "Indonesia Mysticism and Activism." In Gustav E. von Grunebaum (ed.), *Unity and Variety in Muslim Civilization.* Chicago & London: The University of Chicago Press, 1963, 284-310.

Effendy, Bahtiar, *Islam and the State in Indonesia.* Singapore: Institute of Southeast Asian Studies, 2003.

_____, "Islam and the State in Indonesia: Munawir Sjadzali and the Development of a New Theological Underpinning of Political Islam." *Studia Islamika*, vol. 2, no. 2 (1995), pp. 97–121.

Egger, Vernon, *A Fabian in Egypt: Salamah Musa and the Rise of the Professional Classes in Egypt, 1909-1939*. Lanham: University Press of America, 1986.

Eisenstadt, S. N. "Intellectuals and Tradition." *Daedalus*, vol. 101, no.2 (Spring 1972), pp. 1-19.

Elshakry, Marwa, *Reading Darwin in Arabic, 1860-1950*. Chicago: University of Chicago Press, 2014.

Ende, Werner and Udo Steinback (eds.), *Islam in the World Today: A Handbook of Politics, Religion, Culture, and Society*. Ithaca, N.Y.: Cornell University Press, 2010.

Eliraz, Giora, "Distinctive Contemporary Voice: Liberal Islam Thought in Indonesia." *Studia Islamika*, vol. 15, no. 3 (2008), pp. 1-38.

_____, *Islam in Indonesia: Modernism, Radicalism and the Middle East Dimension*. Brighton: Sussex Academic Press, 2004.

_____, "The Social and Cultural Conception of Mustafa Sadiq al-Rafi'i." *Asian and African Studies*, vol. 13 (1979), pp. 101-29.

Faisal, Bakti Andi, "Islam and Modernity; Nurcholish Madjid's Interpretation of Civil Society, Pluralism, Secularization, and Democracy." *Asian Journal of Social Science*, vol. 33, no. 3 (2005), pp. 486 -505.

Federspiel, Howard M., *Islam and Ideology in the Emerging Indonesian State: The Persatuan Islam (PERSIS), 1923 to 1957*. Leiden: Brill, 2001.

_____, "The Muhammadijah: A Study of an Orthodox Islamic Movement in Indonesia." *Indonesia*, 10 (1970), pp. 57–79.

Gelvin, James L. and Nile Green, "Introduction." In James L. Gelvin and Nile Green (eds.), *Global Muslims in the Age of Steam and Print*. Berkeley Los Angeles London: University of California Press, 2014. pp. 1-22.

Gershoni, Israel and James P. Jankowski, *Confronting Fascism in Egypt: Dictatorship versus Democracy in the 1930s*. Stanford: Stanford University Press, 2009.

_____, *Egypt, Islam, and the Arabs: The Search for Egyptian Nationhood, 1900-1930*. Oxford: Oxford University Press, 1986.

_____, *Redefining the Egyptian Nation, 1930-1945*. Cambridge: Cambridge University Press, Cambridge, 1995.

Gershoni, Israel, "Intellectual History in Twentieth-Century Middle Eastern Studies". In Israel Gershoni and Amy Singer (eds.), *Middle East Historiographies: Narrating the Twentieth Century.* Seattle: Washington University Press, 2006, pp. 131-82.

_____, "Reconstructing Tradition — Islam, Modernity, and National Identity in Egyptian Intellectual Discourse, 1930-1952." In Moshe Zuckermann (ed.), *Ethnizität, Moderne und Enttraditionalisierung.* Tel Aviver Jahrbuch für deutsche Geschichte, 2002, 155-211.

_____, "Secondary Intellectuals, Readers, and Readership as Agents of National-Cultural Reproduction in Modern Egypt". In Yaakov Elman and Israel Gershoni (eds.), *Transmitting Jewish Traditions: Orality, Textuality, and Cultural Diffusion.* New Haven: Yale University Press, 2000, pp. 324-48.

Gibb, Hamilton A.R., "The Heritage of Islam in the Modern World." *International Journal of Middle East Studies,* part 3, vol. 2 (1971), pp. 129-47.

_____, *Modern Trends in Islam.* Chicago: The University of Chicago Press, 1947.

_____, *Studies on the Civilization of Islam.* Edited by Stanford J. Shaw and William R. Polk. Boston: Beacon Press, 1962.

Goldschmidt JR, Arthur, Book Review of Gershoni and Jankowski, "Egypt, Islam, and the Arabs: The Search for Egyptian Nationhood, 1900-1930". *International Journal of African Historical Studies,* vol. 20, no. 4 (1987), pp. 730-2.

Goldziher, Ignaz, "Education (Muslim)," *Encyclopaedia of Religion and Ethics,* vol. 5 (1912), pp. 198-201.

Grunebaum, Gustave Edmund von, "I'jaz." *Encyclopedia of Islam.* Leiden: E. J. Brill, 1969, vol. 3, pp. 1018-20.

_____, *Islam: Essays in the Nature and Growth of a Cultural Tradition.* 2nd ed. London: Routledge & Kegan Paul LTD, 1961.

_____, *Medieval Islam: A Study in Cultural Orientation.* Chicago & London: University of Chicago Press, 1953.

_____, *Modern Islam: The Search for Cultural Identity.* New York: Vintage Books, 1964.

Hatina, Meir, *Identity Politics in the Middle East.* London and New York: I.B. Tauris, 2007.

_____, "On the Margins of Consensus: The Call to Separate Religion and State in Modern Egypt." *Middle Eastern Studies,* vol.36, no.1 (January 2000), pp.35-54.

Hayimasae, Numan, "The Intellectual Network of Patani and the Haramayn". In P. Jory (ed.), *The Ghosts of the Past in Southern Thailand; Essays on the History and Historiography of Patani.* Singapore: NUS press, 2013), pp. 110-128.

Hefner, Robert W., *Civil Islam: Muslims and Democratization in Indonesia.* Princeton and Oxford: Princeton University Press, 2000.

_____, "Secularization and Citizenship in Muslim Indonesia". In David Martin, Paul Heelas and Paul Morris (eds.), *Religion, Modernity, and Postmodernity.* Oxford: Blackwell Publishers, 1998, pp. 147-68.

Heyd, Uriel, *Language Reform in Modern Turkey.* Jerusalem: Israel Oriental Society, 1954.

Heyworth-Dunne, J., *An Introduction to the History of Education in Modern Egypt.* London: Taylor & Francis Group, 1968.

Hourani, Albert, *Arabic Thought in the Liberal Age: 1798–1939.* London: Oxford University Press, 1970.

Ibn Khaldun, 'Abd al-Rahman, *The Muqaddimah: An Introduction to History.* Translated by Franz Rosenthal. Princeton: Princeton University Press, 1967, vol. 1.

Ibrahim, Ibrahim A., "Isma'il Mazhar and Husayn Fawzi: Two Muslim 'Radical' Westernizers." *Middle Eastern Studies,* vol.9 (1973), pp. 35-41.

Johns, A.H., "Islam in Southeast Asia". In Mircea Eliade (ed.), *The Encyclopedia of Religion.* New York: Macmillan Publishing Company, 1987, vol. 7, pp. 411–2.

Joll, Christopher M., "Islam's Creole Ambassadors." In P. Jory (ed.), *The Ghosts of the Past in Southern Thailand; Essays on the History and Historiography of Patani.* Singapore: NUS press, 2013, pp. 129-46.

Juynboll, G.H.A., "Ismail Ahmad Adham (1911-1940), the Atheist." *Journal of Arabic Literature,* vol. 3 (1972), pp. 54-71.

Kassab, Elizabeth Suzannen, *Contemporary Arab Thought: Cultural Critique in Comparative Perspective.* New York: Columbia University Press, 2010.

Keddie, Nikki R., "Symbol and Sincerity in Islam." *Studia Islamica,* vol. XIX (1963), pp. 27-63.

Kerr, Malcolm H., *Islamic Reform: The Political and Legal Theories of Muhammad 'Abduh and Rashid Rida.* Berkeley and Los Angeles: University of California Press, 1966.

_____, *Islamic Reform: The Political and Legal Theories of Muhammad 'Abduh and Rashid Rida.* Berkeley and Los Angeles: University of California Press, 1966.

Khaldi, Boutheina, *Egypt Awakening in the Early Twentieth Century: Mayy Ziyadah's Intellectual Circles.* New York: Palgrave Macmillan, 2012.

Kozma, Liat, *Policing Egyptian Women: Law, Sex and Medicine in Khedival Egypt.* Syracuse, Syracuse University Press, 2011.

Khuri-Makdisi, Ilham, " Fin-de-Siècle Egypt: A Nexus for Mediterranean and Global Radical Networks". In James L. Gelvin and Nile Green (eds.), *Global Muslims in the Age of Steam and Print.* Berkeley Los Angeles London: University of California Press, 2014, pp. 78-100.

Kostiner, Joseph, "Impact of the Hadrami Emigrants in the East Indies on Islamic Modernism and Social Change in the Hadramawi during the 20th Century." In Raphael Israeli and Anthony H. Johns (eds.), *Islam in Asia, vol. II: Southeast and East Asia.* Jerusalem: The Magnes Press, 1984, pp. 206–37.

Laffan, Michael, "An Indonesian Community in Cairo: Continuity and Change in a Cosmopolitan Islamic Milieu." *Indonesia,* vol. 77, (April 2004), pp. 1-26.

_____, *Islamic Nationhood and Colonial Indonesia: The Umma Below the Winds.* London and New York: RoutledgeCurzon, 2003.

_____, *The Makings of Indonesian Islam: Orientalism and the Narration of a Sufi Past.* Princeton, NJ: Princeton University Press, 2011.

Lapidus, Ira M., *A History of Islamic Societies,* 3rd ed. Cambridge: Cambridge University Press, 2015.

Lerner, Gerda, *The Creation of Patriarchy.* New York, NY: Oxford University Press, 1986.

Lewis, Bernard, *History: Remembered, Recovered, Invented.* Princeton: Princeton University Press, 1975.

_____, *Islam in History: Ideas, Men and Events in the Middle East.* London: Alcove Press, 1973.

_____, *Islam and the West.* New York and Oxford: Oxford University Press, 1993.

Lockman, Zachary, "Explorations in the Field: Lost Voices and Emerging Practices in Egypt, 1882-1914". In Israeli Gershoni, Hakan Erdem, and Ursula Wokoeck (eds.), *Histories of the Modern Middle East: New Directions.* Boulder: Lynn Rienner Publishers, 2002, pp. 137-153.

Mandal, Sumit K., "Challenging Inequality in a Modern Islamic Idiom: Social Ferment amongst Arabs in Early 20th-century Java. In Eric Tagliacozzo (ed.), *Southeast Asia and the Middle East: Islam, Movement, and the Longue Durée.* Stanford, CA: Stanford University Press, 2009, pp. 156-75.

_____, "Forging a Modern Arab Identity in Java in the Early Twentieth Century". In Huub De Jonge and Nico Kaptein (eds.), *Transcending Borders: Arabs, Politics, Trade and Islam in Southeast Asia.* Leiden: KITLV Press, 2002, pp. 163–84.

_____, "Natural Leaders of Native Muslims: Arab Ethnicity and Politics in Java under Dutch Rule". In Ulrike Freitag and William G. Clarence-Smith (eds.), *Hadhrami Traders, Scholars and Statesmen in the Indian Ocean, 1750s–1960s.* Leiden: Brill, 1997, pp. 185-98

Manger, Leif, *The Hadrami Diaspora: Community-Building on the Indian Ocean Rim Manger.* New York: Berghahn Books, 2010.

Mariscotti, Cathlyn, *Gender and Class in the Egyptian Women's Movement.* New York: Syracuse University Press, 2008.

Melhem, Hisham, "The Barbarians Within Our Gates." *Politico Magazine,* 18 September 2014, http://www.politico.com/magazine/story/2014/09/the-barbarians-within-our-gates-111116 (last accessed, 9 March 2018).

Milner, Anthony, *The Invention of Politics in Colonial Malaya: Contesting Nationalism and the Expansion of the Public Sphere.* Cambridge: Cambridge University Press, 1994.

_____, "Islam and the Muslim State". In M.B. Hooker (ed.), *Islam in Southeast Asia.* Leiden: E.J. Brill, 1993, pp. 23–49.

Mitchell, Richard, *The Society of the Muslim Brethren.* New York and Oxford: Oxford University Press, 1993.

Mobini-Kesheh, Natalie, *The Hadrami Awakening: Community and Identity in the NetherlandsEast Indies, 1900–1942.* Ithaca: Cornell University Press, 1999.

Munhanif, Ali, "Islam and the Struggle for Religious Pluralism in Indonesia: A Political Reading of the Religious Thought of Mukti Ali." *Studia Islamika,* pp. 79-126.

Mutalib, Hussin, *Islam in Malaysia: From Revivalism to Islamic State.* Singapore: Singapore University Press, 1993.

Noer, Deliar, *The Modernist Muslim Movement in Indonesia: 1900–1942.* Oxford: Oxford University Press, 1978.

Osterhammel, Jürgen, *The Transformation of the World: A Global History of the Nineteenth Century.* Translated by Patrick Camiller. Princeton: Princeton University Press, 2014.

Othman, Mohammad Redzuan, "The Origins and Contribution of the Early Arabs in Malaya". In Eric Tagliacozzo (ed.), *Southeast Asia and the Middle East: Islam, Movement, and the Longue Duree.* Stanford: Stanford University Press, 2009.

Quawas, Rula B., "A Sea Captain in Her Own Right: Navigating the Feminist Thought of Huda Shaarawi." *Journal of International Women's Studies,* vol. 8, issue 1, pp. 219-35.

Oudeyer, Pierre-Yves and Frédéric Kaplan, "Language Evolution as a Darwinian Process: Computational Studies." *Cognitive Processing,* vol. 8, no. 1 (2007), pp. 21–35.

Philipp, Thomas. "Feminism and Nationalist Politics in Egypt." In Lois Beck and Nikki Keddie (eds.), *Women in the Muslim World.* Cambridge: Harvard University Press, 1978, pp. 277-95.

Piterberg, Gabriel, "The Tropes of Stagnation and Awakening in Nationalist Historical Consciousness: The Egyptian Case." In James P. Jankowski and Israel Gershoni (eds.), *Rethinking Nationalism in the Arab Middle East.* Columbia University Press, New York, 1997, pp. 42-61.

Radwan, Abu al-Futouh Ahmad, *Old and New Forces in Egyptian Education.* New York: Teachers College Columbia University, 1951.

Ramdani, Nabila, "Women in the 1919 Egyptian Revolution: from feminist awakening to nationalist political activism." *Journal of International Women's Studies,* vol. 14, issue 2 (March 2013). pp. 39-52.

Reid, Donald Malcolm, *Cairo University and the Making of Modern Egypt.* Cambridge University Press, Cambridge, 1990.

_____, "Nationalizing the Pharaonic Past: Egypt 1922-1952,". In James Jankowski and Israel Gershoni (eds.), *Rethinking Nationalism in the Arab Middle East.* New York: Columbia University Press, 1997, pp. 127-67.

Riddell, Peter G., "Arab Migrants and Islamization in the Malay World during the Colonial Period". *Indonesia and the Malay World,* vol. 29, no. 84 (2001), pp. 113–28.

_____, *Islam and the Malay-Indonesian World: Transmission and Responses.* Honolulu: University of Hawai'i Press, 2001.

_____, "Religious Links between Hadhramaut and the Malay-Indonesian World c.1850 to c.1950." In Ulrike Freitag and William G. Clarence-Smith (eds.), *Hadhrami Traders, Scholars and Statesmen in the Indian Ocean, 1750s-1960s.* Leiden: Brill, 1997, pp. 217-230.

Roff, William R., "Indonesian and Malay Students in Cairo in the 1920's". *Indonesia,* vol. 9 (April 1970), pp. 73-87.

_____, "Kaum Muda – Kaum Tua: Innovation and Reaction Amongst the Malays, 1900- 1941". In K. G. Tregonning (ed.), *Papers on Malayan History.* Singapore: Journal South-East Asian History, 1962, pp. 162–92.

_____, *The Origins of Malay Nationalism.* New Haven and London: Yale University Press, 1967.

_____, "South-East Asian Islam in the Nineteenth Century". In P. M. Holt, Ann K. S. Lambton and Bernard Lewis (eds.), *The Cambridge History of Islam, vol. 2: The Further Islamic Lands, Islamic Society and Civilization.* London: Cambridge University Press, 1970, pp. 155–81.

Ryad, Umar, *Islamic Reformism and Christianity: A Critical Reading of the Works of Muhammad Rashid Rida and his Associates (1898-1935).* Leiden: Brill, 2009.

Ryzova, Lucie, "Egyptianizing Modernity through the 'New Effendiya'; Social and Cultural Constructions of the Middle Class in Egypt under the Monarchy". In Arthur Goldschmidt JR, Amy J. Johnson, and Barak A. Salmoni (eds.), *Re-envisioning Egypt 1919-1952.* Cairo; New York : American University in Cairo Press, 2005, pp. 124-63.

Ryzova, Lucie, *The Age of the Efendiyya: Passages to Modernity in National-Colonial Egypt, Oxford Historical Monographs.* New York: Oxford University Press, 2014.

Safran, Nadav, *Egypt in Search of Political Community.* Cambridge, MA: Harvard University Press, 1961.

Scheuerman, William, "Globalization". In Edward N. Zalta (ed.), *The Stanford Encyclopedia of Philosophy* (Summer 2014 Edition), http://plato.stanford.edu/archives/sum2014/entries/globalization/ (last accessed , 20 March 2018).

Semah, David, *Four Egyptian Literary Critics.* Leiden : E. J. Brill, 1974.

Shakry, Omnia, "Schooled Mothers and Structured Play: Child-Rearing in Turn-of-the-Century Egypt." In Lila Abu-Lughod (ed.), *Remaking Women: Feminism and Modernity in the Middle East.* Princeton: Princeton University Press and Cairo: American University in Cairo Press, 1998, pp. 143-8.

Sharabi, Hisham, *Arab Intellectuals and the West: the Formative Years, 1875-1914.* Baltimore and London: Johns Hopkins Press, 1970.

Shavit, Uriya, *Islamism and the West: From "Cultural Attack" to "Missionary Migrant".* London and New York: Routledge, 2014.

Shils, Edward, "Intellectuals, Tradition, and the Traditions of Intellectuals: Some Preliminary Considerations," *Daedalus,* vol. 101, no. 7 (Spring 1972) , pp. 21-34.

Smith, Charles D., "The Crisis of Orientation: The Shift of Egyptian Intellectuals to Islamic Subjects in the 1930s." *IJMES,* vol. 4 (1973), pp. 382-410.

Smith, Wilfred Cantwell, *Islam in Modern History: The Tension between Faith and History in the Islamic World.* New York: Mentor Book/New American Library, 1957.

Stark, Jan, *Malaysia and the Developing World: The Asian Tiger on the Cinnamon Road.* London and New York: Routledge, 2013.

Stetkevych, Jaroslav, *The Modern Arabic Literary Language: Lexical and Stylistic Developments.* Chicago: University of Chicago Press, 1970.

Sulaiman, Yasir, *The Arabic Language and National Identity: A Study in Ideology.* Washington, D.C.: Georgetown University Press, 2003.

Syamsuddin, M. Din, "Islamic Political Thought and Cultural Revival in Modern Indonesia." *Studia Islamika,* vol. 2, no. 4 (1995), pp. 47–68.

_____, *Religion and Politics in Islam: The Case of Muhammadiyah in Indonesia's New Order.* PhD. dissertation, Los Angeles: University of California, 1991, pp. 268-70, 287-88.

_____, "The Muhammadiyah Daʻwah and Allocative Politics in the New Order Indonesia." *Studia Islamika,* vol. 2, no. 2 (1995), pp. 35-71.

Tibawi, A.L., *Islamic Education.* London: Luzac & Co., 1972.

Tingor, Robert L., *Modernization and British Colonial Rule in Egypt, 1882-1914.* Princeton, Princeton University Press, 1966.

Trocki, Carl A., *Singapore: Wealth, Power and the Culture of Control.* New York, NY: Routledge, 2006.

Tschacher, Torsten, "'Walls of Illusion': Information Generation in Colonial Singapore and the Reporting of the Mahdi-Rebellion in Sudan, 1887-1890". In Derek Heng and Syed Muhd Khairudin Aljuneid (eds.), *Singapore in Global History.* Amsterdam: Amsterdam University Press, 2011, pp. 67-88.

Tuker, Judith, *Women in Nineteenth-Century Egypt.* Cambridge: Cambridge University Press, 1985.

Turnbull, C. M., *A History of Modern Singapore 1819-2005,* (published posthumously). Singapore: NUS Press, 2009.

Vatikiotis, P. J, *Arab and Regional Politics in the Middle East.* London & Sydney: Croom Helm, 2001.

_____, *The Modern History of Egypt.* Asia-Africa Series of Modern Histories. London: Weidenfeld and Nicholson, 1969.

Versteegh, Kees, *The Arabic Language.* Edinburgh: Edinburgh University Press, 2014.

von der Mehden, Fred R., *Two Worlds of Islam: Interaction between Southeast Asia and the Middle East.* Gainesville: University Press of Florida, 1993.

Wendell, Charles, *The Evolution of the Egyptian National Image: From its Origins to Ahmad Lutfi al-Sayyid.* Berkeley: University of California Press, 1972.

Whidden, James, "The Generation of 1919". In Arthur Goldschmidt JR, Amy J. Johnson and Barak A. Salmoni (eds.), *Re-envisioning Egypt 1919-1952*. Cairo; New York : American University in Cairo Press, 2005, pp. 19-46.

Yalçınkaya, M. Alper, *Learned Patriots: Debating Science, State, and Society in the Nineteenth-Century Ottoman Empire*. Chicago; London: The University of Chicago Press, 2015.

Yousef, Hoda, "Malak Hifni Nasif: Negotiations of a Feminist Agenda between the European and the Colonial." *Journal of Middle East Women's Studies,* vol. 7, no.1 (Winter 2011), pp. 70–89.

Zakariya, Hafiz, "Cairo and the Printing Press as the Modes in the Dissemination of Muhammad 'Abduh's Reformism to Colonial Malaya." *International Proceedings of Economics Development & Research* (IPEDR), vol. 17 (2011), pp. 121-26.

Zuhur, Sherifa, *Revealing Revealing: Islamist Gender Ideology in Contemporary Egypt*. Albany, State University of New York Press, 1992.

Index

A

Abaza, Fikri, 63
'Abd al-Qadir, Muhammad Zaki, 67, 72
'Abd al-Raziq, 'Ali, 16
'Abduh, Muhammad, 22-3, 25, 31, 39, 49, 55-6, 61, 121-3, 126, 128-30
Abu Shadi, Ahmad Zaki, 96-9
adat, 116, 126
Adham, Isma'il Ahmad, 51-3, 92
al-Afghani, Jamal al-Din, 22, 121, 123
'Alam, Muhammad Mahdi, 50
Amin, Ahmad, 16, 50
Amin, Qasim, 55-6, 61, 65-8, 70, 74-5, 89
Antun, Farah, 12
al-'Aqad, 'Abbas Mahmud, 16
Arslan, Shakib, 136
Ataturk, Mustafa Kemal, 13, 30, 41, 133
al-Azhar, 14, 23-4, 31, 34, 36, 50, 105, 115, 119-20, 125, 134-5
'Azmi, Mahmud, 42
Azra, Azyumardi, 115-6
'Azzam, 'Abd al-Wahhab, 27, 32-3, 40, 45

B

Badawi, Ahmad Ahmad, 111-2
Badran, Margot, 59
Bangsa, 124
Barakat, Bahey al-Din, 107
Batavia, 127
Bayly, C. A., 114
Beirut, 122
bid'a, 24, 99
al-Bishri, 'Abd al-'Aziz, 34, 47-9
Boktor, Amir, 106

C

Caliphate Question, 125
Constantinople, 122
Copts, 41, 51

D

Dar al-Da'wa wa-al-Irshad, 135
Dar al-'Ulum, 33, 36, 50, 77, 88
Darwinism, 12, 87, 89, 132
Dayf, Ahmad, 33, 95
El-Desouky, Ayman A., *83*
Diab, Mohammad Tawfik, 47
Dutch East Indies, Dutch colonial government/rule, 117-8, 122-3, 125

E

Effendiyya, 17
Egyptian University, 23-4, 27, 30-1, 36, 50, 58, 80, 101, 110
Ersoy, Mehmet Akif, 30
Europe, 11-2, 21-2, 26-8, 30-1, 35, 40-2, 46-7, 50-3, 83, 105-6, 114, 121

F

Fahmi, Asma, 76
Fahmi, Mansur, 27-8, 35, 40, 44-5, 50, 54, 65, 88,
Fatwa, 117, 122-3

G

Geertz, Clifford, 117
Gelvin, James L., 19, 114-5
Gershoni, Israel, 16-7
al-Ghamrawi, Muhammad Ahmad, 33, 45-6
Gibb, Hamilton A.R., 54
Green, Nile, 19, 114-5
Grunebaum, Gustave Edmund von, 29

H

Hadramis, Hadramaut, 118, 123, 126-7
al-Hajiri, Muhammad Taha, 112
Hajj, hajji, 116-8, 122
al-Hakim, Tawfiq, 16
halaqa, 126
Hamza, Muhammad 'Abd al-Qadir, 88, 91, 93, 98, 108
al-Harawi, Husayn, 61-2, 67, 81
Haykal, Muhammad Husayn, 16
Hefner, Robert W., 129
Husayn, Taha, 16

I

Ibn Khaldun, 41
i'jaz, 92, 102
ijtihad, 90, 122, 128-9

al-Imam, 123-5
'Imran, Muhammad Basyuni, 135-6
'Inan, Muhammad 'Abdallah, 30, 78
'Isa, Ahmad, 88-9, 102
ishtiqaq, 100-1, 103-4
al-Iskandari, Ahmad, 36, 103-4
Islamic modernism, 25, 119-31, 135
al-Ittiihad, 125
al-Ittihad al-Nisa'i al-Misri, 58-9

J

jahiliyya, jahili, 62, 112, 116
Jam'iyyat al-Islah wa-al-Irshad al-'Arabiyya, 127
Japan, 52-3, 133, 136
Jawa, 116
jihad, 116
Jum'a, Muhammad Lutfi, 81, 93

K

Kamil, Mustafa, 120
Kaum Muda, 127-8
Kaum Tua, 128
kerajaan, 124
Kerr, Malcolm H., 130
Khaki, Ahmad, 88, 90
al-Khuli, Amin, 33

L

Latin, Latinization, 41-2, 95, 97-9, 102, 105
Lebanese, 9, 11-2, 57, 85, 136
Liberalism, Liberal, 13, 15, 49, 86, 123, 130, 132

Liberal Islamic thought, 128-9

Lockman, Zachary, 16

M

Madkur, Ibrahim Bayumi, 36

madrasa, 105-6, 125, 135

Madrasat al-Mu'alimin al-'Ulya, 45

Madrasat al-Qada' al-Shar'i, 33

Mahdist movement, 134

Mahmud, Hafiz, 69-70, 72, 90

majaz, 102, 103

al-Manar, 122-4, 135-6

masakin, 127

mashayikh, 127

Mazhar, Isma'il, 25-6, 38

al-Mazini, Ibrahim 'Abd al-Qadir, 37, 53, 64, 95-6, 106, 112

Mecca, 116-7, 119-22

Medina, 116-7, 120

Melhem, Hisham, 9

Mill, John Stuart, *49*

al-Misri, Ibrahim, 38, 52-3

Mubarak, Zaki, 31, 35-6, 49, 99, 101

Muhammad 'Ali, 10-11, 106

Muhammadiya, 128-9

al-Munir, 124

muqimin, 116

Musa, Nabawiyya, 41, 60, 62, 67, 75-6, 78-9

Musa, Salama, 18, 51, 60, 91, 98, 104-5

Musharrafa, 'Ali Mustafa, 35, 88-89, 102

Muslim Brotherhood, 14, 36, 51

Mustafa, Ibrahim, 110

N

al-Nahda, 11, 57, 83, 85

Nahdlatul Ulama (NU), 129

Naht, 101, 103

Naji, Ibrahim, 70

Nasif, Malak Hifni ("Bahithat al-Badiyya") 56, 60, 67, 70, 75, 79

Nationalism,
 Egyptian, 13, 17, 54, 85-6, 92
 Arab, 42, 85

Nimr, Faris, 12

Noer, Deliar, 121

O

Ottoman Empire, 9, 11, 13, 85, 114, 118-9, 136

P

Padang, 124

Padri movement, 116-7

pan-Islamism, 117, 124

pan-Malayanism, 125

Paris, 33, 36, 121

pesantren, 126

Pilihan Timur, 125

Polygamy, 55-6, 59-62

pondok, 126

Q

al-Qalamawi, Suheir, 80

qiyas, 100

Qutb, Sayyid, 31, 63, 73, 77-8, 80-1

R

Radwan, Abu al-Futuh, Ahmad, 106
al-Rafi'i, Mustafa Sadiq, 26-7, 32, 34, 43, 46-7, 62-3, 62-3, 68, 73, 81, 92
rajas, 123
Rida, Muhammad Rashid, 121-2, 125, 135-6
Roff, William R., 128

S

Sada, 126-7
Sa'id, Nazla al-Hakim, 70-71, 79-80
Salafiyya, Salafist, *al-salaf, salafi,* 14, 38, 51, 89-90, 122, 131
Salam, Mustafa Muhammad, 109
sarf, 107, 110
Sarruf, Yaqub, 12
al-Sayyid, Ahmad Lutfi, 15-16
Seruan Azhar, 125
Sharaf, Muhammad, 89-90, 102-3
al-Sharif, Hassan, 87-8, 91, 101, 110
Sha'rawi, Huda, 58, 60, 62, 67
shari'a, 46, 55-6, 61, 65, 116, 124
Shukri, 'Abd al-Rahman, 37
Singapore, 121-5, 128, 134
Spengler, Oswald, 28
Suez Canal, 117-9
Sumatra, 123, 124

T

Taha, Amina Ahmad, 74
Taine, Hippolyte Adolphe, 49
taqlid, 33, 40, 46, 122

ta'rib, 100, 102, 104
Taymur, Mahmud, 94-5
Tschacher, Torsten, 134
Turkey, 13, 30, 41-3, 52-3, 98, 133

U

'ulama', 14, 116, 117, 124, 129, 135
umma, umat, 46, 116, 122, 124
al-'Urwa al-Wuthqa, 121

V

von der Mehden, Fred R., 121

W

Wasif, Amin, 89

Z

al-Zayyat, Ahmad Hassan, 40, 42, 45-6, 67, 69, 81
Ziyada, Mayy, 57

www.ingramcontent.com/pod-product-compliance
Lightning Source LLC
LaVergne TN
LVHW051556070426
835507LV00021B/2606